CHINA IN
ETHIOPIA

CHINA IN ETHIOPIA
THE LONG-TERM PERSPECTIVE

Aaron Tesfaye

Published by State University of New York Press, Albany

© 2020 State University of New York

All rights reserved

No part of this book may be used or reproduced in any manner whatsoever without written permission. No part of this book may be stored in a retrieval system or transmitted in any form or by any means including electronic, electrostatic, magnetic tape, mechanical, photocopying, recording, or otherwise without the prior permission in writing of the publisher.

For information, contact State University of New York Press, Albany, NY
www.sunypress.edu

Library of Congress Cataloging-in-Publication Data

Names: Tesfaye, Aaron, author.
Title: China in Ethiopia : the long-term perspective / Aaron Tesfaye.
Description: Albany : State University of New York Press, [2020] | Includes bibliographical references and index.
Identifiers: LCCN 2019049097 (print) | LCCN 2019049098 (ebook) | ISBN 9781438478357 (hardcover : alk. paper) | ISBN 9781438478340 (pbk. : alk. paper) | ISBN 9781438478364 (ebook)
Subjects: LCSH: China—Foreign relations—Ethiopia. | Ethiopia—Foreign relations—China. | China—Foreign relations—20th century. | Ethiopia—Foreign relations—1889–1974. | Ethiopia—Foreign relations—1974–1991. | Ethiopia—Foreign relations—1991–
Classification: LCC DS775.8 .T47 2020 (print) | LCC DS775.8 (ebook) | DDC 337.63051—dc23
LC record available at https://lccn.loc.gov/2019049097
LC ebook record available at https://lccn.loc.gov/2019049098

10 9 8 7 6 5 4 3 2 1

Contents

List of Tables — vii

Foreword — ix

Acknowledgments — xi

Abbreviations — xiii

Introduction — 1
    China and Ethiopia: Analytical Framework — 3
    China and Africa: An Overview — 7
    Methodology — 15
    Structure of the Book — 15

Chapter 1. China–Ethiopia Relations: Looking Back and Forward — 17
    Imperial Ethiopia and China: Pragmatic Relations, 1955–1974 — 18
    The Military Regime and China: Fragile Solidarity, 1974–1991 — 23
    China Returns to Ethiopia — 25
    Conclusion — 31

Chapter 2. Contemporary Chinese–Ethiopian Relations — 33
    Chinese Political Interests in Ethiopia — 34
    Chinese Security Interests in Ethiopia — 40
    Ethiopia's Modernization Interest in China — 43
    Conclusion — 49

Chapter 3. China and Ethiopia: Economic Relations	51
Nature of China–Ethiopia Economic Relations	52
Nature of Chinese Investment in Ethiopia	57
China–Ethiopia Trade Relations	66
Conclusion	70
Chapter 4. China and Ethiopia: Strategic Partners	73
Strategic Elements in China–Ethiopia Relations	75
Chinese Foreign Assistance to Ethiopia	79
Ethiopia, China, and the Horn of Africa	85
Conclusion	90
Chapter 5. China and Ethiopia: Long-Term Perspectives	93
Ethiopia and China's Belt and Road Initiative	96
Ethiopia's Development Plan, the BRI, and Regional Integration	98
China and Ethiopia: The Long-Term Perspective	109
Conclusion	114
Chapter 6. Conclusion	117
Notes	127
Bibliography	149
Index	167

Tables

3.1	Licensed Chinese Investment Projects by Region and Status, August 27, 1998 to June 25, 2015	53
3.2	Chinese Investment in Ethiopia by Major Sector, 2017 (in US$)	58
3.3	Chinese Investment and Loans in Ethiopia, 2003–2015 (in US$ million)	59
3.4	Licensed Chinese Investment Projects by Sector and Status, August 27, 1998 to June 25, 2015	61
3.5	Industrial Parks in Ethiopia	63
3.6	Ethiopian Exports to China, 2015	67
3.7	Ethiopia's Balance of Trade with China, 2006–2015 (in US$ million)	69
4.1	Historical Data of Chinese Assistance to Ethiopia (1974–1996)	83
5.1	Ethiopia's GDP Growth from 2005 to 2010 (in %)	99
5.2	Sectoral Distribution of GDP (in %)	101
5.3	Chinese Loan Commitments to Ethiopia by Creditor, 2012–2013	108

Foreword

The study of African engagement with China, sometimes framed as China–Africa relations, is an area which has expanded enormously over the past two decades. From an obscure interest pursued mostly by a narrow ground of scholar and journalists, the subject has blossomed into a well-recognized research field that has taken the lead in explaining and theorizing transnational relations in its many manifestations. Scholars from a diversity of disciplines, from media studies to international relations, have weighed in on topics such as Chinese and African migration, the impact of Chinese development approaches, and fitting Africa–China security into emerging trends in geopolitics. More recently, forays into knowledge construction and post-structuralist readings of the relationship have garnered interest.

While much of the academic work to date has focused on the "meta-level" or "micro-level" of enquiry, there is much value in examining state–state engagement as an appropriate framework for capturing the variety and dynamism of diplomatic, economic, and even sociological phenomena encompassing Africa–China ties. The expansion of bilateral studies, from the work of Jean-Pierre Cabasten on Francophone Africa–China ties to a host of edited volumes such as the one by Marcus Powers and Ana Cristina Alves on Angola–China relations, arguably offer greater depth in terms of content and insight than the broad sweeps that have characterized most scholarship in its first phase of elaboration.

Aaron Tesfaye's book *China in Ethiopia* is one such contribution, investigating the content of a relationship that has an historical context rooted in the Cold War, changing economic and commercial dynamics in the successive era of rapid globalization which have produced new development policies and outcomes that hold implications for state and society. Ethiopia's strategic management of China has, in many ways, provided other African countries with a textbook case of how to extract value from the relationship—albeit not without problems but nonetheless in a fashion that arguably mirrors the experimental approach to development characteristic of Chinese learning. Moreover, its status as the home of the African Union and concurrently its geographic standing in the Horn of Africa puts it at the nexus of regional (and even beyond, on the Arabian Peninsula) security concerns and the continent's own version of the "great game" of geopolitics. In this way, Tesfaye's book is especially important and timely, providing readers with a substantive look at this most important relationship.

Chris Alden
London School of Economics and Political Science (LSE)

Acknowledgments

The idea for this book germinated in 2015 while I was teaching a seminar at the Institute of Peace and Security Studies at Addis Ababa University, Ethiopia, in 2014. I have witnessed, during my yearly visit to Ethiopia, an increasing Chinese presence. Thus, while on a weekend trip in the western part of the country, I encountered an Ethiopian–Chinese roadbuilding crew. I was curious about the international team and I asked the Chinese foreman in English how long they had been working on the project. He didn't speak English and very little Amharic, the national language. Later on, I brought up the issue with my students, which resulted in a lively debate on the pros and cons of the Chinese in Ethiopia.

The Chinese can be found all over Ethiopia engaged in all sorts of projects, from infrastructure building to resource exploration. However, a significant bilateral study of Chinese and Ethiopian affairs that unpacks political, economic, and strategic relations has been lacking. This book is an attempt to fill the gap in the literature in Sino-African relations. It is intended to contribute to knowledge of our understanding of China and Ethiopia as the latter seeks to establish peace, stability, and—in partnership with China—economic development in the volatile region that is the Horn of Africa.

Many scholars assisted in my tentative steps in beginning to understand China and its relations with Ethiopia. Some of these are Chris Alden, London School of Economics and Political Science; Ian Taylor, University of St. Andrews; Li Anshan, Beijing University; Edmond Keller at the University of California, Los Angles and many colleagues at the Chinese in Africa/Africans in China Research Network. At Addis Ababa University, many thanks go to Kay Mathews, whose thoughtful conversation about China–Africa relations encouraged my research. Finally, I am grateful to officials in the Ethiopian Ministry of Foreign Affairs, the Ministry of Finance and Economic Cooperation, and many individuals at the Ethiopian Investment Agency. Any and all shortcomings of the research, of course, are solely mine.

Aaron Tesfaye
William Patterson University

Abbreviations

AASNP	Addis Ababa Schools Net Project
ALF	Algerian Liberation Front
AU	African Union
BRI	Belt and Road Initiative
CADIP	China Association for the Development of Industrial Parks
CCECC	China Civil Engineering Construction Corporation (CCECC)
COMESA	Common Market for East and South Africa
COSEZ	China Overseas Special Economic Zones
CPA	Comprehensive Peace Agreement
EAC	East African Community
EASTBRIG	East African Standby Brigade
EIPDC	Ethiopian Industrial Park Development Corporation
EPRDF	Ethiopian People's Revolutionary Democratic Front
EPRP	Ethiopian People's Revolutionary Party
ERC	Ethiopia Railway Corporation
ETC	Ethiopian Telecommunications Corporation
EXIM	Export Import Bank

FOCAC	Forum on China–Africa Cooperation
GTP	Growth and Transformation Plan
IGAD	Intergovernmental Authority for Development
JECC	Joint Ethiopia–China Commission
LAPSSET	Lamu Port South Sudan Ethiopia Transport Corridor
NEPAD	New Partnership for Africa's Development
OAU	Organization of African Unity
OECD	Organization for European Economic Development
PASDP	Poverty Alleviation and Sustainable Development Program
REC	Regional Economic Community
SEZ	Special Economic Zones
TAZARA	Tanzania–Zambia Railroad Project
TVET	Technical and Vocational Education and Training
UNTAG	United Nations Transition Assistance Group

Introduction

There are now many studies that explore Africa–China/China–Africa relations. But research that explores bilateral relations of African countries with China are becoming increasingly important. This is because such research unpacks political, economic, and security issues. In addition, it attempts to facilitate the examination of African agency: leaders and elites, the state, and everyday people, which better inform the impacts of China's engagement with Africa.[1] This book attempts to do that through exploration of China–Ethiopia relations. The topic was chosen because the China–Ethiopia relationship is unique in Africa. It is well known that China has relations with many African countries, but especially with resource-rich nations such as Angola, the Democratic Republic of the Congo, Nigeria, South Africa, Zambia as it marches forward in its modernization objectives with ambitions to become a global power. But Ethiopia, which has very good relations with China, does not offer such vast resources. Ethiopia is a developing nation where 80% of its total population, now 100,000 million people, are agrarian.

Thus China's interest in Ethiopia is not based on economics, although Ethiopia's large population offers a good market; it is mainly political. This is because Ethiopia offers China (a) Ethiopia's "political resources," which are the African Union (a gleaming complex rebuilt by China at a cost of $200 million) and the UN Economic Commission for Africa (the African Standby Force headquarters are located in Addis Ababa); (b) Ethiopia's geostrategic position in the Horn of Africa and influence in political and economic organizations, such as the Intergovernmental Authority for Development (IGAD) located in Djibouti; (c) the high volume of African security issues in the Greater Horn of Africa and throughout the continent, which interests China as it gets "blue helmeted" and deepens its engagement in UN peacekeeping operations.

In brief, Ethiopia indirectly provides China access to African elites who serve in various corridors of political and economic power on the continent. Ethiopia's interest in China is straightforward: it needs capital and technology in order to deepen its modernization, and China supplies both. Ethiopia is also interested in China's "know-how," its ability to feed its population, and the lifting of millions of its citizens out of poverty. A corollary mutual factor that has influenced China–Ethiopia relations is Beijing's partnership with Chinese corporations to collaborate in its agenda of "going out" into the world, or Zǔchūqū Zhànlüè

This policy also resulted in Chinese capital moving into Ethiopia and coinciding with its Growth and Transformation Plan (GTP). The plan was attractive to China because it became engaged in financing and building large projects in Ethiopia, such as roads, rail, industrial parks, and other infrastructure projects.

In introducing China–Ethiopia relations, it is important to explore the issue of Ethiopian agency. Too often, in the study of China and Africa, the former is seen as the driving force, with very little recognition given to the role of individual actors, sectors, or other entities beyond the level of state elites.[2] In fact, some scholars even entertain the notion of "state capture" by China due to the preponderance of its economic might vis-à-vis African nations.[3] However, a word of caution is in order. Such a view, while recognizing relations between Chinese and African state actors, gives much power to the former and is weak as an explanation of the relationship.[4] The fact is, African relations with China are different from state to state. Clearly, as stated above, China–Ethiopia relations are different. Ethiopian state leaders are rational actors in their calculations based on the national interest.

Such was the case of the former Ethiopian prime minister Meles Zenawi, who ushered in contemporary Ethiopian–Chinese relations in the early 1990s that focused on Ethiopia's economic development by eschewing a neoliberal economy and traditional bilateral donors, such as the World Bank and the International Monetary Fund, as well as political and economic conditionalities.[5] Ethiopian leaders of the period created an autonomous hard state, albeit in the form of a federal republic controlled by the Ethiopian People's Revolutionary Democratic Front (EPRDF)—a coalition of regional national/ethnic groups that defeated the military regime in 1991—and with loans and financing from China implemented the agriculture-led industrialization policy. Nevertheless, the ability of Ethiopian state actors—or African countries, for that matter—to negotiate well with Chinese actors was not and is not equal, nor can it be, given the weakness of Africa institutions. The facts remain that China, as a rising power, defines the terms of engagement, and discussions revolve around its plans and strategies.

China and Ethiopia: Analytical Framework

Although China has a long history of involvement with Ethiopia—diplomatic relations were established in 1970—enhanced Chinese–Ethiopian relations did not begin until the EPRDF assumed political power in 1991. The impetus for the closer relationship came about when the Ethiopian Government wanted to recalibrate its relations with the West and readjust its foreign policy with Russia and China. In 1995, Prime Minister Zenawi visited China, and subsequently the Chinese president, Jiang Zemin, stopped in Addis Ababa as part of an extensive tour of Africa. These visits culminated in the signing of a trade, economic, and technical cooperation agreement between the two nations. In the agreement, China bestowed on Ethiopia most-favored-nation status, and Addis Ababa was chosen to host the first Forum on China–Africa Cooperation (FOCAC), in 2000. Since then, China has been actively engaged in Ethiopia's economic development, offering loans and skilled manpower and helping to build highly visible infrastructure, roads, and railway systems in Addis Ababa and elsewhere. In short, for Ethiopia, China's rapprochement with Africa coincided with the efforts of the ruling party in implementing its Growth and Transformation Plan (GTP), which was part and parcel of its agriculture-led industrial development strategy for transforming the ancient polity.[6]

This study is a mid-level analysis of China–Ethiopia relations and addresses a number of questions. First, what are China's interests in Ethiopia? Is there a hierarchy of interests, with some greater than others? What are China's short-term and long-term objectives? China's interest is related to economy, security—particularly energy, and diplomacy. In terms of hierarchy, in the long term, China is primarily interested in Ethiopia because of security in terms of resources in the Greater Horn of Africa region, which includes Djibouti, Eritrea, Ethiopia, Kenya, Somalia, Sudan, South Sudan, Uganda, and, just across the Red Sea, Yemen. Ethiopia, a nation of 90 million people, is located in an unstable region. That is, the region is diverse and the problems of the different nations are interlinked; events in one country affects others, and the problems of one nation can be solved only with the involvement of others. As a consequence, for any of the nations, social, economic, and political development can be achieved only in a climate of enhanced security and stability for all. At the same time, the Horn of Africa is an important geostrategic region located just across the oil fields of the Middle East, where there has always been great power rivalry and where there is now the emergence of regional powers such as Saudi Arabia and, to an extent, Qatar.

However, it is widely believed that Ethiopia and some nations in the Horn of Africa are on the verge of an oil-driven economic revolution. This is because the hydrocarbon potential in the Horn of Africa includes yet-to-be-commercialized gas, as well as oil prospects in the early stages of investigation in Ethiopia and potential oil resources offshore from Somalia. In addition, oil resources in Uganda, Kenya, and South Sudan and emerging fossil hydrocarbon potential have piqued the interest not only of China but also of global and national companies that are building pipelines and port facilities in the Greater Horn of Africa region.[7]

In addition, the Chinese are interested in Ethiopia because it is an important player in the Horn of Africa. As a member of IGAD, it has been engaged in helping reconstruct the failed state of Somalia and has played a major role in helping achieve a fragile peace between warring elites of South Sudan, where China has a significant oil investment. Ethiopia's capital, Addis Ababa, is home to the headquarters of the African Union, built by China to the tune of $200 million and an important political institution on the continent. It is also the primary location of other important international organization such as the African Standby Force and the United Nations Commission for Africa. In brief, Ethiopia offers China an entry point in terms of its immediate long-term objectives of diplomacy with African nations.

A second set of questions includes how China leverages its relations with Ethiopia to secure its interests in the Horn of Africa region and environs. Does China have long-term interest objectives? If so, are some countries more important to China than others? The answers to some of these questions are significant because China has also forged military relations with Ethiopia. It has a military attaché in its embassy in Ethiopia, the first in sub-Saharan Africa. China supports the mediation efforts of IGAD in South Sudan, in which Ethiopia is a significant player. At the same time, as a permanent member of the UN Security

Council, China has begun to dispatch its blue-helmeted UN troops to troubled places such as Darfur, Western Sahara, Mali, and South Sudan in order to provide peace and security.[8] These interactions of China with African nations have created ideal conditions for developing its military presence overseas, which is essential in safeguarding its global investments, undergirded by its professed policy of nonalignment, respect for international boundaries, and noninterference in other countries' internal affairs.

In the Greater Horn of Africa and environs, there are now great political tensions as nations reassert their security interests. The Nile River and Ethiopia's construction of its hydroelectric project, the Great Renaissance Dam, are bones of contention that may be leading Cairo to secure the partnership of Eritrea and Somalia to secure its interests in the region. In the past, Egypt and Ethiopia backed rival forces in Somalia, prolonging Somalia's civil war. In addition, since 2015, Saudi Arabia has begun to project its power and its influence in the Greater Horn of Africa with its intervention in Yemen to crush the Iranian-backed Houthi rebels. It has also begun to build a coalition of combat units from Egypt, Sudan, and Eritrea to secure the entire African shore of the Red Sea.

It is in this complex and volatile area that China has established interim technical service stops in Oman and Sudan and has also entered an agreement to establish either a military base or a facility in Djibouti, a strategic chokepoint at the narrow strait of Bab el-Mandeb in the Red Sea.[9] But there are others who have established a foothold in the Red Sea littoral—including Turkey in Suakin Island, Sudan; Qatar in Eritrea; UAR in Somalia and Somaliland—while India and Russia are also exploring relations with countries in the region.[10]

According to a white paper produced by the Chinese government, China viewed the military base as necessary to protect its national interests:

> Its national security is more vulnerable to international and regional turmoil, terrorism, piracy, serious natural disasters and epidemics, and the security of overseas interests concerning energy and resources, strategic sea lines of communication (SLOCs), as well as institutions, personnel and assets abroad, has become an imminent issue.[11]

A final set of questions in the research concerns what obstacles China encounters in the pursuit of its national interests. Is there rivalry between China and big powers in the Greater Horn of Africa region? If so, how is China engaged in overcoming these obstacles? Is it seeking alliances in the short term? If so, with which nations in the region? The great powers are present in the Horn of Africa and its environs. The United States recently renewed its lease on Camp Lemonnier, a naval expeditionary base, for another ten years. It is using the base not only to combat terrorism in the region but also as a satellite center to monitor developments in the Middle East in which it has a national interest. France also has a military presence in Djibouti, and Japan's self-defense forces have a base for anti-piracy operations, which is expected to be bolstered to include the dispatch of patrol aircraft and the rescue of Japanese civilians in Middle East emergencies. China's presence in Djibouti is ostensibly explained by the rationale of combatting piracy, but clearly there is now a great power rivalry for control of the Red Sea shipping lanes and influence in the Greater Horn of Africa region. Ethiopia is important to China because it has the ability to project its power and influence neighbors, such as Somalia and especially South Sudan, in which China has substantial investments in oil.

Finally, China's cooperation with Ethiopia differs fundamentally from Western types of relations and is multilayered. First, the traditional relationships of Ethiopia with the industrialized nations are North to South whereas China's relationships are South to South, allowing for a two-way approach and, at least in theory, the relationships are seen by China as "win-win." Second, China's development assistance to Ethiopia, ranging from infrastructure construction to development loans, comes with no official conditionality, perhaps a legacy of its own experiences and ideology of equity. Third, relations between China and Ethiopia are bilateral, with FOCAC serving as a multilateral forum for engagement in areas related to economic, diplomatic, and social agendas. The importance of the forum was underlined by a white paper released by the Chinese state in 2006 that set forth its long-term strategic plan for deepening and increasing cooperation and consultation with African countries.

Nevertheless, China's relationship with Ethiopia is asymmetric, and for now China needs Ethiopia because it is an anchor state in the Horn of Africa, it has a strong and battle-hardened military, and it offers political stability and a large market—Ethiopia's population is expected to be 170 million by 2050. Ethiopia is one of the few nations in Africa that is on track to achieve many of the Millennium Development Goal targets set by the UN. Since 2004, Ethiopia's economy has grown by an unprecedented average of 10% a year and is expected to grow by 6.5% in the period 2016–2020.[12] For Ethiopian leaders, China is a model of a late industrializer practicing a socialist market economy, from which Ethiopia wants to learn. As a result, there have been significant exchanges of experts, scholars, and military professionals between the two countries. Courses in Cantonese and Mandarin are offered at universities in Ethiopia, and Amharic and other Ethiopian languages are taught at Chinese universities.

China's relationship with Ethiopia is not based, as one scholar claimed, on "authoritarian affinities,"[13] but rather on strategic pragmatism. After all, China has also formed relationships with other African nations that are not authoritarian, such as Botswana, Mauritius, and Tanzania, and also, for that matter, with Mexico and Australia. But then again, the United States also has a good relationship with Ethiopia because it considers the African country a strong security partner; the two nations collaborate on issues of counterterrorism and regional conflicts in Sudan and South Sudan, and U.S. drones patrol East Africa, especially Somalia. However, U.S. policy against counterterrorism in the Horn of Africa is being quickly eclipsed by the presence of China in the Red Sea littoral, including the Chinese military base in Djibouti. While the United States has a base in Djibouti, Camp Lemonnier, others such as Turkey and Qatar have military bases in Sudan and Eritrea, with Russia and India exploring the possibilities of an anchor in the area. The recent overture by Arab states and renewed interest by the United States in 2019 demonstrated by significant loans and investment is indicative of the importance of Ethiopia in the Horn of Africa.

China and Africa: An Overview

Africa–China relations have been a source of both hope and anxiety on the African continent. The hope is that China, in the spirit of the long history of African solidarity, could offer the continent a new and truly genuine partnership that would increase the prospects that the continent will achieve its developmental aspirations. However, there are anxieties about the possibility that China may end up conducting itself like Africa's traditional partners, who have been focused more on their own interests than those of Africa. Indeed, it is difficult to predict how China will use its newfound power and influence.

It is important to point out that China has viewed Africa since 1949 through a strong ideological lens.[14] This was because "the earliest independent African states (Egypt, Ethiopia, Liberia and South Africa, were pro-western at that time . . . with Ethiopia and South Africa even participating in the UN military operations in Korea to fight Chinese-backed forces in 1950–54."[15] China was not a member of the UN and Taiwan claimed it was the legitimate representative of the Chinese people. When Beijing launched the "five principles of peaceful coexistence," it began to court newly independent African countries, which it considered natural allies. During the period of the struggle for African independence, China offered military, intelligence, weapons, and training to freedom fighters ranging from Algeria to Namibia to South Africa. China's policy appealed to many African nationalists. During these heady years of good Sino-African relations, China also offered direct economic assistance in the form of low-interest loans for public projects. The most important of these was the Tanzania–Zambia Railroad Project (TAZARA).[16] The close relations in the 1950s stand in marked contrast to China's marginalization of Africa in the 1980s, when during the reforms of Deng Xiaoping, Africa was "seen as largely irrelevant . . . [as China was focused] firmly towards Japan and the United States."[17] During this period, China viewed the roots of Africa's economic crisis during the so-called "lost decade" as internal and blamed some African leaders for their uncritical embrace of socialism.[18] A major change came in 1989, when China under Jiang Zemin (1989–2002) separated foreign policy from ideology.

In the post-Tiananmen period, China, facing severe criticism from the West for its violations of human rights, underwent a major shift in its foreign policy. It openly began courting African nations, as some African leaders were in support of the Chinese state quelling the "counterrevolution." The support emanated from the principled stand that China and Africa faced twin enemies, imperialism and neo-imperialism, and that the call by the West for greater attention to human rights in China was an attempt to derail Chinese modernization and industrialization.[19] Subsequently, under the leadership of Hu Jintao (2002–2012), China began the process of improving its national security by emphasizing its responsible role in the international system and expanding its soft power globally.[20]

Thus, after Tiananmen, Beijing started a diplomatic and economic assistance offensive, first to reward African nations that had stood by

China and later to court the remaining countries. This effort enabled China to be influential in international organizations and to resist Western hegemony during the last days of the cold war.[21] Since that time, China has rapidly increased its aid to Africa, cancelled many debts, and seen a boom in China–Africa trade, with a strategic Chinese focus on oil.[22] China has become Africa's second biggest trading partner, after the United States. China has presented African nations with an attractive alternative to conditional Western aid and gained valuable diplomatic support as it has defined its international interests. This is because China has put great effort into building an overall positive image through the notion of "South–South" relations and the promotion of a "win-win" strategy based on mutual economic gain.

However, as one scholar noted, China's investment—which in most instances is a combination of loans, investment, and aid—in some African countries has been attractive because it does not embed pressures on African leaders to reform and strengthen participatory democracy, good governance, and human rights; rather, it emphasizes the principles of sovereignty in states' internal affairs, a concept that has undergirded self-perceptions of African political elites since decolonization.[23] A secondary attraction may be that Chinese development assistance is implemented faster and more efficiently than aid from the West because "the multilateral aid platform has become increasingly dysfunctional and uncoordinated, leading to wide frustration among recipient countries."[24] The question of whose aid is better is complex because aid means many things to different groups, with historical, political, economic, and cultural underpinnings.

China's role as an emerging donor in Africa has polarized actors within the developmental regime, and some have criticized China's "productivist" approach as "driven less by notions of citizenship and social rights and more in terms of accumulation functions while others welcome it as an opportunity to explore new ideas about social development."[25] In any case, China's influence is growing in Africa and raising the possibility of the emergence of its "soft power." Such a concept, of course, is descriptive rather than normative, and at times is not fully under the control of the state and may not, in some instances, deliver desirable outcomes.[26] But some Chinese scholars interpret the concept to mean more than cultural and ideological attractiveness, arguing that the main source of Beijing's soft power in Africa is the model of Chinese development combined with multilateral diplomacy and overseas assistance programs.[27] But the nature of such assistance in Africa, discussed in the Ethiopian case study in subsequent chapters, and "tied loans," which involve Chinese corporations and workers tied to African projects, has been found to be problematic.

The significance of China–Africa relationships was underscored in 1996, when President Jiang Zemin toured Africa, leading to the establishment in 2000 of FOCAC, which has become an important framework for a new type of China–Africa partnership. This platform was in turn strengthened by the Beijing Declaration, which pledged to promote the common development of China and Africa and to vigorously promote cooperation in many areas, including economics, trade, finance, agriculture, public health, science and technology, culture, education, transportation, environment, and tourism. FOCAC is a major coming-out effort by China, aimed at building mutually beneficial trade, economic, development, and political relations with Africa based on principles of "South–South" cooperation, and as a result China is making a bigger impact in Africa in terms of economic growth.

The January 2006 white paper "China's African Policy" defined China's political and economic agenda in Africa. It established the one-China principle as the political foundation for China's relations with African nations and regional organizations. Since its establishment, FOCAC has held seven ministerial summits: in 2000, in Beijing; in 2003, in Addis Ababa; in 2006, in Beijing; in 2009, in Sharm el-Sheikh Egypt; in 2013, in Lusaka, Zambia; in 2014, in Beijing; and in 2015, in Johannesburg. The Beijing Declaration, signed by China and 44 African states, is a founding document of FOCAC. Its aim is to favor the emergence of a new, just, and equitable political and economic world order in which developing countries have more effective participation in the international process of decision-making.

China's image in Africa, once viewed with suspicion, is now changing. Indeed, Chinese competition in farming, retail, and petty trade is significant, and some nations such as Malawi, Tanzania, Uganda, and Zambia have set new rules that restrict the industries or areas in which Chinese can operate; however, an increasing number of Africans say that Chinese create jobs.[28] The deepening ties between China and Africa have led some scholars to express concern over whether China is a competitor, a development partner, or an emerging hegemon.[29] Some claim that China is not genuinely interested in Africa for its development so much as for its raw materials, and its sojourners and settlers in Africa are the vanguard of a new imperialism.[30] Others are cautious and dismiss the "voracious dragon" and the "scramble for Africa" paradigms; taking a middle ground, they claim that China–Africa relations are merely driven by the self-interests of all parties.[31] The answer may be that Chinese involvement on the continent can be understood only by exploring the range of economic, diplomatic, and security rationales as well as the response of African elites to China's entreaties.[32]

In terms of economic rationale, China needs African markets for its exports. Africa imports manufacturing products from China and, since 2004, sub-Saharan Africa has recorded growth "in the 5–6 percent range, making the region an increasingly attractive market for investment and consumer goods."[33] In addition, the increase in trade and capital flows between China and Africa may also have to do with China's membership in the WTO and with trade liberalization. Also, regional free trade arrangements in Africa have enabled Chinese traders and investors to exploit economies of scale.

A secondary reason for the growing role of China in Africa is Africa's demand for infrastructure. It is an established fact that two of the major challenges in Africa are transportation and energy bottlenecks, which stifle productivity and growth. Sub-Saharan Africa has the world's least sufficient infrastructure—roads, rail links, bridges, harbors, and airports—translating to poor economic efficiencies.[34] It is widely recognized that poor infrastructure hinders agricultural performance, inhibits diversification of exports, and inhibits moving up the value chain to achieve economic growth.[35] Meeting the continental demand for improved infrastructure requires financing and technical expertise, both of which are lacking by and large in Africa, and the demand has been beneficial for China, especially in light of the minuscule amount of aid in this sector from traditional donors.

Chinese involvement in Africa is a mixture of economic assistance, investment, debt relief, and expanding markets, and Beijing is often perceived as dominating these relationships. This is because the Chinese government has created policy banks to facilitate its foreign economic activities, such as the Chinese Development Bank, the China Export-Import (Exim) Bank, and the China Agriculture Development Bank. These entities facilitate "tied" commercial investments and foreign aid. That is, these banks play a major role in selecting and supporting certain Chinese firms based on long-term strategy which is not "very different from the other Asian economies, Japan, Korea and Chinese Taiwan, which also used development finance to support certain strategic industries."[36]

It is this type of "industrial aid" to Africa that China refers to as a "win-win." China considers this aid a win for both parties because it has enabled several industries in China to mature while helping the industrial sector in Africa, which has long been neglected as most Western foreign aid focused on the social sector. It was this industrialization of Africa as an arena of investment that interested China because it wanted to shift abroad some of its industries that had matured, and Africa in many ways was an ideal partner, given China's relations with the continent since Bandung in 1955, the site of the first large-scale conference of Asian and African nations, most of which were newly independent, which took place from April 18 to 24, in Indonesia. This, however, does not mean the interests of the political and business leaders of China necessarily coincide in terms of the grand strategy in Africa. As scholars have pointed out, while the bureaucrats in Beijing are tasked with advancing China's national interests and creating a positive image of China, the objectives of Chinese corporations, in pursuit of returns on investment, may result in different outcomes.[37]

In any case, the China–Africa "win-win" scenario has been a cause of concern. As one scholar noted, "The policy of a win-win outcome may be undercut by the fact that although African leaders have openly welcomed Beijing's courtship, they have been slow to formulate strategies that will ensure that Africa and Africans benefit from the unfolding partnerships."[38] In addition, China's multifaceted relationship with African elites has raised the question of African agency, which until recently had not been considered. In other words, China's renewed interest and engagement in Africa was the main driving force behind its activities, and no recognition was given to African actors. That is, most studies focus on relations between Chinese and African state actors, resulting in crediting China with much of the power compared to Africa.[39] But recently scholars have noted that while it is true there is an interaction between Chinese and African state elites, there have also been examples of African agency, particularly in Angola, Nigeria, and Ghana.[40]

One important plank of China's increasing role in Africa is its approach to financing, which is very different from that of multilateral and bilateral institutions. Instead of undertaking whole projects, as it did in the 1960s, China now separates social services and business development projects, using aid to facilitate investments. While it does finance public goods and social services, it aids other projects that are supposed to generate revenue by providing trade credit and commercial loans through its Exim Bank, linked to output of the project, thereby aligning debt financing with repayment capacity. In other words, "China's official financing in Africa aligns debt financing of commercial projects using aid to leverage finance from nongovernment sources, and focus(es) on capital expenditure and development of the productive sectors,"[41] which explains the mix of Chinese investments in Africa.

While Chinese investments in Africa facilitate development, the biggest criticism regarding China's presence in Africa is that in its quest for resources it turns a blind eye to human rights abuses. China's noninterference policy derives from its five principles of peaceful coexistence: mutual respect for sovereignty and territorial integrity, mutual nonaggression, noninterference in others' internal affairs, equality and mutual benefit, and peaceful coexistence as set down by Premier Zhou Enlai at the Bandung Peace Conference in 1955.[42] While this policy is championed by some African leaders looking for economic growth without political preconditions, China for its part has not undermined democratic institutions or conventions and continues to work with both authoritarian and nonauthoritarian regimes. China has also not taken sides with warring factions nor stoked armed conflict, but has on occasion played peacemaker out of self-interest, such as in the South Sudan crisis.

There is also the optimistic view that looks at China–Africa relations as win-win. One positive view is that the dependence of African countries on Chinese capital goods may lead to economic growth, particularly in the form of technology transfers, provided that African countries undertake trade liberalization, which is critical in attracting Chinese capital on a nonpreferential basis, and that the policy also include openness, political stability, and good fiscal policy.[43] A similar view, with a caveat, claims that in any type of trade both positive and negative effects exist, and it is up to African leaders to mitigate the negative effect.[44]

In a similar vein, some argue that trade with China diversifies the economy of African countries and offers the possibility of a developmental state focused on reducing both urban and rural poverty.[45] But this argument is weak; economic transformation depends on many variables—not just trade—including the consensus and commitment of elites to the development agenda, the ideology of development, the institutions that can be used, and bureaucratic capacity, just to mention a few. Some scholars are blunt in their assessment of China–Africa relations, viewing the rise of Asian economies and the restructuring of the global order as a unique opportunity for Africa. They caution that the dependency theory of the past is outmoded, lacking explanatory power in today's global economy, and that the emerging global order of the 21st century offers many possibilities.[46]

Finally, there are scholars who eschew the pessimistic and/or new colonialism thesis of China–Africa relations and simply argue that the interactions are the inevitable result of globalization and processes to which Africa must respond because it has no choice.[47] Such a view underlines the fact that Chinese companies are no different from their Western counterparts; they use the same market-driven model advocated by the West, and their motivations are no different from those of Western corporations in Africa—namely, the extraction of resources and receipt of a return on investments.[48] Thus, while Chinese private investment in Africa is market-driven, it is highly competitive within China and exhibits a strong spirit of entrepreneurship; on the whole, the relationship involves a historical evolution and one should also focus on how Chinese direct investment is linked to economic cooperation.[49]

What has been missing in the above discussions, arguments, and explanations regarding China–African relations is that Africa sees China as the driving force with very little recognition given to the role of African agency beyond the level of state elites.[50] In fact, some scholars even entertain the notion of "state capture" by China due to the preponderance of its economic might vis-à-vis African nations.[51] However, others caution that such a view, while recognizing relations between Chinese and African state actors, gives too much power to the former and is weak as an explanation of the relations.[52] Their argument is that African relations with China are different from state to state, that African state elites are rational actors and in some instances have managed to create "a hybrid set of institutions to broker Chinese investment projects . . . and that social actors have influenced and derived benefits of Chinese migrants" in some African nations.[53] While the form and content of negotiations between China and Ethiopia warrants more research, in general, the ability of African state actors to negotiate with Chinese actors is not even. This is because African politics and institutions across the continent are weak, giving China the upper hand as a rising power. As a result, China defines the terms of engagement and discussions revolve around its plans and strategies.

Introduction

Methodology

This book is the result of field research in Addis Ababa, Ethiopia and its environs over a period of three years (2015–2018.) It is based on primary sources from the archives of the Investment Commission, the Ministry of Trade, and the Ministry of Finance and Economic Cooperation of the Federal Democratic Republic of Ethiopia, and interviews of officials in the above institutions. In addition, information and data from various officials and project analysts in Ethiopia's regional states were collected. Archival documents are used in this study from various government ministries in Ethiopia, as well as secondary sources from William Paterson University and other institutions in the US including insights gathered from various colleagues at international conferences who are scholars of Chinese in Africa/Africans in China Research Network

Structure of the Book

The introduction includes an analytical framework of relations between China and Ethiopia. Chapter 1 deals with Chinese–Ethiopian relations from the 1960s to the 1990s and the end of the Cold War. It describes the complex relations of Ethiopia with the great power rivalry in the Horn of Africa, China's role in the rivalry, and eventual establishment of diplomatic relations with Ethiopia. It traces the difficult relationship between China and Ethiopia during the period of military rule in Ethiopia (1974–1991), when the left-leaning military regime allied with the Soviet Union, straining Chinese–Ethiopian relations. Finally, the chapter discusses the beginning of a new relationship between China and the Federal Democratic Republic of Ethiopia, leading China to become a major player in Ethiopia's GTP, active in the building of infrastructure, electric power, and telecommunications and the realties that activity involves.

Chapter 2 focuses on contemporary Chinese–Ethiopian relations. It explores Chinese security interests in Ethiopia and in the Greater Horn of Africa. It discusses the importance of Ethiopia in the geopolitics of the region; explains why Ethiopia is important to China in light of its agreement to establish a military base/facility in Djibouti, located at the chokepoint of the Red Sea shipping lane of the strait of Bab el-Mandeb; and details the implications of the big power rivalry. This chapter also discusses Chinese diplomatic interests in Ethiopia, where the African Union and other important African and international organizations are located.

Chapter 3 is devoted to an analysis of Chinese–Ethiopian economic relations. It provides an overview of the nature of these relations and discusses whether the relations, which some have described as South–South, are likely to have a "win-win" outcome compared to outcomes with Ethiopia's traditional development partners.[54] It then explores the nature of Chinese investments in Ethiopia—investment volume, manufacturing sectors in certain industries, special economic zones (SEZs)—and examines what attracts Chinese companies to invest in Ethiopia. The chapter also explores Ethiopia's interest in China as a potential model of modernization. The discussion addresses the appropriateness of the Chinese model of economic development for Ethiopia and whether aspects of the model are transferable.

Chapter 4 investigates China–Ethiopia strategic partnerships. It begins by analyzing strategic elements in China–Ethiopia relations. It argues that China is interested in Ethiopia because it offers political resources. Addis Ababa is an African capital and the headquarters of many international organizations; the text details why these facts are important to China. It discusses how China–Ethiopia cooperation is different from traditional relations with the global North, which are based on dependency. The chapter discusses Chinese foreign assistance to Ethiopia. It explores the types and forms of assistance and why it is different from that of traditional donors. Finally, the chapter examines Chinese and Ethiopian interests in the Horn of Africa, showing how they overlap.

Chapter 5 explores Ethiopia and China's Belt and Road Initiative by discussing the role of China in building the Addis Ababa–Djibouti Railway as the first leg of the BRI in the Horn and Eastern Africa. It outlines Ethiopia's economic development plan and potential for regional integration with Horn and Eastern African nations as China embarks to connect it via Djibouti to the Lamu port in Kenya and on to Bagamoyo in Tanzania, then via the TAZAR to Zambia and South Africa.

Chapter 6 is the concluding chapter. It summarizes the main arguments and findings. It provides an overview of information discovered in China–Ethiopia relations as well as areas for further development and research.

CHAPTER 1

China–Ethiopia Relations

Looking Back and Forward

China and Ethiopia are ancient empires that experienced political and social upheavals in the 20th century. In a survey of scholarship on China's relationship with Africa, more specifically with Ethiopia, an astute scholar lists a number of similarities between China and Ethiopia that were identified by early Chinese scholars:

> First, both China and Ethiopia were ancient civilizations, they had a political organization undergoing a transformation from a feudal to a modern system, both suffered from capitalist invasion and the decline of handicraft industries, and both were victims of imperialism.[1]

While Ethiopia's revolution was usurped by the military because of a divided left, China was able to complete its revolution and assert its sovereignty under Mao Zedong (1949–1976). Subsequently, in the late 1970s and 1980s, it reformed its command economy under Deng Xiaoping, encouraging private enterprise. Later, after a period of rapprochement during the Nixon presidency, China established full diplomatic relations with the United States.

It is important to note that in the 1950s and 1960s China fully supported the struggles of colonial peoples around the world. The Chinese Revolution was a model for peasant revolts and various liberation fronts in Africa, Asia, and Latin America. But the development of China's relations with African nations was complicated by the international power struggles of the Cold War period, and China's affiliation with the Communist bloc resulted in its isolation in the 1950s. Chinese relations with Africa were made difficult by the influence of colonial powers.

As to Ethiopia, signing the Mutual Defense Assistance Agreement with the United States in 1953 and permitting the establishment of Kagnew Station in Eritrea, with listening capabilities deep into the Soviet Union, placed it decidedly in the Western camp.[2] In return, it was rewarded with infrastructure and institution building as well as with a relatively large military and economic package that made it the primary recipient of U.S. foreign aid in Africa. However, faced with the realities of African anticolonial struggles, particularly the establishment of the Organization of African Unity (OAU) in 1963, of which Ethiopia was a main founder, Ethiopia established diplomatic relations with China.

During the post–World War II period, China and Ethiopia adhered to the principle of collective security established by the UN, designed to counter any action that endangered global peace and security by agreeing that such action would lead to an appropriate collective response.[3] This principle was tested when the Korean War erupted in 1950. The United States pursued two postwar doctrines to prevent conflict. The first was collective security as defined and enshrined by the newly established UN; the second was the policy of containment of the Soviet Union and its allies. Subsequently, the UN passed a resolution to organize a UN command to intervene in the Korean conflict. This resolution led Emperor Haile Selassie I to send Ethiopian troops, equipped by the United States, to do battle with the Chinese in Korea.[4] Some scholars have suggested that the decision of Ethiopia to commit its troops in the Korean conflict may have been influenced by the calculation that such support would result in the further equipping of its army by the United States, thereby improving Ethiopia's leverage in future discussions over regions in the Horn of Africa.[5]

Imperial Ethiopia and China: Pragmatic Relations, 1955–1974

Chinese–Ethiopian relations did not begin until China stepped into the international arena in the 1950s. That is because the "country that captured Ethiopia's attention in (East) Asia in the imperial period

(1923–74) was Japan [and] for historical and ideological reasons, China was perceived as the 'other,' and this image persisted . . . until 1964."⁶ The main reason for Ethiopia's interest in Japan was the influence of a young generation of Ethiopians, living at the turn of the 19th century who wanted to solve the problems of underdevelopment by emulating the Japanese model of industrialization because it had provided its people peace, prosperity, and independence while Ethiopia's underdevelopment had produced the opposite.⁷ These Ethiopian modernizers advocated— their influence peaking in the 1920s and 1930s—a non-Western model of economic development based on the Meiji transformation (1868–1912).⁸ However, beginning in the late 1930s, as fascism reared its head in the world and Japan invaded China, there was "great sympathy by the Chinese towards the Ethiopian people in their struggle against the Italian invasion."⁹ The Nationalist Party (Kuomintang) of the National Government of the Republic of China led by General Chiang Kai-shek strongly opposed the 1935 Italian aggression toward Ethiopia.

The modern relationship between China and Ethiopia began at the first Asia–Africa Conference, held in Bandung, Indonesia, in 1955. The Bandung event has been characterized as an anticapitalist conference.¹⁰ But in fact it was a gathering of newly independent countries and had a major influence on the global nonaligned movement. The conference was seen as being anti-Western and antiuniversalist but was in reality a major postwar event for articulation of the norms of human rights and universal organization.¹¹ That is, the objectives of Bandung were

> [to get] rid of the sphere-of-influence politics and the Cold War by enabling Africa–Asia to take the leading role in actively responding to, and overcoming, barriers stemming from being incorporated into the Cold War after liberation from colonial power. In this way, the conference's final communiqué promotes world peace, economic and cultural cooperation, human rights and self-determination, as well as concerns for subordinated people.¹²

The spirit of Bandung was not realized because, given Cold War realities, some nations wanted to blaze independent paths and sought to use the nonaligned movement to advance their agendas.¹³ China embarked on spreading Mao Zedong's revolutionary ambitions worldwide. As one scholar observed,

> [China] as a country ... itself had experienced the heavy weight of imperialism, [and] the Chinese government was attuned to African sensitivities on this point. This approach set the Chinese apart from Soviet and other European communists, who were often keen to meddle in African countries' internal affairs as part of their own policies of cultivating satellite states, just as the capitalist ex-colonial bloc did.[14]

But some nations such as Egypt saw the movement as an opportunity to advance Pan-Arabism in the Middle East, and India set its own direction in international relations, focusing after its conflict with China (1962) on building its defense sector and securing its immediate neighborhood.

Nevertheless, it was at the Bandung Conference that Zhou Enlai, the premier of China and the leader of the Chinese delegation, sought common ground that was widely accepted by the participants and led to relations with African countries and the establishment of a Chinese embassy in Egypt. There is no evidence that during this period China and Ethiopia entered into any formal relationship, but the conference laid the groundwork for solidarity and cooperation. In 1956, China sent a cultural delegation to Africa, which was received by the Ethiopian emperor Haile Selassie. Although Ethiopian and Chinese delegates met again from December 26, 1957 to January 1, 1958 at the Afro-Asian Solidarity Conference held in Cairo, Ethiopia did not support China's entry into the UN and it abstained during the UN General Assembly vote on Resolution 505 in 1952 because of its close alliance with the United States, which, along with others, opposed the admission of China to the UN following the Korean War, supporting instead the Republic of China, based in Taiwan, which kept its membership in the international body until 1971.

It was not until the later years of the 1950s that Ethiopia began to assert an independent foreign relations policy, as nationalism and anticolonial struggles began to spread following the Accra Summit in 1958. The Summit, led by Kwame Nkrumah of Ghana, was the first conference of independent African states. Although there were initial differences among delegates on the thorny issues of whether to open the conference to nationalist liberation fronts, such as the Algerian Liberation Front (ALF), that were still engaged in armed struggle against colonialism and of the recognition of the Palestine Liberation Organization (PLO), in the end there was a wide measure of agreement in supporting the independence of African nationalism in all its manifestations. Thus, Ethiopia finally abandoned its traditionally aloof attitude to African affairs and swung right into the mainstream of African nationalism.

A secondary reason that swayed Ethiopia to begin to craft an independent foreign policy may have been the fact that the United States provided financial assistance for Egypt to build the Aswan Dam over the Nile River without consulting Ethiopia. Egypt's plans did not bear fruit with the World Bank because President Nasser of Egypt attempted to strike a deal with the United States in the aftermath of the Suez conflict of 1956 that did not work out. U.S.–Egyptian relations were ruptured for two reasons. First, Egypt and Syria took steps toward a larger pan-Arab state and because the newly created "United Arab Republic (UAR) was viewed as an anti-Western entity."[15] As advocate of pan-Arabism, Nasser supported Iraqi nationalism, which was beginning to weaken Britain's influence in the Middle East. The upshot was that Ethiopia recalibrated its foreign policy, resulting in a visit by the emperor to the Soviet Union in 1959, and soon after supported China's entry to the UN.

Ethiopia's process of establishing diplomatic relations with China was complicated by at least three factors. First, China was a socialist country and Ethiopia a monarchy, and the able Ethiopian foreign ministry professionals who advised the emperor were wary of the consequences of relations between the two. Second, China's support for the Eritrean Liberation Front, which was seeking Eritrea's independence from Ethiopia, complicated Ethiopian–Chinese relations. Eritrea's President Isayas Afeworki, then head of the Eritrean People's Liberation Front, had obtained his military training in 1966–1967 at the Nanjing Army Command College in Nanjing, China. The third complication was the Mutual Defense Agreement that was signed with the United States in 1942, by which the United States equipped and trained the Ethiopian armed forces.[16]

But during this period China had established full diplomatic relations with Ethiopia's neighbor Sudan and Beijing was wooing Ethiopia through several educational and cultural visits. There was also a flurry of letters between China's chairman Liu Shaoqi and Emperor Haile Selassie, eventually culminating in the latter sending a cultural delegation to China in 1962. The situation was further complicated by Taiwan's desire to establish diplomatic relations with Ethiopia, but this desire did not mature.

It was not until 1963–1964, when Premier Zhou Enlai embarked on an African tour, that relations between China and Ethiopia began to show some results. Although Ethiopia was not on the list of counties to be visited, Haile Selassie—quickly emerging as a continental leader—invited Zhou to visit Ethiopia. But to avoid offending his U.S. ally and to ensure continued U.S. foreign aid, the emperor decided the visit would be in Asmara, at that time a province of Eritrea, a plan to which the astute diplomat Zhou agreed.[17] The main concern of Ethiopia at the meeting was Chinese neutrality in the Ethiopia–Somalia dispute; this disagreement was to remain a stumbling block to the establishment of full diplomatic relations. It is also important to note that Zhou's stopover was preceded by the emperor's second visit to the United States, in October 1963, during which Ethiopia requested that the Kennedy administration provide more military assistance to combat adherents of "Greater Somalia." The request was granted because of U.S. concerns of "increased communist activity [in the region] . . . and appreciation of the emperor's moderating influence in Africa"; as a result, the Kagnew Station was expanded.[18]

The 1960s witnessed an open ideological rift between China and the Soviet Union stemming from their divergent national interests and different interpretations of Marxism–Leninism. The split had to do with competition for who should lead world communism. Africa became a Cold War zone where China, the Soviet Union, and the United States collided. The Congo crises of 1961–1965 set the stage for Cold War politics in Africa and provided some clue to China's interest in Africa during Africa's first decade of independence struggles for those countries that were still colonized.[19] But Taiwan was also courting Africa, and its ambassador to Ethiopia managed to get an audience with Haile Selassie in 1960, who agreed in principle to establish diplomatic relations. However, the fast-developing diplomatic overtures of the People's Republic of China toward Ethiopia scuttled Taiwan's efforts. During this period, the ideological split between China and the Soviet Union, early in the 1960s, and ensuing nationalism resulted in confrontation over Damansky or Zhenbao Island.[20] Although a major conflict was averted, the dispute opened an opportunity for the United States, during the Nixon administration, to establish rapprochement with China in order to isolate the Soviet Union.[21]

The Sino-Soviet ideological split did not directly affect Ethiopia—the left did not fully emerge until the mid-1970s—but the winds of change in the Cold War period created a diplomatic opening. A stumbling block to diplomatic relations was Chinese military aid to the Eritrean Liberation Front, which came at the same time Soviet arms were flowing to the Eritrean People's Liberation Front. After China completely stopped its provision of arms to the group, Ethiopia and China established full diplomatic relations in 1970.[22] Soon after, perhaps indirectly influenced by Ethiopia, other African nations began to take similar steps. In 1971, 26 African countries, including Ethiopia, voted in favor of UN General Assembly Resolution 2758 recognizing the People's Republic of China as the sole legitimate representative of the Chinese people at the UN and restoring Beijing's seat in the UN Security Council.

In the same year, Haile Selassie and Mao met in Beijing and formed several trade and economic agreements by which China allocated interest-free loans, built various factories and projects, and dispatched many teams of Chinese experts to assist in rural electrification as well as provide technical cooperation that led Ethiopian airlines to establish a full air transportation service. But by and large, Chinese–Ethiopian trade relations were very limited due to the differing natures of their economies. Still, the political winds of change had begun in Ethiopia, sparked by its great famine in 1973 as well as a global oil crisis; the result was the tottering of the ancien régime and its eventual collapse in 1974.

The Military Regime and China: Fragile Solidarity, 1974–1991

During the decade and a half of the military regime (1974–1990), Ethiopia–China relations continued with China genuinely interested initially in the socialist aspect of the Ethiopian revolution, particularly its land nationalization policies. Several educational and cultural exchanges took place between the two countries. But by the late 1970s, the military regime, beleaguered by the urban guerrilla warfare conducted by the left, Eritrean nationalists, and Somali irredentists, eventually succeeded in establishing a modicum of political stability with the assistance and influence of the Soviet Union and Cuba. In 1984, the Chinese Xinhua News Agency representatives were expelled, and Ethiopia increasingly fell under the influence of the Soviet Union and the Eastern bloc nations.[23]

In general, Chinese–Ethiopian relations were amicable during the early years of the military regime (1974–1978), but after that complications set in because of China's policy in Somalia, which invaded Ethiopia in 1977; China supported the Western Somali Liberation Front in the

Ogaden region of Ethiopia. The politics of "Greater Somalia" and the irredentist ambitions of its leaders during this period is treated elsewhere.[24] But suffice it to note that soon after the invasion, Somalia's President Siad Barre visited China and was provided with a loan of $28 million for the purpose of road construction, although China pledged it was neutral in the conflict and would abide by the UN and OAU decision on the matter. This and other Chinese activity, such as sending military aircraft to Egypt, did not go over well with the Ethiopian government. But perhaps the final straw in Sino-Ethiopian relations under the military regime was Ethiopia's alliance with the Soviet Union, at that time China's enemy.

The immediate concern of Ethiopia during this period was to win the conflict in Eritrea and the war with Somalia. Achieving both depended on maintaining internal political stability through a strong military and creating a structure conducive to socialist development. These required an alliance that would guarantee an immediate and massive inflow of armaments. In the 1970s, China provided the Eritrean Liberation Front with weapons. Ethiopia and China also had different strategies on rebel insurgency in Sudan; Ethiopia supported the southern insurgents because Sudan was supporting Eritrean guerrillas, and China backed the national government in Khartoum for one important reason: "it was buying oil at a price discounted by Sudan because of its limited market and lack of refining capabilities."[25] During this period, a new Ethiopia proclaimed support for and solidarity with socialist countries. It branded China as reactionary in order to curry favor with Fidel Castro, who was visiting Ethiopia and was a staunch ally of the Soviet Union.[26] The upshot was that by 1977 Ethiopian–U.S. relations were ruptured and the military government terminated the Ethio-U.S. Mutual Defense Agreement due to promises of massive flow of arms from the Soviet Union.

During this period, the Soviets were very much involved in Somalia, with relations beginning in 1974; they were engaged in irrigation and dam-building projects. In Ethiopia, the Eritrean nationalist fronts scored major victories and in the Ogaden the Western Somalia Liberation Front often disrupted rail lines from Djibouti. In Addis Ababa itself and in other major urban areas, there was significant urban guerilla warfare between the Ethiopian People's Revolutionary Party (EPRP), an underground Marxist group, and the military, recounted elsewhere. After this period of upheaval in 1978, the Soviets stopped their support of Somalia and began to supply arms to Ethiopia.

The alliance with the Soviets and the Eastern bloc, especially with Cuba, whose troops fought in the Ogaden, eventually payed dividends at least in terms of increasing Ethiopia's military capabilities. The Ethiopian military regime's growing relations with the Soviet Union and increasing distance from China were based on its national interests. Ethiopian leaders believed China was helping its enemies—Somalia, the Eritrean Liberation Front, and the EPRP. Nevertheless, in 1978, China built a diesel power station at Bonga in southwestern Ethiopia, and by 1982 it had constructed a 186 miles-long highway between Woldeya (capital of north Wollo) and Werota (in the Gondar zone of the Amhara region), which is still known today as the "China Road." Meanwhile, in 1978, the leader of the Ethiopian military regime, Colonel Mengistu Haile Mariam, visited Moscow and signed the Treaty of Friendship and Cooperation and condemned China. In 1979, Ethiopia ordered the ambassador of China to close the Xinhua News Agency office in Addis Ababa.

In the 1980s, Ethiopia considered ending its diplomatic relations with China. However, cooler heads prevailed as a rupture in relations would have canceled several economic and trade relations and would simply have led China to side with Somalia. In 1982, with the beginning of new Sino-Soviet relations, Chinese–Ethiopian relations began to improve, especially after China provided food assistance in Ethiopia's 1980 famine and dispatched medical teams to affected areas. Finally, in 1987, with the formal establishment of the People's Democratic Republic of Ethiopia, Mengistu visited China and met with Deng Xiaoping, who had led China's economic reform and export-led growth, beginning in 1978. But when Mengistu returned from China, his military regime faced stiff resistance from popular regional forces and urban dwellers. By 1989, the Ethiopian military regime, under assault by both the Ethiopian People's Revolutionary Democratic Front (EPRDF) and its ally, the Eritrean People's Liberation Front, as well as others, began to totter. In 1991, the EPRDF marched into Addis Ababa and established the Transitional Government of Ethiopia (1991–1994.)

China Returns to Ethiopia

It is important to note that contemporary China's interest in Ethiopia, in fact in Africa, did not begin until the ascendency of Jiang Zemin to political power (1989–2002). From its revolution in 1949 until Jiang's tenure, China saw Africa through a strong ideological lens.[27] In time, under the leadership of Hu Jintao, China began the process of improving its national security by emphasizing its responsible role in the international system and expanding its soft power globally.[28] This ushered in important changes, and China became pragmatic, separating foreign policy from ideology.

In Ethiopia, too, important changes had taken place. In May 1991, the EPRDF established a transitional government and in 1993 Eritrea declared its independence. Subsequently, Ethiopia reordered state–society relations, ending the unitary state in favor of federalism based on self-determination of its nationalities; it established a federal government made up of fourteen regions. Five of the regions subsequently merged to become the Southern Region, thereby guaranteeing a modicum of peace in the ten regions that made up the country.[29] These changes in Ethiopia coincided with the end of the Cold War, and the new leaders, once ardent Marxists but now faced with the realities of globalization, recalibrated Ethiopia's foreign policy to include Russia and began sending feelers to China. As a result, Beijing sent a new ambassador to Addis Ababa.[30]

During this period, China initiated its policy of "going out" into the world. China would utilize international resources and markets and emphasize an export-oriented economy, which would eventually establish good economic relations with other nations.[31] The intent of this "opening up" program (*gaige kaifang*) was to integrate China into global capitalism as a means of reviving its former prosperity, which, after protracted internal upheaval, had been destroyed by a series of foreign interventions and civil wars spanning the 19th and early 20th centuries. In this era of hope and optimism, in 1995, the late prime minister of Ethiopia, Meles Zenawi, visited China, and Jiang subsequently stopped in Addis Ababa as part of an extensive tour of Africa.

For Ethiopia, rehabilitating the national economy and devastated communities was a central plank of its development objectives. In order to achieve these objectives, it set out to build links with industrial nations to attract foreign investment as well as technology. A link was created with China when Jiang visited Ethiopia in 1996 and signed the Fourth Agreement on Economic and Trade Cooperation. The agreement bestowed on Ethiopia most-favored-nation status. In 1998, a Joint Ethiopia–China Commission (JECC) was established between the two governments. Since then, China has been actively engaged in Ethiopia's economic development, offering loans and skilled manpower and helping to build highly visible infrastructure, roads, and railway systems in Addis Ababa and elsewhere. In return, Ethiopia underlined its political support of China on the Taiwan issue and expressed its appreciation of China's noninterference policy.

This is because Ethiopia's ruling party, the EPRDF, was faced with domestic and external challenges—Ethiopian diaspora—to its one-party system. During the first multiparty election held in 1995 the winner was the ruling party, but the May 2005 election was the most significant in the country to date. This is because, the election gave a more credible opportunity to Ethiopians to participate en masse, and was one of the rare instances in which poorly organized political organizations outside state power mounted a considerable electoral challenge to the EPRDF, which allowed its opponents to campaign relatively freely and openly. As the events of the 2005 election unfolded, it soon became obvious the opposition was riven by internal rivalry. The opposition was defeated. In the immediate aftermath of the 2010 elections, opposition parties claimed Ethiopia faced the prospect of one-party rule for the foreseeable future. The 2010 and 2015 elections have created a situation where the opposition has gone from winning some seats in parliament to losing all of them. The 2010 result clearly reasserted the EPRDF's domination of the Ethiopian political landscape, in 2015, the EPRDF won again, raising many questions about the future of multiparty politics in the country.

In any case, the strengthening of China–Ethiopia relations coincided with the efforts of the ruling party, the EPRDF, to transform the nation through the implementation of the Growth and Transformation Plan (GTP), an agriculture-led industrial development strategy.[32] The major plank of the strategy, the growth of the agricultural sector, required substantial external investment, including investment in new, large-scale commercial farming operations, as well as major improvements in market systems and infrastructure. Toward this end, China established a technological training center that cost $6.4 million under the economic and technological cooperation agreements signed in 2006 and 2007. The main purpose of the center was to promote the transfer of physical agricultural technologies and knowledge to enhance local capacity building through demonstration and training.[33]

The economic relations between China and Ethiopia were buttressed with military cooperation, which began in 1994 when Qian Qichen, vice premier of China, visited Ethiopia and began talks on growing the existing military relations. The visit was reciprocated with a high-level

Ethiopian military delegation to Beijing. In 1997, China appointed a military attaché to its embassy in Ethiopia. In 2000, Ethiopia was co-chair of the Forum on China–Africa Cooperation (FOCAC). The forum is an institutional framework for cooperation because Africa is interested in, among other things, natural resources, markets, and support in the international arena. FOCAC offers African states an alternative in terms of South–South cooperation in economic and political fields.[34] But there are imbalances in China–Africa relations. China is much more coherent in its African agenda, whereas African nations face difficulty due to the diverse interests and lack of a common strategy among their leaders.[35]

Ethiopia hosted the second ministerial conference of FOCAC, which met December 15–16, 2003, in Addis Ababa, the headquarters of the African Union. Present at the opening ceremony were Chinese premier Wen Jiabao; Ethiopian prime minister Meles Zenawi; the president of the African Union, Alpha Oumar Konare; six African presidents; and a representative of the UN. The major agenda at the conference was how to achieve and strengthen mutually beneficial pragmatic cooperation, while the main achievement was the *Forum on China–Africa Cooperation and Addis Ababa Action Plan 2004–2006*, a declaration in which China outlined several principles and measures it would undertake in its relations with Africa. The areas of cooperation included peace and security on the continent; multilateral cooperation in international affairs, including with the African Union and the New Partnership for African Development; economic development involving agriculture, infrastructure building, trade, and tourism; debt relief; social development; medical/public health; and cultural exchanges.[36]

At this conference, China underlined the importance of Africa's developing mineral and energy sectors for mutual benefit and access to Africa's markets for Chinese-manufactured products that cost less than products produced in Africa yet were of reasonable quality. Second, the conference offered new opportunities for China to export to Africa's growing consumer markets as well as investment opportunities in African economies that would benefit both countries in areas such as mineral extraction, construction, and telecommunications. Finally, China emphasized the spirit and objectives of internationalism, the importance of African votes in the UN, and promotion of equal treatment in international relations as well as advancing the one-China policy, which insists that Taiwan and mainland China are inseparable parts of a single China.

Ethiopia's objective during the conference was to fully utilize China's development experience and possibilities for technical know-how assistance, and at the same time secure markets in China for Ethiopian products. After the conference, Chinese–Ethiopian relations accelerated in terms of both trade and investments. The reasons for the close relationship were many. One was Ethiopia's GTP, an ambitious industrial policy that aimed to foster broad and sustained development. The major plank of the GTP was agriculture-led development, but the hope was that in time the contribution of the industrial sector would increase.[37] However, although transformation of the economy did occur, sustained growth was made difficult by extensive budget shortfalls inherited from the past military regime's control of the economy and war spending.[38] In practice, this had meant dependence on external borrowing and inflows of grant-in-aid. But today China provides "soft" loans and has provisioned road and rail construction as well as installation of larger electric power stations, a topic discussed in a subsequent chapter.

China–Ethiopia economic relations have been bolstered by political support from the governments of the two countries. The ruling party of Ethiopia has shown significant interest in the Asian model of development and anticipates learning from many of China's experiences to deepen its own growth and transformation objectives. One scholar underlined that fact:

> Ethiopia is one case where China's post-reform development trajectory has indeed been influential in shaping policymakers' developmental goals and strategies. . . . The final seven years of former Prime Minister Meles Zenawi's rule, in particular, were marked by a clear desire to draw broad lessons from China's success.[39]

There is however some debate on the "Beijing Consensus," which asserts that China's post-reform development experiences transformed global development practices by encouraging imitation abroad.[40] In the case of Ethiopia, there may be constraints in the total transferability, primarily due to Ethiopia's institutional contexts and environments, but there may also be opportunities.[41] Nevertheless, to achieve its objectives, Ethiopia has provided incentives for foreign direct investment, such as tax relief for foreign direct investment capital imports, and China has provided generous incentives to its firms investing in Ethiopia, particularly for those in manufacturing industries.[42]

In 2001, China signed an agreement with Ethiopia to strengthen Ethiopia's Technical and Vocational Education and Training (TVET) institutions, considered key in developing human resources, particularly in the agricultural sector and rural development. The TVET initiative is involved in agricultural vocational education; it involves curriculum planning and China sending teachers to Ethiopian agricultural schools.

China–Ethiopia relations have also been strengthened by exchanges of teachers and students. The Chinese Young Volunteers Serving Africa program started in 2000 with a few hundred students but grew to number in the thousands, with the first batch of volunteers arriving in Ethiopia in 2006.[43] Educational exchange has been augmented by long-term scholarships offered to Ethiopians attending school in China, with graduates returning to Ethiopia as instructors in the Ethio-China Polytechnic College. China has also established a Confucius Institute in Ethiopia, which provides special Chinese courses to Ethiopian diplomats and offers scholarships at *Hanban*, its headquarters in Beijing.[44]

China and Ethiopia have also forged military relations, and the military relationship has undergone noteworthy developments. Since 1998, there have been high-level visits of military leaders between the two nations with the objective of promoting cooperation. Some Ethiopian military personnel have been trained in China, but whether this leads to specific agreements between China and Ethiopia has not as yet been established.

China–Ethiopia relations can be divided into three distinct periods: the period of initial diplomatic relations (1970–1974), the time of fragile relations under Ethiopia's military regime and its ally the Soviet Union (1974–1990), and new and deeper relations under the EPRDF government. The first periods of Chinese–Ethiopian relations were characterized by caution, given that China was highly ideological, and Ethiopia was a conservative empire. But overall China's establishment of diplomatic relations with Ethiopia in 1970 paid dividends for both countries because Ethiopia was a major supporter of Africa's independence movements and a founding partner of the OAU in 1963. Formal relations between China and Ethiopia eventually facilitated the support of many African states for the one-China principle. In the second period (1974–1990), China–Ethiopia relations were strained due to Cold War politics and Chinese competition in the Horn of Africa with the Soviet Union and the United States, especially its involvement in Somalia in the late 1970s.

The third phase of China–Ethiopia relations began in 1991, when the EPRDF overthrew the military regime in Ethiopia and recalibrated its foreign policy at the end of the Cold War. China–Ethiopia relations have deepened for a variety of reasons, which are detailed in subsequent chapters. First, China is interested in Ethiopia because it is an anchor state with influence in most of the Horn of Africa nations in which China has economic interests. The region has become the new frontier for oil and gas exploration, with many global companies positioning themselves there.[45] China is also interested in Ethiopia for strategic reasons, and the agreement to establish a military/naval base in Djibouti, across the strait of Bab el-Mandeb, which controls the Red Sea lane, means China needs a strong military ally in the region.

Ethiopia, for its part, is interested in China because of China's accomplishments as a late modernizer. While the Ethiopia regime has its supporters and detractors, China is heavily invested in Ethiopia in terms of providing loans, building infrastructure, and sharing technical know-how, and China has begun a robust exchange of experts and is involved in knowledge transfers to Ethiopia. But are China–Ethiopia relations a new form of cooperation based on South–South solidarity or a new form of dependency? An attempt will be made to answer this question and others in subsequent chapters.

Conclusion

This chapter traced Chinese and Ethiopian relations going back to the imperial era of the Emperor Haile Selassie, continuing into the subsequent military regime that overthrew the feudal order, and including contemporary relationships. It explained how China under Mao Zedong, isolated after the Korean War of 1952 and at the height of the Cold War, was highly ideological, encouraged independence movements in Africa and Asia, and met with Ethiopian delegates at the 1955 Bandung Conference in Indonesia. It underlined how relations between China and Ethiopia were made difficult as the latter entered into a Mutual Defense Agreement with the United States. Other complications in terms of establishing diplomatic relations were that China was governed by the Communist Party while Ethiopia was governed by a monarchy and the intelligentsia in the foreign ministry advised caution. An additional issue was China's support for the Eritrean Liberation Front and Chinese neutrality in the Ethiopian–Somali dispute and Mogadishu's vison for

"Greater Somalia." The situation was further complicated by Taiwan's desire to establish diplomatic relations with Ethiopia. The chapter also discussed how the Sino-Soviet ideological split and the winds of change during the Cold War created a diplomatic opening leading to a thawing of Chinese–U.S. relations and 26 African nations at the UN recognizing China as the sole legitimate representative of the Chinese people; this led to the restoration of China's seat on the UN Security Council. Finally, the chapter explained how the Sino-Soviet split facilitated U.S.–Chinese relations and eventually led to Sino-Ethiopian diplomatic relations.

But the chapter also noted that such diplomatic relations were fragile and the military regime that overthrew Ethiopia's feudal order, faced with two rebellions—in Eritrea and in the Ogaden—and an urban uprising by a faction of the Ethiopian left, entered fully into the Soviet sphere of influence, which provided it with weapons to establish political order. Although the military regime of Ethiopia still had full diplomatic relations with China, with the signing of the Treaty of Friendship and Cooperation with the USSR, Sino-Ethiopian relations were very restrained. The chapter underlined how Ethiopia's nationalities led by the Ethiopian People's Revolutionary Democratic Front (EPRDF) and the Eritrean People's Liberation Front, were able to defeat the military regime, leading in 1993 to the de facto independence of Eritrea and in 1995 to the establishment of a federal republic in Ethiopia.

Finally, the chapter provided an outline of China's return to Ethiopia with the ascendancy to power of President Jiang Zemin (1993–2003) and the sending of a new Chinese ambassador to Ethiopia. The end of the Cold War in the 1990s also saw the recalibration of Ethiopia's foreign policy, which coincided with China's "opening up" program, which began to integrate its economy into global capitalism as a means of reviving its prosperity, leading to visits of Ethiopia's former prime minister Meles Zenawi to China and subsequent visits to Ethiopia by Jiang. These visits culminated in 1998 with Ethiopia's support of China on the Taiwan issue and China granting Ethiopia most-favored-nation trading status. Subsequently, this led to the signing of the JECC, paving the way for political, economic, and social relations between the two nations. The next chapter unpacks and discusses contemporary Chinese–Ethiopian relations. Specifically, it focuses on Chinese diplomatic and security interests and Ethiopia's interest in learning about China's rapid industrialization.

CHAPTER 2

Contemporary Chinese–Ethiopian Relations

Contemporary relations between China and Ethiopia began soon after the Ethiopian People's Revolutionary Democratic Front (EPRDF) gained control of state power in 1991. While the previous military regime of Ethiopia was allied with the former Soviet Union, the end of the Cold War along with the Soviet Union's collapse opened a path and new opportunities for Ethiopia to expand its diplomatic and economic relations globally. However, it is also important to underline that Ethiopia and China had enjoyed 35 years of diplomatic relations and had at various international forums, such as the Non-Aligned Movement and the UN, advanced the interests of developing nations.

    China is interested in Ethiopia for diplomatic, security, and economic reasons as the latter is a key player not only in the Horn of Africa but in the African Union (AU) as well. Ethiopia places economic diplomacy at the helm of its foreign policy and gives importance to drawing relevant lessons from the emerging Asian powers, particularly in the economic realm. China's fast-track industrialization in the last three decades, its ability to feed its population through the green revolution and lift more than two hundred million of its citizens out of poverty, and its economic reform and policy of "Four Modernizations" under Deng Xiaoping are important milestones. As Ethiopia embarks on a deepening of its modernization process, China's mix of a command and market economy and state-led development seems an attractive model to emulate.

    Scholars are, of course, divided as to the appropriateness of the Asian model in Africa, arguing that development is a long process and questioning whether the cultural experiences of Asia are relevant to

Africa.[1] Some like the idea of "self-directed development," such as was undertaken in Singapore under Lee Kuan Yew and South Korea under Syngman Rhee.[2] Whatever the different views may be, the Ethiopian state has exhibited in the last decade rapid economic growth, and the World Bank claims its agriculture-led industrialization policy will transform the ancient polity into a middle-income nation by 2050.[3] In any case, Ethiopia has undertaken a proactive policy to strengthen its relations with China, while the latter has shown readiness to share with Ethiopia its developmental experiences. China and Ethiopia are proponents of South–South cooperation, which is founded upon "first, sincerity, friendship and equality; second, mutual benefit, reciprocity and common prosperity; third, mutual support and close coordination; and fourth, learning from each other and seeking common development."[4]

The Chinese model of development based on these precepts, which promote economic and social development with cautious political reform, has appealed to Ethiopian leaders. As a result, there have been high-level visits by the former prime minister of Ethiopia, Meles Zenawi, to China in 1995 and 2004 as well as visits to Ethiopia by former president of China Jiang Zemin in 1996 and Premier Wen Jiabao in 2003, leading to dialogue and the strengthening of relations between the two countries. In addition, it is important to note that the launching of the 2000 Forum on China–Africa Cooperation, on the initiative of China, was highly instrumental in revitalizing the decades-old relations between China and Ethiopia, with the latter seizing the opportunity by hosting the second ministerial conference forum in Addis Ababa.

China–Ethiopia cooperation is multifaceted; the two nations have put in place important instruments that promote economic cooperation. Several bilateral agreements have been signed regarding developmental assistance, agriculture, trade, investment promotion and protection, and education and tourism. The fleshing out of these agreements is conducted by the Trade, Economic, and Technical Committee of the Joint Ministerial Commission established by the two nations.

Chinese Political Interests in Ethiopia

There are several factors to consider in China's diplomatic interests in Ethiopia. One obvious fact is that Addis Ababa is an intercontinental diplomatic hub hosting (a) the AU, whose headquarters was renovated and built by China; (b) the UN Economic Commission for Africa; and (c) the Intergovernmental Authority for Development (IGAD) located in nearby Djibouti. Additionally, plans are underway for the AU to move the headquarters of the New Partnership for Africa's Development (NEPAD) from South Africa to Addis Ababa. It is important to note that China's policy of noninterference in the domestic politics of African nations is key to its relationships with African leaders. This policy is not new but goes back to the Bandung Conference of 1955. The only official condition China has set on this relationship is the following:

> The one-China principle is the political precondition and foundation for the establishment and development of China's relations with African countries and regional organizations. . . . The overwhelming majority of African countries abide by the one-China principle, refuse to have official relations and contacts with Taiwan, and support China's great cause of reunification.[5]

In any case, the above continental and regional organizations offer China an opportunity for close contact with African leaders as well as with eminent personages who influence the domestic and foreign policies of individual African nations.

A second variable is the reality that Ethiopia, with the largest standing army in sub-Saharan Africa, at 130,000 strong, is a force for stability in the Horn of Africa but is also strategically located there. Although Ethiopia is still influential in Mogadishu, having helped establish the Federal Government of Somalia, it also has close relations with Somaliland, with its capital city Hargeisa. Although unrecognized by the international community, Somaliland has been a self-declared de facto sovereign state since 1991. It has not been recognized internationally because it is considered an autonomous region of Somalia. Ethiopia's interest in Somaliland is tied to the port of Berbera because it needs to reduce its dependence on Djibouti,[6] and its close relations with Hargeisa may have opened the opportunity for a major Chinese business group to visit Somaliland and engage in talks regarding expanding the port on the Indian Ocean.

Ethiopia is also deeply involved with its western neighbors in the Republic of South Sudan, which is now plagued with on-again, off-again civil war fueled by competition for the levers of state power with the objective of commanding the nation's resources.[7] Ethiopia has concerns for the security of its federal form of governance due to a rebel Nilotic ethnic group that straddles the Ethiopia–South Sudan border, the Anuak militants. This group, which lives in western Ethiopia and South Sudan, has established a liberation front.[8] China and Ethiopia thus have a common interest in political stability in South Sudan. The oil being refined there by China that is critical for its energy needs is also critical to Ethiopia, which is landlocked and would like to acquire it through a cross-border pipeline. But both China and Ethiopia have had to contend with the politics of two Sudans because at present South Sudan's oil flows through Port Sudan in the north.[9]

Thus, Chinese and Ethiopian interests in the Horn of Africa have led to a close partnership that includes military cooperation, with Beijing supplying Ethiopia with artillery, light armored vehicles, and troop transport. These relations have also resulted in several Ethiopian officers visiting China for training. This military relationship was cemented when Ethiopia signed a military cooperation agreement with Beijing in 2005 for training, exchange of technologies, and joint peacekeeping missions.[10] This close cooperation is buttressed by the presence of a military attaché, one of the few on the continent, in the Chinese embassy in Addis Ababa. In 2016, Fan Changlong, vice chairman of China's Military Commission, visited Ethiopia, met with the Ethiopian president and high-level military officials, and discussed ways to strengthen relations and conduct high-level exchanges of military officers between the two nations.[11]

China is also interested in Ethiopia because of the latter's influence on the Republic of Sudan and Egypt due to its control of the Blue Nile River, which supplies some 80% of the water that reaches the Republic of Sudan and Egypt. The Blue Nile is critical to Egypt's agriculture and to Sudan because of the Gezira Scheme, a massive area of cotton production; for both nations, the Blue Nile is a lifeline. Ethiopia's Grand Renaissance Dam is expected to revitalize the impoverished region with 6,000 MW of electricity annually, and Ethiopia intends to exploit its invaluable water sources to achieve the status of a middle-income country. To achieve its long-term objective to become a regional energy supplier to nations such as Djibouti, Kenya, Sudan, and Yemen, Ethiopia initiated its 25-year master plan building hydroelectric dams along its vast waterways in twelve river basins. Five of the six proposed dam projects are with Chinese firms; the sixth, the Grand Renaissance Dam, is solely an Ethiopian project.

China has recognized the important rise of Ethiopia and has set its sights on bolstering a country historically known for its resistance to European colonization. In terms of the grand politics of the Nile basin, Ethiopia has explicitly stated that it has no allegiance to the 1929 colonial agreement between Britain and Egypt and that it has no problem allowing China to be present in the region. Ethiopia's Grand Renaissance Dam 25 miles east of its border with Sudan will be the largest hydroelectric power plant in Africa when completed. The potential impacts of the dam and the methods Ethiopia will use in sharing the waters of the Nile have been sources of basin-wide as well as regional controversy.[12]

Egypt, too, is beginning to recognize the facts on the ground; it seems to have acquiesced, has toned down its belligerence, and appears to be seeking an amicable arrangement with Ethiopia.[13] However, since 2019 Egypt has become more strident in its demands. Although China is not entirely financing the construction of the dam, the Chinese Electric Power Equipment and Technology Company is covering 85% of the cost of the transmission lines (or $1 billion) while the balance is being financed by the Ethiopian Electric Power Corporation.[14] But China is not the only nation courting Ethiopia. India, Brazil, and Turkey are busy on the continent and have formed economic and investment relations with Ethiopia. It is not a stretch to argue that China's and India's recent fast economic development may be due to Africa's export of resources and raw materials, surpassing members of the Organisation for Economic Co-operation and Development in direct investment, indicating a growing trend in South–South relations.[15]

While Ethiopian leaders have focused on the New Partnership for Economic Development (NEPAD) and, like much of Africa, have been bound with rich nations of the global North, the increasing involvement of the BRIC nations, especially China and India, poses both an opportunity and a challenge.[16] First, while both the AU and NEPAD have emphasized the need for the continent to speak with one voice, such solidarity is more rhetoric than real due to African leaders' perceptions of benefits and costs in their respective asymmetric relations with China. Second, some African nations are also still under the influence of powerful former colonial governments, making it difficult to craft a continent-wide China–Africa policy.

As discussed in Chapter 1, China has a long relationship with Ethiopia, and formal relations go back to 1971. But this relationship is different from China's relationship with resource-rich sub-Saharan African countries. Ethiopia is a large country with tremendous growth potential and a leading player in the region and is thus considered creditworthy and safe for investment. But more important to Ethiopia's economic growth, China's development assistance is critical for sustaining its agriculture-led industrialization.[17] It is no exaggeration to state that in terms of infrastructure transformation, no country in Africa has been impacted by Chinese capital as much as Ethiopia. As in many African countries, Chinese cooperation in Ethiopia includes soft loans, grants, and technical assistance. China's nature of engagement with Ethiopia is based mostly on semicommercial projects via Chinese contractors in the infrastructure sector. While it is difficult to pin down the volume of Chinese development assistance in Ethiopia—that is, to delineate which loans are concessional and which ones are outright grants—it seems that many Ethiopian public projects have been undertaken by Chinese construction companies with loan financing from China. Such arrangements are unique in sub-Saharan Africa, where resources for "take-off" exchange are embedded in agreements or where official Chinese assistance is linked to direct foreign investment.

The emergence of China as a development financer is something new in Africa, with funds issued on nonconcessional terms to fund Ethiopian infrastructure projects such as roads and dams. An exception is the telecommunications sector, where it was felt the Chinese have a comparative advantage. Thus, while it is difficult to categorize different forms of Chinese development assistance, most of the development activities have followed Chinese investments. Although there is now the beginning and the expansion of corporate social responsibility activities (hospitals, medical missions, etc.), by and large such projects are either negligible or small, the exception being vocational training centers established via bilateral efforts with Ethiopia beginning in 2009.

But perhaps the stronger ties that are developing between China and Ethiopia can be seen in the political area, particularly regarding the Taiwan issue. As Chinese influence grows in Africa, Taiwan struggles to maintain its grip on its partners in Africa. Beijing has won the diplomatic race in gaining adherents in Africa to its one-China principle. Only Swaziland maintain diplomatic relations with Taiwan and recognizes it as an independent entity. In 2005, the Ethiopian parliament passed a resolution in support of China's Anti-Secession Law and the Ethiopian government made its position clear on the matter:

Ethiopia has been one of the African countries that had supported the rightful restoration of China's seat at the UN Security Council in 1971. It also supports the "One China Principle." China has advocated for the voice of developing countries to be heard in matters concerning the UN and its Security Council. Ethiopia has always counted on China's support in this regard.[18]

In addition, in 2007, Ethiopia joined some African nations in voting down a resolution of the UN Human Rights Commission that condemned China's human rights practices.[19] For its part, as with other African nations, China never comments on the internal politics of Ethiopia. But this could change in the future as China consolidates its emerging international power and begins to act as a "responsible" nation; it may start to address governance issues in Africa. But naturally for China to do that, it might have to tackle its own governance issues.

In addition to governmental relations, China and Ethiopia have established institutional relationships. The Chinese Communist Party and Ethiopia's EPDRF have a solid working relationship. This is because China has worked very hard to engage the Ethiopian state across a broad range of departments with the objectives of increasing understanding and sharing knowledge, skills, and experience. Many Ethiopian officials were educated in China, including the past president, Dr. Mulatu Teshome, and key department heads have routinely visited China. Most seem optimistic about the benefits of mutual engagement and what China could bring in terms of technology transfer, skills, trade, and investment.

There is no doubt that the relationship of the EPDRF to China's Communist Party as well as its business elites and their investments has buoyed the economy and strengthened the hand of state leaders in Ethiopia. But it is far from reasonable to extrapolate from this, without any verifiable evidence, that the Chinese were behind the success of the 2010 Ethiopian election that the EPDRF won. As one U.S. foreign affairs expert claimed, "it was the Chinese Communist Party which advised the EPDRF in its drive to recruit five million new members [in Ethiopia] between 2005 and 2010 and has [as a result] developed deep party-to-party ties."[20] Such a claim is highly partisan and seems designed to create a wedge in state–society relations in Ethiopia. It does not advance knowledge of China–Africa relations, but rather paints China as an interloper in the domestic politics of Ethiopia despite China's well-known policy of noninterference in the affairs of African nations. In a similar vein, another scholar sees China as a rival of the United States in Africa, claiming that

> Africa Command would do best not to oppose or undermine Chinese activities in Africa. Pressuring countries to choose between the United States and China would be a losing proposition: first, the United States would not always win (and where the United States did not win, its influence would de-cline precipitously, while that of China would rise proportionately); second, where the United States did win, China would be encouraged to subvert the system.[21]

However, two scholars—one of whom is a seasoned former U.S. diplomat—differ from the above view; they succinctly state that "American and Chinese interests in Africa are different, but not substantiality so. There are more areas where the two countries can cooperate for the benefit of Africans than there are issues of disagreement and potential competition."[22]

Finally, China and Ethiopia share many similar experiences: they are both ancient polities with a feudal past, and both underwent a violent revolution, subsequently reconstructing their respective societies (for better or worse). Fundamentally, China's relationship with Ethiopia is for now more political and strategic than economic as the latter is the launching pad for China's continent-wide diplomatic onslaught and economic penetration of a continent of about one billion people. Thus, while trade and investment relations with China are good for Ethiopia, they may not necessarily be converted into growth and poverty reduction. The questions of growing the Ethiopian economy is ultimately a domestic issue. But what relations with China, however asymmetrical, have produced is an understanding that an agrarian society could develop given the right mix of leadership, economic assistance, and focus.

Chinese Security Interests in Ethiopia

There are two reasons behind China has security interests in Ethiopia. First is Ethiopia's strategic location in the Horn of Africa combined with its possession of the largest army there. Second, Ethiopia and the Greater Horn of Africa region have as-yet untapped vast oil reserves. At the same time, the politics of the region are complex and fraught with ongoing conflicts: (a) the fragmentation and now recovery of Somalia and the effects of the military intervention of its neighbors and global actors, (b) the separation of South Sudan from Sudan, (c) the unsolved dispute between Ethiopia and Eritrea, and (d) the recent internal conflict in South Sudan. Despite the above challenges, the region has the potential to become an economic hub.

An important Chinese energy security interest lies in the fact that the region is on the verge of an oil-driven economic revolution. Today, a combination of improved technologies and higher oil prices make small oil fields in frontier areas of the region commercially viable. To reduce dependence on costly petroleum product imports, Ethiopia, as well as the region, can look forward to supplying its own needs and becoming a net exporter to international markets.

In seeking energy security, China is interested in Ethiopia's hydrocarbon potential, which includes yet-to-be-commercialized gas, as well as oil prospects in the early stages of investigation in Ethiopia and potential oil resources offshore from Somalia. In addition, oil resources in Uganda, Kenya, and South Sudan need access to export markets; for this, both regional connectivity and economic cooperation will be needed, and the Chinese could be potential partners in this endeavor. The emerging fossil hydrocarbon potential has piqued the interest of Chinese and other national and global companies that are taking positions in potential pipeline and port facility development in the region.

Thus, Chinese companies are busy exploring for minerals and oil in Ethiopia's Ogaden region near Somalia. In 2007, separatist rebels stormed a Chinese-run oil facility, killing more than seventy people including nine Chinese petroleum engineers from Zhongyuan Petroleum Exploration Bureau. The Ogaden Liberation Front, a militant group fighting for independence for part of eastern Ethiopia, immediately took responsibility. While Ethiopia's intervention in Somalia in 2006 may have sparked the rebel attack, the Chinese have not left the region. In fact, soon after the incident, China-owned GCL POLY Petroleum Investment signed an agreement with Djibouti to construct a pipeline to transport natural gas from the Ogaden to Djibouti through Dire Dawa. In 2011, a Chinese delegation visited Somaliland, and soon after a trilateral agreement worth $4 billion was signed by China, Ethiopia, and Somaliland with Chinese PetroTrans of China, permitting the company to explore and develop gas and oil reserves in the Ogaden region of Ethiopia and ship them through Berbera.[23]

China is also interested in developing the port of Berbera in Somaliland for export of its energy needs from the region. Berbera is located strategically at the mouth of the Red Sea and is the center of Asia, Africa, and the Middle East. The Somaliland government in Hargeisa is interested in leasing the port to Hong Kong–based Hutchison Port Holdings, with Ethiopian Shipping Lines becoming one of the main shareholders.[24] The port of Berbera is expected to become the main port for Somaliland and Ethiopia, a landlocked nation. Many in the region believe that if the port of Berbera is well managed by China and given a full face-lift, its traffic could exceed that of its rival neighbor, Djibouti.

But China is also making its presence felt in Djibouti. The Republic of Djibouti is wedged between Ethiopia, Eritrea, and Somalia. What is more, it is strategically located in the Red Sea and oversees the narrow Bab el-Mandeb Strait, the channel separating Africa from Arabia and one of the busiest shipping lanes in the world, leading into the Red Sea and northwards to the Mediterranean. Camp Lemonnier hosts U.S. Special Forces, fighter planes, and helicopters and is a major base for drone operations in Yemen and Somalia in the War on Terror. In 2014, Somali al-Qaeda–linked militants attacked Djibouti, saying the attack was to punish the East African state for contributing to an AU force in Somalia. In 2015, the United States renewed its lease of the base for ten years with an option to extend for another ten.[25] But the United States was in for a surprise; Djibouti signed a military agreement with Beijing in February 2014 allowing the Chinese navy to use its port, and China later made its presence felt when one of its warships docked at the port and a senior Djibouti military official toured the ship.[26]

Djibouti's links with China are strong. Former president Hassan Gouled Aptidon made four trips to China during his tenure in office; the gestures were reciprocated by Chinese deputy foreign minister Ji Peiding's visit to Djibouti in 1999 to discuss economic matters. In March 2001, President Guelleh made his first trip to China to strengthen economic and trade cooperation and addressed the China–Djibouti Economic and Trade Seminar in Beijing, attended by about 100 Chinese and Djibouti entrepreneurs. This was followed in 2002 by President Guelleh meeting with Chinese vice foreign minister Qiao Zonghuai in Djibouti to discuss bilateral relations which was reciprocated by President Guelleh's visit to China in 2017. Since then, relations between China and Djibouti have been on a fast track. In 2015, China announced it would establish its first military base in Africa in the strategic port of Djibouti, raising the prospect of U.S. and Chinese bases side by side in the tiny Horn of Africa nation.[27] It is obvious that in its dealings with Djibouti, China has a much stronger strategic advantage. This is because maritime ports are Djibouti's only major economic asset apart from its military and logistical facilities currently in use by France and the United States. Thus, China's plan to spend significant capital on upgrading its ports and infrastructure is an offer Djibouti cannot refuse. France also bases the Fifth Overseas Interarms Regiment of the French Army, as well as fighter aircraft, in Djibouti.

As for the United States, it was at first very concerned about the China–Djibouti pact and China's intention to build a base in the northern port city of Obock. The United States understood the tremendous financial incentive China offered Djibouti—namely, the purchase by China Merchant Holdings, an important state-owned enterprise, of a majority share in the vital port of Djibouti with the purpose of making it a "Silk Road Station" that will expand the country's trade and logistics capabilities. China plans to invest $7 billion to redesign the infrastructure of the port, which includes a vital rail link to Ethiopia.[28] At this stage, it is hard to gauge Chinese intentions, whether the Obock region will serve as a full-blown military base or a staging ground for projecting China's power in the Horn of Africa, the Red Sea, and beyond.

But for now, it is believed that China hopes the center could ease difficulties in refueling and replenishing Chinese navy ships and provide recreation for officers and sailors taking part in antipiracy missions in the Gulf of Aden. This does seem plausible as China sent more than 60 ships to the waters off the coast of Somalia on 21 separate missions between December 2008 and November 2015.[29]

Ethiopia's Modernization Interest in China

Ethiopia's ruling party grew out of a peasant-supported guerilla movement and has been strongly influenced by these roots; the party shares the broad contours of the Chinese Revolution. Ethiopia's federal government institutions, such as the prime minister's office and the EPDRF's Central Committee, play central roles in setting national policy. This system at times bypasses representative institutions and puts significant responsibility for policy implementation on regional, zonal, and local (*woreda*) institutions. This is because of the state-centered view of development and the need to decentralize decision-making to win public support. Thus, while governance and administration may be increasingly decentralized, national policy and decision-making structures remain highly centralized.[30]

Ethiopia's interest in China is based on pragmatism and is primarily economic. While there are historical parallels between China and Ethiopia, in the evolution of their indigenous states and revolutions—successful in the former but not in the latter—Ethiopia sees in China what it can become with the right mix of political-social control and state-led development in a mixed economy. The fact that Deng Xiaoping's economic reform in China, among other factors, was the foundation for China's prosperity has not been lost on Ethiopia's state leaders, who as guerrillas had once adopted a Marxist ideology but became practical with the end of the Cold War and the challenges of globalization.

But Ethiopia also has certain resemblances to China in terms of social control. Like Communist China, Ethiopia is ruled by a single party. Land belongs to the state; urban-dwelling associations and peasant associations are the order of the day. Although there have been some reforms and the Ethiopian state does not have a monopoly of the commanding heights of the economy, certain sectors are off-limits both to private and foreign capital. This includes Ethiopian Airlines and telecommunications sector. However, as of 2019 there have been talks that new leadership in Ethiopia is planning to open these sectors to both national and international investors.

Thus, despite the above manifestations of political power, in practical terms, Ethiopia sees China as a source of economic assistance, investments, and inexpensive technologies that would lift millions of small entrepreneurs out of poverty through access to farm machinery and transport. This is because state policy-makers in Ethiopia have grasped that economic growth cannot be achieved without sustained technological and industrial upgrading and structural transformation of the country's economic activities. Thus, Ethiopia sees China's investments in the country's infrastructure projects—highways, railways, bridges, and inputs into power-generating plants—as transforming the ancient polity. It also considers China a vast market for its agricultural commodities.

Ethiopian policy-makers also seem to grasp the fact that the East Asian tigers—which achieved rapid economic growth due to a combination of export-led growth, disciplining of labor, and state investment in key industries—have in the past three decades been slowly losing their comparative advantage due to increased costs of production: land, stricter regulatory compliance, and high labor costs. Ethiopia, with abundant labor, domestic and regional markets, and access to high-income markets, seems poised to step in and fill the breach, promoting itself as an alternative hub in which the Chinese can find new and favorable production centers.[31] This prospect is very attractive because China is transitioning from low-skilled manufacturing to a higher stage, opening an opportunity. China's evolution from low-skilled manufacturing has freed jobs, and Ethiopia, with its huge population and low labor costs, can fill them.[32]

Ethiopia sees its agriculture sector playing a key role in the acceleration of the country's industrial development. The rationale is that since the sector accounts for over 50% of the gross domestic product (GDP), the development and expansion of agriculture will act as a catalyst in driving growth in trade and industry through its strong forward linkages. That is, an increase in food production implies a greater supply of raw materials for production and higher incomes for the agricultural population; higher incomes, in turn, mean increases in consumption of industrial goods, which will boost economic growth as well as capital formation. Thus, while China is active in Ethiopia's agricultural sector, Ethiopia's leaders for their part are carefully considering the Chinese model that involves a combination of policy reform; state support; access to and development of new technologies, irrigation systems, seed varieties, and fertilizers; and the use of hybrid crops that have aided China in feeding its growing population.

Although Chinese cannot legally own land in Ethiopia, they have brought in bulldozers and trucks to improve existing roads and build new ones, an action that has earned them good will with Ethiopian policy-makers and peasant farmers because better roads allow farmers to get their goods from farm to market more easily. In northern Ethiopia, the Chinese have built more than 93 miles of roads and provided cell phones to peasant farmers, allowing them for the first time ever to check prices before they go to market and call ahead for supplies and materials.[33] The Chinese are also leasing huge amounts of land for isolated compounds for road engineers, land that is stocked with prefabricated homes, complete with satellite TVs and Chinese cooks. But this investment may not be entirely altruistic. China is concerned with its ability to feed its own population today and in the future, and it may be buying up Ethiopian-grown cabbage, carrots, and other crops to ship back home. While such purchases are good for China, Ethiopia may need to guarantee food security first to its own people, who in the recent past suffered two great famines.

To understand China's involvement in Ethiopia, one has first to discern Ethiopia's development objective, which is to transform the ancient polity into a middle-income country by the mid-21st century. Ethiopia's leaders recognize that, although other factors facilitate this transformation, foreign direct investment is the key. Thus, Ethiopia has been pursuing a multipronged approach to achieving its development objective. First, it is pursuing scaled-up aid from traditional donors, appealing to them on grounds of achieving the Millennium Development Goals. Second, it is seeking support from nontraditional donors, such as China, which, the government hopes, will provide financing with fewer conditions affecting domestic politics than imposed by traditional donors. The upshot has been that donor assistance and Chinese investments and grants have helped shift Ethiopia's economy from complete dependence on the export of agricultural commodities to utilizing its abundant labor and cheap power to begin developing a manufacturing industry and building its infrastructure.[34]

Although the ruling party in Ethiopia has transformed the once-moribund command economy of garrison socialism to a private one, it is careful not to adopt full-blown laissez-faire capitalism. The Ethiopian state maintains a monopoly in strategic industries such as banking and telecommunications, land remains nationalized, and Ethiopian peasants have usufruct but not property rights. That is, Ethiopia today operates a state-led economy and it is prioritizing investment in infrastructure as it seeks to continue to rise from its status as a poor nation.

In Ethiopia, there is clear evidence of improvements in infrastructure, health care, education, and poverty alleviation as well as reductions in the infant mortality rate. The impact of this economic growth, however, has led to only slight improvements in the plight of the urban poor. While significant steps have been achieved with measurable economic gains, there are still undeniable obstacles within the federal system: prevailing patron–client relationships, constraints on state capacity to efficiently and effectively implement policy, and bureaucratic rent-seeking in the provision of public goods. These problems will have to be resolved before Ethiopia's political economy can reach the stage of sustainable development.[35]

Although Ethiopia's state leaders have not articulated a specific policy regarding their preferences of a country-specific development model, what one can garner from the increasing flow of investments and technology, the relocation of branch firms, the acceptance of foreign assistance, and the immigration of innumerable Ethiopians to Asia, the preferred model is China, followed by South Korea. As some scholars have noted, "Ethiopia's political leadership has, from the mid-1990s onwards, increasingly been inspired by China's example of developing without following prescriptions from the outside. [China is] playing an important role in Ethiopia's development ideology and overall structure."[36]

China's model appeals to Ethiopia for several reasons. China, and to a lesser extent South Korea, established its independence first through its revolution and second through its reform policy. After the Cultural Revolution, China was able to provide economic goods to its citizens when it selectively adopted capitalism, opening its markets to foreign investors and accumulating the capital needed for industrialization. Second, both nations were ancient empires that went through revolutions that reordered state–society relations.[37] Third, the political culture of both countries has been and still is authoritarian; the one-party state has been the motor for the development process in Ethiopia and industrialization in China. Fourth, China's insistence on noninterference in domestic politics and attaching no strings in terms of loans and grants is an attractive aspect of China–Ethiopia relations.

China's development assistance to Ethiopia has been in the form of grant assistance and interest-free loans. The eight principles of China's foreign aid announced during Premier Zhou Enlai's Africa visit in the early 1960s are very relevant in China–Ethiopia cooperation. Ethiopia has been receiving development assistance from China since the signing of the Agreement of Economic, Technical, Scientific and Trade Cooperation in 1971. The first project completed with Chinese assistance in Ethiopia was the Woldeya-Woreta Road, which has been quite beneficial in linking two remote parts of Ethiopia. A more recent accomplishment has been the completion of the Addis Ababa Ring Road, about 14 miles long, on a contractual basis with partial financial assistance from the Chinese government. Construction of light industries; irrigation, infrastructure, and water projects; low-cost housing; and human resource development are some of the ventures completed using Chinese assistance. Ethiopia has also benefited from the debt cancellation scheme the Chinese government extended to Africa as announced in the first ministerial meeting of the China–Africa Cooperation Forum in 2002.

Ethiopia is an agrarian nation with 85% of its population employed in rural areas. The nation is keen to learn from China's experience regarding the development and modernization of agriculture. In this regard, China has been forthcoming in arranging several study tours for Ethiopian experts over the years. Ethiopia is at present drawing meaningful lessons from China's modernization of its agricultural systems by employing Chinese teachers as trainers of Ethiopian agriculture experts at various agricultural, technical, and vocational training colleges. China has been providing short- and long-term scholarship opportunities for Ethiopians as well as arranging customized programs in agriculture, infrastructure, health, and light industry fields such as textiles, which has led human resource development in Ethiopia.

For Ethiopia, China's support and cooperation in technology transfer, research, and education is very important. In this regard, two Chinese telecommunications companies, Huawei and ZTE, have been very active in Africa beginning in 1998, especially in education-related projects. In 2015, in Ethiopia, Huawei began to be involved in a project aimed at sharing resources to promote education in the Addis Ababa School Net Project (AASNP). The purpose of the AASNP is to "create connectivity among 65 educational institutions, including 64 secondary schools and one university college through ICT infrastructure . . . which was implemented by the Addis Ababa Educational Bureau . . . at a cost of 11.5 million dollars."[38]

Since Ethiopia plans to become a middle-income country, cooperation in human resource development is a significant channel for China–Ethiopia relations. Thus, China's support and assistance in furnishing Ethiopia's higher learning institutions and their laboratories with required state-of-the-art equipment, facilities, and teaching materials stand out. Ethiopia anticipates the assistance from China will play a significant role in building the human power of Ethiopia's educational institutions. As noted by one journalist, "The statistics from Tsinghua University provide an insight. In the 2015–2016 academic year, most of the university's 111 African students came from Zimbabwe, Ethiopia, Tanzania, Morocco, Eritrea, and Cameroon—slightly favoring East Africa."[39]

Ethiopia's interest in China as a model of development was strengthened when it officially sought a strategic relationship in some economic areas where the former had built pockets of efficiency. This has resulted in China being willing to share its successful management system in aviation and tourism. Such arrangements highlight Sino-Ethiopian strategic relationships and cooperation in various spheres such as regional peace and stability; utilization of the Addis Ababa–Djibouti Railway, discussed in Chapter 3; and collaboration in international arenas. This was stressed by China's minister of foreign affairs, Wang Yi, who noted, "We will support Ethiopia to be a force of stability in East Africa and to maintain stability in the region and play an important role in the resolution of regional hostile issues."[40] One can infer from such statements that China seems committed to supporting Ethiopia's economic objectives.

Conclusion

This chapter explored contemporary Chinese–Ethiopian relations. First, it outlined Chinese diplomatic interests in Ethiopia, arguing that Ethiopia, as a founding member of the Organization of African Unity, now the African Union, is a formidable player not only in African politics but in the Horn of Africa as well. Ethiopia offers China much-needed political resources. In addition, the location of numerous international organizations, including African institutions, in Ethiopia provides China with a way to work its diplomacy. It allows China to demonstrate that as a member of the UN Security Council it is a responsible emerging global power delivering a "global good" by participating in UN peacekeeping operations and securing peace in parts of conflict-ridden Africa.

Second, the chapter discussed China's security interest in Ethiopia. It underlined that while Ethiopia does not offer China resources compared to better endowed African nations, it has a vast potential in oil and gas reserves, which straddle countries in the Horn of Africa region. In addition to China's exploration for resources in the Ogaden region of Ethiopia, Addis Ababa has assisted China in making connections with Somaliland, with the objective of rebuilding the port of Berbera, not only to facilitate Ethiopia's exports but also as a key installation to support China's ambitions in the Horn of Africa region.

Finally, the chapter discussed Ethiopia's modernization interest in China. It outlined the vision of the ruling party to transform Ethiopia through its Growth and Transformation Plan to become a middle-income country by 2050. It discussed how the Asian model of development, with a mix of strong state control and selected interventions, has produced economic growth in Ethiopia. It argued that many aspects of China's rise from poverty to become the second-largest economy in the world in just three decades has resonated among Ethiopian leaders. However, while Ethiopia has emulated aspects of China's state-led economic reforms that it finds appealing, its prioritization of stability over an active civil society has been a concern. The next chapter will deepen the above discussions by exploring the nature of Chinese and Ethiopian economic relations, the nature of Chinese investments in Ethiopia, and trade relations between the two countries.

CHAPTER 3

China and Ethiopia

Economic Relations

Ethiopia is fast becoming one of the continent's success stories in terms of economic development. The country is also experiencing success in the political and diplomatic spheres. Despite its lack of natural resources, between 2005 and 2015, Ethiopia's economy grew at an average rate of 10% a year; its overall gross domestic product (GDP) amounted to $54.8 billion in 2014. The remarkable economic growth, a modicum of political stability, a large market, and a population of close to 90 million people have attracted investors from Turkey, the Netherlands, the United States, and India, but the largest and most significant investor and economic partner of Ethiopia has been China. According to one authoritative source, Beijing has poured more than $20.6 billion into Ethiopia since 2005, much of it in low-interest loans to build infrastructure, such as roads, rail lines, and telecommunications.[1]

Broadly speaking, China's economic relations with Ethiopia has several characteristics and its investments in Ethiopia are very selective. First are Chinese investments in megaprojects such as rail lines and huge dams. Second, China is also involved in several smaller projects, ranging from agriculture to construction contracting, including water-well drilling. While a newly built and very visible example of Sino-African relationships is the new and gleaming Africa Union headquarters in the sprawling capital city of Addis Ababa, most of China's investments are in rural Ethiopia. A cursory look at these investments indicate that many projects are in the regional state of Oromia and in Addis Ababa

(Table 3.1). These locations are not accidental. The state of Oromia is the largest and best-endowed region in Ethiopia, and Addis Ababa and its environs have historically held the lion's share of investments because its infrastructure is relatively well developed. Thus, among the nine regional states of Ethiopia, Chinese investments are found in all except the Somali regional state, where, according to government data, a project is in the works.[2]

China is economically attracted to Ethiopia because of the latter's market and strategic location in the Horn of Africa. The location is significant even now due to the direct rail link, discussed subsequently, built by China—the Addis Ababa–Djibouti railway—and the fact that it offers access to the sea. A secondary reason for Chinese economic interest in Ethiopia is that Ethiopia is implementing its second five-year (2015–2020) Growth and Transformation Plan (GTP). It envisions an annual GDP base-case scenario of 11% and a high-case growth scenario of 14.9%. China wants to be part of this growth, and its private companies see an opportunity in Ethiopia's second GTP.

Ethiopia is in the process of improving the quality of its social services and infrastructure and enhancing productivity in agriculture and manufacturing, both of which are major objectives of the plan. In brief, to accomplish the above, Ethiopia will need massive inflows of foreign direct investment as it continues to encourage investment in the export-oriented sectors of textiles/garments, leather/leather products, cut flowers, fruits and vegetables, and agro-processing. Chinese firms are also attracted to Ethiopia because the latter has eliminated most of the discriminatory tax, credit, and foreign trade treatment of the private sector, simplified administrative procedures, and established guidelines regulating business activities. In other words, Ethiopia has made the investment climate attractive, and foreign investors do not face unfavorable tax treatment, denial of licenses, discriminatory import or export policies, or inequitable tariff and nontariff barriers.

Nature of China–Ethiopia Economic Relations

Contemporary China–Ethiopia relations date to 1988, predating the Forum on Africa China Cooperation (FOCAC). In 2000, the two nations formed the Joint Ethiopian–China Commission (JECC) and reached an economic agreement that included the protection and promotion

Table 3.1. Licensed Chinese Investment Projects by Region and Status, August 27, 1998 to June 25, 2015

Region	Total no.	Preimplementation no.	Implementation no.	Operation			
				No.	Capital in birr (000)	Perm. empl.	Temp. empl.
Addis Ababa	620	217	60	343	7,673,959	22,470	35,327
Afar	2			2	1,800	5	35
Amhara	18	10	4	4	68,929	1,213	74
B.Gumuz*	1	1					
Dire Dawa	7	2	3	2	178,426	550	50
Gambella	1	1					
Multiregional	44	3	5	36	399,993	1,728	2,451
Oromia	286	114	42	130	10,640,653	15,400	8,957
SNNPR**	7	2	1	4	134,867	450	401
Somali	1	1					
Tigray	6	2		4	110,097	110	63
Total	993	353	115	525	19,208,725	41,926	47,358

Source: Federal Democratic Republic of Ethiopia, Investment Agency. (2017). Addis Ababa: Author.
*Benishangul-Gumuz
**Southern Nations Nationalities People's Region

of investments. The difference today is that China is transplanting to Ethiopia its labor-intensive industries, such as textiles and shoe manufacturing, because wage levels have risen in China and Chinese companies want to take advantage of the cheap labor in Ethiopia. China is building Ethiopia's infrastructure and training its people because it is interested not only in the local market but also in the global one since it has developed a market chain. Thus, Ethiopia is becoming a springboard to both African and global markets.

This development has led China to exercise its soft power by providing loans and grants, technical cooperation, and human resources development without being visible in the architecture of donor–recipient relations because China sees itself engaged principally in South–South cooperation. The nature of China's economic relationship with Ethiopia, as in much of Africa, is based on the demand for supplies, and as a result its trade with Ethiopia has gone up significantly. Its investment in Ethiopia has also increased considerably—as a 2012 World Bank survey indicates, from "virtually zero in 2004 to an annual amount of US $58.5 million in 2010. Behind the figure is a growing and vibrant Chinese business community represented by the Chinese Chamber of Commerce in Ethiopia."[3] While the bulk of China's foreign direct investment is mostly concentrated in the manufacturing sector, Chinese companies are also engaged in other economic activities, particularly in the renewal or building of infrastructure in partnership with government agencies such as the Ethiopian Road Authority, the Ethiopian Electric and Power Corporation, and the Ethiopian Telecommunications Corporation.

Four kinds of Chinese investments in Ethiopia began in the 1980s; construction companies at first dominated investments followed by the manufacturing sector in the 1990s. Chinese companies are engaged in a broad range of market-enhancing manufactured products, such as textiles and shoes; manufacturing currently accounts for 50% of Chinese investments in Ethiopia, with around 60 active business in 2007 valued at approximately $60 million. At present, Ethiopia hosts 95 registered Chinese companies with investments valued at $117 million.[4] It is important to note that in terms of the retail sector, Chinese businesses are prohibited from retailing in Ethiopia the products they manufacture. This is because Ethiopia strictly enforces investment laws preventing all foreign companies from engaging in retail.

The third type of Chinese investment is in the extractive industries, namely oil and gas; examples are in the Ogaden region of Ethiopia. The fourth type is efficiency seeking, particularly in agriculture or sectors that produce inputs efficiently for use by producers based in China. In 2015, 17 efficiency-seeking projects were planned, ranging from dairy to animal husbandry and cash crops. While 13 projects were at the preimplementation stage in 2015, four agricultural projects were functioning. At present, China is mostly interested in agro-processing. To this end, it assisted Ethiopia in building and financing agricultural vocational training centers, and has been providing experts to transform and modernize the sector, and has been conducting workshops on extension programs.[5] In addition, since Ethiopia has vast numbers of livestock, China is particularly interested in modernizing this activity because in the long term it is interested in importing meat from Ethiopia.

China is involved in production of wind energy in 21 countries, including Ethiopia. China's involvement in this area has been linked to global outreach as part of its "going out" process and part of developing nations' priorities in developing their energy sectors.[6] But some scholars claim China's motive is based on status and the desire to bolster its image in developing counties as a "can-do" nation in mitigating climate change and in building its reputation in green energy technology.[7]

Whatever the motive, China is involved in the energy sector in Ethiopia, which has vast hydro, wind, solar, and geothermal renewable energy potential. It has the second-largest hydropower potential in Africa. The country's total exploitable reserves of hydro and wind energy are 45 and 10 GW, respectively. So far only about 5% of its hydropower resources and less than 1% of its wind power resources have been exploited.[8] Plans to develop wind energy capacity in Ethiopia started in 2006 with a grant from Germany, and the Ethiopian government identified several potential sites, including Adama, Ashgoda, and Mesebo-Harena. This was followed by a loan from France to develop a wind farm in Ashgoda near Makale. In 2008, the Ethiopian Electric Power Corporation signed a contract of $289.7 million to develop a 120-MW wind farm in Ashgoda. The project was financed by the French Development Bank and Bank BNP Paribas.

In 2009, HydroChina, financed by a grant from the Chinese government, began a survey of solar and wind power in Ethiopia. It eventually signed a contract with Ethiopia to develop a 51-MW wind farm at Adama, some 59 miles from Addis Ababa. The project, which cost $117 million, was financed by the Export Import Bank of China through a preferred export buyer's credit. In 2015, Adama Phase II with a generation capacity of 135 MW was inaugurated with the China Exim Bank financing 85% of the cost of the project. Ethiopia and China have also signed an arrangement for a $1 billion power transmission line that will bring electricity from a hydropower plant to the capital, Addis Ababa.[9] The 318-mile link from the 6,000-MW Grand Renaissance Dam on the Blue Nile River will be constructed over three years by China Electric Power Equipment and Technology with funding coming primarily from the China Exim Bank. It hopes to finish the $5 billion Renaissance Dam project by 2018. China has also built electrical mechanisms and transmissions for the Gibe II Dam in southwest Ethiopia. In terms of wind power, it has collaborated with Ethiopia in building Adama I and II, which provide 204 MW of electricity, and it provided training and assistance in the construction of Aysha (120 MW) and Genale Dawa III.

Finally, China is involved in construction contracting and water-well drilling activities as well as real estate development and machinery and equipment rental, with 34 projects in the former area and 31 in the latter. Both the service and the construction sectors are booming in Ethiopia, and Chinese companies are active in the service sector in collaboration with the Ethiopian government, which is building infrastructure, while China is beginning to dominate the real estate market because Ethiopian firms often have difficulty raising capital.[10] Thus, close coordination of Chinese aid, trade, and investments means that all three activities are concentrated in just a few sectors in Ethiopia. One can therefore assume that one aspect of Chinese economic and foreign policy in Ethiopia is focused on facilitating the above foreign investments.

The economic cooperation between China and Ethiopia has been facilitated by their respective governments. Ethiopia has provided several incentives to Chinese firms wanting to invest in Ethiopia because it is focused on transforming the nation via its GTP for 2010–2015 as well as on making Ethiopia a middle-income country. As a result, it provides a variety of incentives, such as tax relief and tariff-free policies, for Chinese foreign direct investment projects.

In terms of Chinese development cooperation with Ethiopia, several factors differentiate it from Western development cooperation. First, Chinese assistance is based on "its principle of non-interference and its desire to provide an alternative to Western-style, conditional giving and investments under the Washington Consensus."[11] And Chinese assistance is commercially oriented. China's noninterference encompasses the following principles: (a) support Arab and African peoples in their struggle to oppose imperialism; (b) pursue a policy of peace, neutrality, and nonalignment; (c) support the Arab and African peoples to achieve unity and diversity in manners of their own choosing; (d) encourage people to settle their disputes by their own efforts; and (e) support the ideas that the sovereignty of Arab and African peoples should be respected by all countries and that encroachment and interference from any quarters should be opposed. But one scholar observed that China "has become more assertive in the field of regional stability," and as a result "has come to understand that peace and security dynamics are so intertwined that [often] they cannot be resolved independently of each other."[12]

Second, Ethiopia's cooperation with China is carefully managed and coordinated in line with the national GTP. While Ethiopia is still dependent on donors for its economic transformation, it is not a passive recipient of foreign assistance, but has been able to craft the framework for aid and investment policy.[13]

While direct figures for Chinese aid are difficult to obtain, the total value of aid can be estimated by adding the total value of completed Chinese projects in Ethiopia, which in 2012 was $3.612 billion.[14] In terms of loans from China, Ethiopia ranked second in Africa, receiving a total of $13 billion from 2006 to 2015.[15] Several scholars have criticized Chinese "tied aid," which hampers the development of local suppliers.[16] One U.S. diplomat has labeled Chinese lending policy in Africa as "predatory" and stated that "China encourages dependency using opaque contracts, predatory loan practices, and corrupt deals that mire nations in debt and undercut their sovereignty, denying them their long-term, self-sustaining growth."[17] But such statements ring hollow considering the Third World debt crisis, beginning with the oil crisis of 1970s, which contributed to the "lost decade" of the 1980s in Africa when many nations fell into a debt trap to Western countries.[18] Other criticisms are Chinese companies' practice of staffing projects at the professional level with their employees from China. In addition, some scholars have questioned the practice of Chinese firms underbidding contracts to get a future foothold and shut out the competition, particularly in telecommunications and road and power plant construction.[19]

Nature of Chinese Investment in Ethiopia

Chinese companies began to relocate to Ethiopia in the 1980s, although it was not until the beginning of the 1990s, after the ruling party in Ethiopia had consolidated political power, that they began to invest significantly. It has been suggested that initial Chinese investments in

Ethiopia mirrored Chinese investment patterns in other parts of the African continent, with construction dominating the early investment initiatives.[20] In 2017, as Table 3.2 demonstrates, Chinese investments in Ethiopia totaled about $23 billion. Most Chinese investments in Ethiopia (69%) are in privately owned businesses, followed by 15% in Chinese–Ethiopian joint ventures, 13% in Chinese state-owned enterprises, and the remaining 3% in other ventures.[21]

There is no systematic analysis of the amount of Chinese economic assistance to Ethiopia; lacking data, there have been various estimates that have attempted to distinguish between interest-free loans and grants (see Table 3.3). According to one scholar, Chinese interest-free loans to Ethiopia have totaled $78.6 million since 1995 and total grants were $22.7 million.[22] Researchers estimate that Chinese assistance made up 14% of total aid to Ethiopia in 2006–2007 and was linked mostly to the construction of the modern Ethio-China Friendship Road system in Addis Ababa.[23] But recent data seem to permit separation of China's foreign direct investments from its loans to Ethiopia.

It is important to note that Chinese investment in Ethiopia initially focused on construction, but now the lion's share is in manufacturing. Chinese companies are engaged in the production of a broad range of goods such as steel, pharmaceuticals, textiles, paper, glass, and others. One of the biggest Chinese manufacturers is the Huajian Group, a company that makes shoes, which indicated in 2014 that it planned to invest $2

Table 3.2. Chinese Investment in Ethiopia by Major Sector, 2017 (in US$)

Sector	Investment in US$
Agriculture	2.2 billion
Chemicals	700 million
Energy	6.7 billion
Entertainment	120 million
Real estate	2.2 billion
Technology	3.2 billion
Transport	3.2 billion
Total	22.96 billion

Source: American Enterprise Institute. (2017). *China global investment tracker* [Data set]. Retrieved from https://www.aei.org/china-global-investment-tracker/

billion over a decade building a new manufacturing zone in Debre Zeit/ Bishoftu on the outskirts of Addis Ababa.

The major Chinese investments in Ethiopia are in manufacturing. As Table 3.3 illustrates, by 2015, China had planned 664 major manufacturing projects in Ethiopia; 254 are in the preimplementation stage while 78 are operational and provide employment to about 27,000 Ethiopians. After manufacturing, China's investments in Ethiopia are largely in construction, followed by consultancy, which includes advising on projects in Ethiopia's telecommunications sector.

In Ethiopia, foreign direct investment in the communications industry is forbidden by law. The Ethiopian Telecommunication Corporation (ETC) has evolved through many structural changes. It has two distinct branches: the Ethiopian Telecommunications Authority and the Ethiopian Telecommunications Corporation. The ETC has always been a government-owned state enterprise with no plans to privatize; the Ethiopian state maintains strict control over its functions and contracts to modernize it for security reasons. This situation could change in the future.

Table 3.3. Chinese Investment and Loans in Ethiopia, 2003–2015 (in US$ million)

Year	Foreign direct investment stock	Loans to government
2003	4.78	
2004	7.87	
2005	29.82	
2006	95.60	1,500
2007	108.88	207
2008	126.45	—
2009	283.44	266
2010	368.06	2,052
2011	426.79	79
2012	606.55	6,324
2013	771.84	1,007
2014	941.62	1,013
2015	1,130.13	13,067.51
Total	4,874.83	25,515.51

Source: China–Africa Research Initiative. n.d. *Chinese loans to Africa* [Data set]. Retrieved from http://www.sais-cari.org/data-chinese-loans-and-aid-to-africa

In 2013, Ethiopia signed an $800 million deal with China's ZTE and Huawei Technology Company to expand mobile phone infrastructure and introduce a high-speed broadband network in the country. ZTE, is China's second-largest telecommunications equipment maker and Huawei is a Chinese multinational technology company that provides telecommunications equipment. Both ZTE and Huawei have been awarded a $1.6 billion project to build telecommunications infrastructure in Ethiopia and an agreement was signed with the Ethiopian Telecommunication corporation in 2015.

In terms of regional distributions in Ethiopia, the greatest share of Chinese investments is in and around the capital city of Addis Ababa, and the second-largest share is in the state of Oromia (Table 3.4). The industrial belt surrounding Addis Ababa was begun during the imperial era, circa 1960s and 1970s, and was involved mostly with state enterprises in manufacturing textiles, leather goods, food, and beverages. It was characterized by high dependency on imported raw materials and intermediate goods; this has remained the distinguishing feature of the Ethiopian manufacturing sector. Various factors—including the lack of basic infrastructure, private and public investment, and any consistent public policy aimed at promoting industrial development—contributed to the insignificance of manufacturing. But today, the same area is a beehive of activity, with firms engaged in light manufacturing in apparel, leather products, and wood and metal products.[24]

In terms of rail construction, while China is involved in many megaprojects, the China–Ethiopia light rail that began functioning in Addis Ababa in 2016 was expected to relieve traffic congestion in the capital city, which is home to an estimated 4 million people. But it has not been smooth due to increases in rural urban migration. In addition, the China Railway Group and China Overseas Engineering Group (COEG) built the Addis Ababa–Djibouti railway, with service beginning in 2015, the first modern electrified railway line in the Horn of Africa. The project, 468 miles in length, is jointly owned by the governments of Ethiopia and Djibouti and provides the former, a landlocked nation, with access to the Red Sea. The railway connecting Addis Ababa to Djibouti via Dire Dawa on a 780-km meter-gauge line was built in 1917 by the French but deteriorated due to a lack of maintenance and management. It was modernized by the Chinese, who replaced the meter-gauge section with 1,435-mm gauge track and electrified it to accommodate trains traveling at 75 miles/h. The new line was constructed in compliance with Chinese

Table 3.4. Licensed Chinese Investment Projects by Sector and Status, August 27, 1998 to June 25, 2015

Sector	Total No. of Proj.	Preimplementation No. of Proj.	Implementation No. of Proj.	Operation			
				No. of Proj.	Capital in birr (000)	Perm. empl.	Temp. empl.
Agriculture	17	13	2	2	4,849	40	40
Manufacturing	664	254	78	332	14,257,891	27,005	11,938
Mining	5	1	1	3	36,500	58	42
Education	1			1	530	6	4
Health	13	2	1	10	15,417	55	42
Hotels (including resort hotels, motels and lodges) and restaurants	43	17	3	23	59,030	360	195
Tour operation, transport and comm.	7	1	2	4	7,326	177	45
Real estate, machinery and equipment rental, and consultancy svs.	122	31	8	83	835,192	6,092	7,077
Construction contracting including water well drilling	118	34	19	65	3,939,988	8,073	27,735
Others*	3		1	2	52,000	60	240
Total	993	353	115	525	19,208,725	41,926	47,358

Source: Federal Democratic Republic of Ethiopia, Investment Agency. (2017). Addis Ababa: Author.

*tantalite, columbite, gold, copper & gemstone exports, imports of chemicals for leather industry/through bonded warehouse system, etc.

electrified railway standards. The total cost for the construction was $4 billion; the Ethiopian section of the line, costing $3.4 billion, was financed by China Exim Bank (70%) and the Ethiopian government (30%).

In addition, Chinese Overseas Special Economic Zones (COSEZ) have also been selected to operate in Ethiopia based on its market and investment environment and its capacity to implement industrialization.[25] Several zones have been planned for Ethiopia, and some are operating fully, with Chinese companies producing electric machinery, steel and other metal, and construction materials. Ethiopia has established the Bole Lemi Industrial Zone, which covers 385 acres, designed to enable agro-processors, pharmaceutical makers, and textile manufacturers to produce and sell value-added goods, boosting revenue from exports.[26] The Ethiopian state is building infrastructure in this zone to facilitate commerce and is also offering tax incentives for industries based there. As one important scholar noted,

> as of December 2012, the cumulative value of contracts signed by Chinese companies in Ethiopia stood at $18.82 billion, with $9.71 billion of work delivered. . . . These include: $350 million for the development of wind energy; $500 million for the purchase of new Boeing aircraft by the national carrier, Ethiopian Airlines; $5 billion for the construction of the Addis Ababa–Djibouti rail line; and a plan to establish six industrial zones during the Second Growth and Transformation Plan (GTP2) period. The first of such zones—the Awassa Industrial Zone—is currently under construction and is expected to be up and running by August 2016.[27]

Ethiopian leaders envision the country becoming a leading manufacturing hub in Africa by 2025; they are placing a high priority on industrial park development and expansion. Ethiopia's Industrial Parks Development Corporation (EIPDC) signed an agreement with the China Association for Development of Industrial Parks (CADIP) to build Ethiopia's industrial parks. One of the largest and most impressive, the Hawassa Industrial Park, was completed in 2017, built by China Civil Engineering Construction Corporation (CCECC) at a cost of $246 million.[28] At present, there are several industrial parks in Ethiopia (Table 3.5). Others, at various stages of establishment, are in Bahar Dar, Jimma, and Aysha.

These industrial parks are open for the private sector, both domestic and international, and are located along key economic corridors connected

Table 3.5. Industrial Parks in Ethiopia

Location	Area	Cluster specialization
Adama	130 ha	Textiles, apparel, footwear, machinery fabrication
Arerti	130 ha	Building materials, furniture
Bole Lemi I	156 ha	Textiles, apparel, leather
Bole Lemi II	186 ha	Textiles, apparel, leather
Debre Berhan	10 million ha	Agro-processing
Dire Dawa	300 ha	Open for multiple sectors, closest port is Djibouti
Hawassa (Phase I)	130 ha	Apparel
Klinto	337 ha	Pharmaceuticals
Kombolcha	300 ha	Textiles, apparel, footwear, leather products
Mekelle	100 ha	Textiles, apparel, footwear, leather, leather products

Source: Federal Democratic Republic of Ethiopia, Investment Commission. (2017). *Industrial parks in Ethiopia*. Addis Ababa: Author.

by ports, roads, and electric railway lines with proximity to large labor pools. They are essentially ready for use, with basic amenities such as roads, electricity, water supply, and sanitation provided by the government in order to make them as attractive possible. In terms of export promotion, the state is providing the industrial parks with incentives targeted at increasing export performance and competitiveness. Industrial park developers and enterprises benefit from a special tax and other financial packages that are coupled with efficiency-enhancing facilitation support and investment protections. The Ethiopian government hopes these industrial parks will enhance forward and backward linkages in the economy.

In addition to the Ethiopian industrial parks, China has established or is establishing its own special economic zones (SEZs.) The Eastern and Hujian industrial parks, owned by Chinese companies, are located near Dukem on the outskirts of Addis Ababa. The others are the Ayka Assis and George Shoes industrial parks. While there may be several positive elements in China's ongoing relationship with Ethiopia, a main concern has to do with the profitability, viability, and fate of some small and medium-sized enterprises in Ethiopia and the establishment of Chinese SEZs. A fact to consider is that these enterprises in Africa are nodes of employment and livelihood.[29] Following criticism at the Forum on China–Africa Cooperation in 2006, China pledged to support and include the creation of the SEZs in Ethiopia. This action could benefit Ethiopia by preventing SEZs from simply becoming Chinese investments.

Another issue in Ethio-Chinese economic relations is the impact of Chinese imports. Two manufacturing sectors that have been impacted are textiles and shoes. Historically, the nascent textile industry was established, in the era of Emperor Haile Selassie, at Akaki on the outskirts of Addis Ababa by Ethiopia and some South Asian entrepreneurs. Although the supply was not adequate, particularly for the urban market that required finer imported fabrics, by and large the textile sector was dynamic and held great potential. But its growth, like that of most sectors, was stifled by the nationalization of the commanding heights of the economy by the subsequent military regime. Today in Ethiopia, under a liberalized trade regime, new and cheap clothing imports from Asia, particularly China, are beginning to knock out the burgeoning apparel industry. And whereas small and medium-sized tailoring enterprises used to exist in Ethiopia, providing livelihoods for many, they are increasingly being marginalized due to ready-made cheap clothing flooding the country from China. Ethiopia's invitation to foreign investors to develop the cotton and textile industries in Ethiopia is a sound policy,[30] but it should be tempered by a concern for incipient local enterprises that are critical to livelihoods.

Chinese firms are attracted to Ethiopia because of its cheap labor, large plots of land, and growing market of 90 million people; therefore, China has invested $2.5 billion in the country, mostly in infrastructure.[31] This investment is complemented by Ethiopia's ambitious plan to build 2,947 miles of electrified railway lines at a cost of $5.9 billion as it seeks to reduce road transport costs that have constrained the continent's fast-growing, non-oil-producing economy over the past decade; these costs have averaged around 8.7% over the past five years. Ethiopia planned to lay more than 1,242 miles of standard-gauge railway track under its five-year national growth plan that ended in mid-2015. The China Civil Engineering Construction Corporation (CCECC) and China Railway Group are working on sections costing more than $1 billion each along Ethiopia's main stretch of 407 miles near the capital.[32]

Another manufacturing sector impacted by Chinese imports consists of small-scale footwear enterprises. On the other hand, small-scale factories have also found niches in exporting for foreign markets.[33] Some of these small operations are now being impacted by the economy of scale of Chinese producers and exporters to Ethiopia. The footwear industry is an important sector in Ethiopia's GTP and has been given a priority.[34] Sales of leather and leather products generated $220 million. The state plans to upgrade 74 unfinished-leather processing factories to produce finished-leather products. To enhance this sector, the state has established the Leather Industry Technology Institute. Thus, the Ethiopian state seems committed to upgrading its leather industry. As a result, although some factories are state owned, much of the industry is made up of private, often medium-scale, local enterprises employing 30–40 people and small-scale ventures of 15–20 employees that produce low-quality footwear due to lack of capital and technology; these cater to rural traders and farmers.[35]

However, a Chinese giant footwear producer, Huajian, which operates in the Eastern Industrial Zone in Ethiopia, has been granted additional land for industrial investment.[36] Huajian is currently exporting its products from its plant in Ethiopia to Western markets. It has a projected production rate of 3,000 pairs of shoes daily for export purposes. Although Huajian's expertise may have a spin-off effect in enhancing the finished-leather sector in Ethiopia, its impact on small local producers has not as yet been measured. Clearly then, while small and medium-scale shoe producers in Ethiopia will eventually be eclipsed by a national modern leather and shoe-producing sector, the future of the national shoe industry does not seem bright. That industry may be losing ground quickly to Chinese products produced in Ethiopia or imported from China and often priced at the low end to gain entry and secure a large share of the market.

The Chinese foothold in some Ethiopian industries, such as construction and shoe manufacturing, is of major concern as these industries, particularly the latter, affect small and medium-scale Ethiopian firms that offer livelihoods to people. As for the apparel industry, it is commonly assumed that the Chinese are flooding the *Merkato*—the largest open-air market in Africa—in Addis Ababa with clothing. But the growth of the apparel market in Ethiopia is also attributable to Ethiopian traders who source goods from China because they have a better understanding of the local markets in Ethiopia. As one scholar observed,

> little scholarship has been devoted to the role of African entrepreneurs in trade between China and Ethiopia. African immigrants form part of a new wave of foreigners who arrive in China to take advantage of the country's fast economic growth and commercial opportunities [in places such as Guangzhou].[37]

In the past, Chinese entrepreneurs and companies engaged in the apparel retail industry did not come to Ethiopia because the county had strict investment laws regarding foreigners investing and engaging in this industry but has now pushed the retail door ajar to foreigners.[38] But in 2018, several large Chinese companies invested in the SEZs and are very much engaged in Ethiopia's textile and apparel industries. The apparel factories are a result of China outsourcing its labor-intensive industries to Ethiopia and becoming the middleman for ramping up production for such global firms as Guess, Levi Strauss, and H&M. These SEZs are attractive to Chinese companies because the Ethiopian government has created several incentives, such as exemption from income tax for the first five years of business and no duty or low taxes on the importation of capital goods and construction supplies. In exchange, the Ethiopian economy got a shot in the arm to the tune of $10.7 billion in loans from China from 2010 to 2015.[39] The Ethiopian Investment Commission is currently targeting large companies in China that can create jobs quickly, and these overtures have attracted organizations such as Jiangsu Sunshine Group, which plans to invest nearly $1 billion in Ethiopia.[40]

Ethiopia has experienced strong economic growth in recent years. With real GDP growth at or near double-digit levels since 2004, the country has consistently outperformed most other countries in Africa and expanded much faster than the continent-wide average. Indeed, the rapid acceleration in Ethiopia's growth has been a key factor in the reduction of poverty, and the nation achieved the UN Millennium Development goal of cutting the mortality rate for children under the age of five ahead of the 2015 deadline.[41] The economic growth undeniably has provided a modicum of political stability (1990–2018) and contributed to a diplomatic and strategic convergence between Beijing and Addis Ababa.

China–Ethiopia Trade Relations

Beginning in the 1980s, China improved its integration into the world trading system and has become a manufacturing hub. Its trade, once dominated by physical planning resulted in an irrational pattern of exports, has been replaced by a decentralized and market-determined trading system. Several studies in the past few years have explored China–Africa trade relations, which have grown strong in the past two decades.[42] China's trade with Africa is highly concentrated. About 60% of Chinese exports to Africa are destined for only six countries: South Africa (21%), Egypt (12%), Nigeria (10%), Algeria (7%), Morocco (6%), and Benin (5%). At the same time, over 70% of Chinese imports originate from just four countries: Angola (34%), South Africa (20%), Sudan (11%), and Republic of the Congo (8%).[43] The high concentration of China's imports from these specific countries in part reflects the importance of crude oil (70% from Africa), explaining Sudan and Angola as key oil exporters.

Some scholars consider China–Ethiopia economic relations an anomaly in light of resource-rich African countries.[44] This is because Ethiopia is one of the few African countries that does not have, at present, oil and mineral resources, and its trade is highly dependent on the export of agricultural products (see Table 3.6). Coffee exports account for approximately 65% of Ethiopia's foreign exchange. Per the 2005

Table 3.6. Ethiopian Exports to China, 2015

Rank	Goods	Value (US$)	Share of exports (%)
1	Sesame seeds	1.3 billion	85.91
2	Leather prepared after tanning/crusting, including parchment-dressed leather	44 million	2.88
3	Niobium, tantalum, and vanadium ores & concentrates	34 million	2.24
4	Titanium ores & concentrates	30 million	1.96
5	Tanned/crust hides/skins of goats or kids in dry state (crust)	22 million	1.50
6	Tanned/crust skins of goats/kids in wet state (wet-blue)	22 million	1.44
7	Natural gums, resins, gum resins, natural oleoresins/balsams	19 million	1.28
8	Tanned/crust skins of sheep, lambs in dry state (crust)	18 million	1.24
9	Other oil seeds and oleaginous fruits	12 million	0.79
10	Oil cake and other solid residues of colza seeds	12 million	0.76

Source: Zewde, Getahun. (2017). Post-2006 Ethiopia–China trade relation: Challenges and prospects. *Asian Research Journal of Arts & Social Sciences, 2*(1), 1–11.

estimates, coffee production engaged almost 25% of the working population and contributed 10% to the national production data. But lately there has been a shift in Ethiopia's exporting pattern, with preferential treatment given to agro-processing; this has led to the exportation of sesame seeds, cut flowers, dried chickpeas, dried beans, vegetables, and bovines. Sesame seeds, exported mainly to China, now account for about 15% of total exports. Another important export commodity is leather, which historically has been exported to Italy. But "Ethiopia's export of leather to China grew at a compound annual average growth rate of 41%, from USD 1.2 million in 2004 to USD 1912 million in 1912."[45]

After sesame seeds, the next largest export of Ethiopia is livestock. In terms of world livestock production, Ethiopia holds the 10th position.[46] A major portion of the livestock production is exported to neighboring countries. Because of an abundance of livestock, Ethiopia's leather industry has witnessed tremendous growth since 2005, mostly due to large-scale private investment, and the country is now exporting raw leather as well as luxury leather products.[47] Floriculture is also expected to rise due to massive investment in the sector. If the growth in floriculture is sustained, Ethiopia can become one of the largest exporters of flowers and plants in the world.

Ethiopia's trade imports include food, animals, machinery, transport equipment, fuel, cereals, vehicles, and textiles. China is the largest import partner for Ethiopia; in 2016, it accounted for over 18% of the total import volume.[48] Owing to heavy importation of petroleum products, Ethiopia does not enjoy a favorable balance of trade. But this could change with the liberalization of trade practices and, in the future, with the maturity of its industrial parks. Ethiopia looks poised to achieve higher levels of exports, and it has chosen certain export products for selective state intervention. At present, given the limited size of local markets and the need to generate foreign exchange, there is a clear focus on export industries, and emphasis in this sector is on high-value agriculture (horticulture) and agro-processing industries (leather products). Export industries benefit from favorable land lease rates, soft loans, tax incentives, subsidies for participation in trade fairs and international missions, and other services. In addition, differential interest rates are offered for various products such as horticulture and leather products, which qualify for soft loans as long as export targets are agreed upon for individual firms. In addition, the Ethiopian currency, the birr, which has been devalued significantly since 1991, has helped to increase export competitiveness and resolve foreign exchange crises but it has also led to several structural challenges, namely an increase in the prices of imported inputs critical to development, particularly food items.

China and Ethiopia signed the Sino-Ethiopian Trade Agreement in 1996, but the trade balance between the two countries has remained in favor of China. One study found that even though China–Ethiopia trade has grown rapidly, it is focused on Chinese exportation of telecommunications, installations of electric power stations, and manufactured goods.[49] One unique way China finances such projects is through its preferential export buyers' credit, in which Western firms are unwilling to participate. As one scholar noted,

> China's Eximbank has provided commercial loans for electricity distribution lines, cement factories, and other projects, secured (and repaid) out of Ethiopia's exports to China: mainly sesame seeds. These credits are known (in Chinese) as *hu hui dai kuan*, or "mutual benefit loan." A Chinese company gets the business, Ethiopia gets finance for development.[50]

Table 3.7 demonstrates Ethiopia's balance of trade with China. As expected, the trade is asymmetrical, favoring China. One obvious solution is, of course, for Ethiopia to increase its exports to China, but increasing

Table 3.7. Ethiopia's Balance of Trade with China, 2006–2015 (in US$ million)

Year	Ethiopian exports	Ethiopian imports	Trade balance
2006	78.9	551	–472
2007	71.6	663	–591
2008	67.6	663	–952
2009	80.6	1,688	–1,608
2010	211.0	1,847	–1,635
2011	228.0	2,021	–1,793
2012	280.0	1,673	–1,393
2013	315.0	2,432	–2,117
2014	308.0	2,952	–2,664
2015	456.0	5,018	–4,561

Source: Post-2006 Ethiopia–China trade relations. *Asian Research Journal of Arts & Social Sciences*, 2(1), 1–11.

the volume will not mitigate the challenge because the trade imbalance is a structural problem. The trade statistics show that the value of imports from China is growing faster than the receipts from exports, thereby resulting in the negative trade balance for Ethiopia. As one scholar noted, one of the reasons for the massive trade imbalance is competition from Chinese imports, particularly in "plastic and textile manufacturing sectors, [which] have severely affected domestic production."[51]

In any case, China–Ethiopia trade relations offers both challenges and opportunities. Clearly one challenge for Ethiopia is the impact on some domestic producers and small-scale business owners engaged in self-employment in some sectors of the Ethiopian economy. But at same time, some businesses benefit from China's cheap prices and low-cost machinery—so much so that they engage in "business practices such as illegally laminating on items imported from Europe with the words 'made in China' in order to evade import taxes."[52] Such rent-seeking could be avoided if Ethiopia develops appropriate import tariffs, but Ethiopia is not, while China is, a member of the World Trade Organization. Ethiopia is dependent for the most part on bilateral agreements and at times has opportunities and access to major export markets but these short-term arrangements may not be viable in the future.

Conclusion

This chapter discussed economic relations, including trade relations, between China and Ethiopia. It outlined the nature and character of those relations. It underscored the fact that although a body of literature characterizes China's interest in Africa as based on the hunger for resources, China's interest in Ethiopia has been an exception. Developing Ethiopia's resources, mainly oil and gas, required long-term investment. China's economic interest in Ethiopia sprang from Ethiopia's market and its strategic location in the Horn of Africa. Most importantly, as the chapter pointed out, China's "going out" process coincided with the implementation of Ethiopia's GTP, which offered Chinese companies investment opportunities and provided Ethiopia with infrastructure and energy, enhancing productivity in agriculture and manufacturing, a major objective of the GTP. The chapter noted that Chinese investment in Ethiopia was facilitated by vendor financing for projects and although the financing was based on market rates, it was conditioned on Chinese firms taking jobs and often bringing their own employees from China to the disadvantage of local labor. Chinese investment was facilitated also by low bidding, demonstrating overall that the success of Chinese firms has been tied to political connections to the governments of China and Ethiopia.

In terms of Ethiopia's trade relations with China, the chapter emphasized that the relationship has been asymmetrical. From 2006 through 2015, Ethiopia imported $19.8 billion worth of goods from China and exported $2 billion to China; the huge gap between imports and exports resulted in a trade imbalance that favored China. This large and growing imbalance in trade is the result of Chinese exports to Ethiopia, which have impacted the shoe, plastic, and textile sectors. While Ethiopia is for the most part an agrarian society, its exports have begun to grow rapidly, particularly coffee but also other high-value commodities such as cut flowers, dried chick peas, and bovines. These have begun to make inroads and Ethiopia's exports to China from 2000 to 2012, particularly sesame seeds, have undergone significant changes. But overall the China–Ethiopia trade imbalance is due to the fact that the former is now the major source of capital goods and transport equipment for Ethiopia and these goods, such as vehicles, building structures and parts, mechanical shovels, and telecommunications parts and accessories, are critical factors in Ethiopia's industrialization.

CHAPTER 4

China and Ethiopia

Strategic Partners

China's Africa strategy involves many variables other than natural resources.[1] While it is true that Chinese economic growth coupled with dwindling domestic oil production and mineral deposits has forced the nation to look abroad for resources, Chinese engaged in business are also looking to open new markets for their products and have been relatively successful, establishing enterprises in some of the most unstable nations in Africa.[2] China has been able to obtain resources, build trade, and win African nations to its side through various mechanisms. First, China was able to increase its aid and economic support to Africa, often with no strings attached. Second, it has increasingly used foreign aid—to the tune of $2 billion in development assistance—to support infrastructure creation that helps Chinese companies get deals with African governments.[3] Third, China has used the instrument of debt relief to African nations; in 2000, China wrote off $1.2 billion in African debt.[4] Fourth, China's strategic initiatives across Africa are designed to safeguard its international forums and institutions, which often have overlooked human rights abuses in African nations. The final strategy involves China's soft power, which includes the establishment of Confucius Institutes; the promotion of Chinese cultural and language studies on the continent; and scholarship programs for African students, who may in the future be opinion leaders on the continent, to study in China.[5]

In terms of a partnership between China and Ethiopia, the latter is a pivotal state in the Horn of Africa, which includes Djibouti, Eritrea, and Somalia as well as the Greater Horn region, the countries of Kenya,

Sudan, South Sudan, Uganda, and Yemen across the narrow strait of Bab el-Mandeb in the Red Sea. Ethiopia's importance is simply its geography. When necessary, it has projected its power to the borderlands and beyond in its national interest. Consequently, Ethiopia's strategic position in the unstable, terrorism-prone Horn of Africa makes it a key state in the region, playing important roles in mediation in the South Sudan conflict, helping reconstruct Somalia, and enjoying good relations with Somaliland, a de facto state that has yet to be recognized by the international community.

As discussed in Chapter 1, while in the Cold War years China's attempt to build relations with Ethiopia was stymied by the Ethio-U.S. military agreement of 1953, later, at the Bandung Conference, China found an ideal opportunity to develop relations with the participating countries, including Ethiopia. China was later to use the Bandung experience to deepen relations with Ethiopia, leading to cultural exchange between the two nations. In 1958, Ethiopia broadened and diversified its relations to include the Eastern bloc, which supported anticolonial movements in Africa.[6] In the 1960s, a pro-Ethiopia foreign policy led the United States to recognize Ethiopia as the most important state actor in the Horn of Africa, and it played a major role in shaping U.S. policy in the region.[7] However, after the Ethiopian Revolution (1974–1977) Ethiopia's relations with the United States became strained when Ethiopia, under the nationalist military regime of Colonel Mengistu Haile Mariam (1974–1990), came under the sphere of influence of the Soviet Union.

During the initial years of the Ethiopian Revolution, there was a good relationship between China and Ethiopia, leading to frequent exchanges of delegates in many economic fields. Ethiopia's embrace of socialism, particularly its land reform, interested China, leading to cooperation in the field of agriculture, but overall relations were not smooth and eventually began to deteriorate because of Somalia's 1977 invasion of Ethiopia. While China announced that it was simply abiding by the decision made by the UN and the Organization of African Unity (OAU) regarding the mediation of the conflict, this did not convince the Ethiopian military regime, which threw its lot with the Soviet Union because it was bedeviled by war on two fronts—with Eritrea and Somalia—as well as an internal insurrection from the Ethiopian left and began to closely identify itself with the causes of the Soviet Union and its socialist allies.[8] In 1995, closer relations with China began when the leaders of the Federal Democratic Republic of Ethiopia decided to recalibrate foreign relations globally, but particularly with China as it was a rapidly modernizing nation.[9]

Strategic Elements in China–Ethiopia Relations

Over the last two decades, the relationship between China and Ethiopia has reached a greater level and the two nations are in the process of strengthening strategic partnerships, with China willing to share with Ethiopia experiences of a successful "governance system, aviation, and tourism," and Ethiopia cooperating with China "in various spheres such as regional peace and stability, utilization of Addis Ababa–Djibouti railway, and collaboration in international arenas."[10] The following was stated by the foreign ministers of China and Ethiopia on June 21, 2017:

> [China] will not only be able to improve the infrastructure facilities in Ethiopia, but we will also work together for regional connectivity, including establishment of transportation networks, electricity and telecommunication links. Thirdly, the two countries will be able to tap into the great potential for cooperation in the fields of agriculture and mining and energy, especially green, clean, sustainable energy, and upgrade our cooperation to a fully-fledged strategic partnership.[11]

The strength of the relationship is underscored by the fact that Chinese president Xi Jinping has made clear his nation's desire to strategize its partnership with Ethiopia. Such close cooperation makes both China and Ethiopia important players in the Greater Horn of Africa, considering Chinese interests in Sudan, South Sudan, Somaliland, as well as Djibouti, which is a gate for Ethiopia's trade and home to a new Chinese military base, which could be critical to China's Belt and Road Initiative (BRI) Red Sea portion. The BRI, coupled with the completion of the Ethio-Djibouti Railway, will catalyze import-export trade in Ethiopia. The BRI also aims at creating deeper economic ties between certain groups of countries and plans to connect Ethiopia, Kenya, and Tanzania through a broadband regional plan. This is envisioned as intensifying trade and investment flows and lending a new dynamism to the development trajectories of African counties, but it is not without its challenges.[12]

In addition, Ethiopia is investing to make its capital, Addis Ababa, a Chinese-friendly airport hub for the African continent, and China has decided to make Ethiopia an aviation center. Beginning in 2019 Ethiopia has the major share of 13% of the total international cargo transportation at Baiyun International Airport in China. The importance of Ethiopian Airlines to China is evidenced by the award it received in cargo and logistics services at a customers' symposium organized by Guangzhou Baiyun International Airport in China in February 2018.[13]

It is important to note that, as with any other nation, China's foreign relations seek to serve its domestic objectives and are geared to the maintenance of its institutions and core interests (*hexin liyi*) and, by extension, its internal stability. While this ultimate objective has remained the same under various leaders, China has formulated foreign policies designed to fit historical and regional contexts, such as in Africa. Thus Ethiopia–China cooperation differs fundamentally from the Western type of relations because it is multilayered. First, Ethiopia's traditional relationships with the West are South to North whereas its relationship with China is South to South, allowing for a two-way approach; this relationship is, at least in theory, mutual. That is, China sees the quality and the quantity of its assistance to Ethiopia as furthering its national interests, which are political economic security, whereas Ethiopia's interest in China is to support an accelerated industrialization and build capacity for independent development.

Second, while China's development assistance to Ethiopia, ranging from infrastructure construction to development loans, it comes with no official conditions, it is deeply intertwined with Chinese business interests, which range from project financing to importation of Chinese labor. This is because there are multiple foreign policy actors in China, whose interests may or may not be consonant with those of Beijing; these interests have their own objectives, which may not reflect China's foreign policy interests, "leading to an increasing set of tensions and contradictions."[14] Thus, China's engagement in Ethiopia, as in much of Africa, is

> multivariate, involving a multiplicity of agencies, operating at different levels, structures, and processes with sometimes contrary interests and goals. . . . These relations are, in practice, heterogeneous, as a result of the state being disaggregated into a multiplicity of provincial relations and central state agencies, and tensions arising between commercial market and political interests.[15]

Third, relations between China and Ethiopia are bilateral, with the Forum on China–Africa Cooperation (FOCAC) serving as a multilateral forum for engagement in areas related to economic, diplomatic, and social agendas. The importance of the forum was underscored in a white paper released by the Chinese state in 2006 that set forth its long-term strategic plan for deepening cooperation and consultation with African countries. Ethiopia is the largest EU aid recipient in Africa, and aid is the major instrument in European cooperation.[16] For China, in contrast, Ethiopia is not primarily an aid recipient, but an important economic and political ally in its new Africa policy. This is evidenced by the newly built gleaming steel-and-glass tower in Addis Ababa funded by China at a cost of $200 million as a gift to the African Union (AU), which continues to strengthen Beijing's influence in Africa. Thus, contrary to widespread assumptions that China primarily engages with resource-rich countries in Africa such as Zambia, Angola, Democratic Republic of the Congo, Mozambique, and South Africa, Ethiopia has become one of the largest recipients of official flows of Chinese money.

In 1995, the late prime minister of Ethiopia, Meles Zenawi, visited China and subsequently President Jiang Zemin stopped in Addis Ababa as part of an extensive tour of Africa. The visits culminated in the signing of a trade, economic, and technical cooperation agreement between the two nations. The agreement gave Ethiopia most-favored-nation status and shortly afterward, in 2000, Addis Ababa was selected as host for the first FOCAC meeting. Since then, China has been actively engaged in Ethiopia's economic development, offering loans and skilled manpower and helping to build highly visible infrastructure, roads, and railway systems in Addis Ababa and elsewhere.

China's rapprochement in Africa coincided with Ethiopia's implementation of its Growth and Transformation Plan (GTP), which is part and parcel of its agriculture-led industrial development strategy for transforming the nation.[17] In practical terms, Ethiopia's interest in China is based on what works and is primarily economic. As one scholar noted, there are historical parallels between China and Ethiopia in the evolution of their indigenous states and revolutions.[18] Ethiopia's state leaders, aware of the accomplishments of China that began under Deng Xiaoping's (1981–1989) economic reform, see in China what Ethiopia can become with the right mix of political-social control and state-led development in a mixed economy.

As a result, there has been a close partnership between China and Ethiopia that includes military cooperation, with Beijing supplying

Ethiopia with artillery, light armored vehicles, and troop transport. These relations have also resulted in many Ethiopian officers visiting China for training. This military relationship was cemented when Ethiopia signed a military cooperation agreement with Beijing in 2005 for training, exchange of technologies, and joint peacekeeping missions.[19] This close cooperation also includes a military attaché in the Chinese embassy in Addis Ababa, very rare in Africa. The military cooperation is in line with China's aim to act in the world as a "responsible state" (*fuzeren guojia*) under the banner of its "new historic mission" announced in 2004.

In the Horn of Africa, China is beginning to strengthen its relationship with regional organizations. The key regional institutions in the Horn of Africa are (a) IGAD, (b) the East Africa Economic Community and (c) the AU's Peace and Security Council, which has been considerably more engaged with the situation in the Horn than in other parts of Africa. All these organizations are intertwined and interact in enabling peace and development in the Horn of Africa Region. IGAD was established in 1983 by Djibouti, Ethiopia, Kenya, Somalia, Sudan, and Uganda for development and drought control in the region, with Eritrea becoming a member in 1993 after attaining independence. In 1996, a revitalized IGAD expanded into areas of regional cooperation.

In 2015, China contributed $100,000 to the secretariat in Djibouti to support the organizational costs of the institution.[20] IGAD is deeply involved in helping reconstruct the state of Somalia and mediating in the South Sudan conflict, an area in which China has substantial investments. IGAD is important in terms of peace and security because there is an international consensus that regional organizations should play a key role in maintaining international order.[21]

China's diplomatic efforts seem designed to work within the overall IGAD peace process. This was made evident in 2006, when its ambassador of African affairs, Zhong Jianhua, held talks with officials in South Sudan and Ethiopia to appeal for the protection of Chinese nationals and investments in rebel-held areas in South Sudan.[22] Such efforts become more important to China after the IGAD talks in Addis Ababa on March 5, 2015, failed to obtain a lasting cease-fire in South Sudan, leading one scholar to suggest China was attempting to upstage Western powers in the peace process, namely the United States, the United Kingdom, and Norway.[23]

Chinese Foreign Assistance to Ethiopia

Foreign assistance is an instrument of the state for achieving foreign policy objectives. It refers to government funding to poor nations in support of economic and social development. In the past, the developmental regime was dominated mostly by Western nations that defined a set of operational attributes that constituted foreign aid as concessional public resource transfers from one government to another or to international organizations or NGOs. But today there are new emerging donors, including China, United Arab Emirates, Saudi Arabia, South Korea, India, and Brazil, which are inconspicuously beginning to change the rules of the game

China's foreign assistance to Africa is based on its Eight Principles for Economic Aid and Technical Assistance to Other Countries. The principles, grounded in sovereignty, equality, and mutual respect, have guided China's foreign aid since the 1960s.[24] In addition, noninterference in the domestic politics of African nations, meaning lack of political conditionality, has been a distinctive feature of Chinese aid to Africa. The eight principles were announced in 1964 by Zhou Enlai, foreign minister of the People's Republic of China under Mao Zedong.[25] In those turbulent years of the African independence period, China adopted, due to its direct experiences, a strongly anti-imperialist rhetoric in its foreign assistance policy, which resonated with many African nations and their struggles against colonialism.

Contemporary China's foreign assistance is driven by three main factors. These are first, economic, meaning the securing of resources such as raw materials, oil, and minerals to undergird its fast modernization and industrialization. Second is a political motive; China needs friends in international organizations as it aspires to become a global power. It is also in the process of establishing strategic diplomacy. The third motive is ideology—not the rhetoric of Third World solidarity, but rather the extension of Chinese ideals and culture through the establishment of Confucius Institutes in Africa. In 2014, China explicitly stated its foreign assistance objectives:

> In providing foreign assistance, China adheres to the principles of not imposing any political conditions, not interfering in the internal affairs of the recipient countries and fully

respecting their right to independently choose their own paths and models of development. The basic principles China upholds in providing foreign assistance are mutual respect, equality, keeping promises, mutual benefits and win-win."[26]

In many ways, Chinese foreign assistance is attractive to African nations because it eschews policies imposed by traditional donor nations with which they disagree. In the late 1980s and 1990s, donor assistance from the West carried political and economic conditions and promoted distinct values. African nations find Chinese foreign assistance more appealing because of its distinctive feature of noninterference in domestic politics. Therefore, China has expanded both the volume and geographic reach of its foreign assistance in Africa, and its emergence as a major player in the foreign aid and development regime has raised some important questions about whether Chinese foreign assistance is a monster or a messiah.[27]

However, a more nuanced observation may be that it is part and parcel of Beijing's objective to become a major global power and that Africa serves its national interests, not only as a source of needed raw materials and new markets, but also to bolster its own position on the international stage. As one astute scholar of Chinese and African affairs observed, while China has rapidly increased its foreign aid to Africa, using the nebulous term of "friendship," it is now a relatively major player in the developmental assistance regime, but little is known regarding how it delivers its foreign aid, and even less about how this foreign aid actually works in the recipient countries.[28] This has raised concerns by traditional donor nations, and consternation and the lack of transparency have generated a jaundiced view of China–Africa relations. As one scholar noted:

> The international community largely perceives the Chinese approach to foreign aid as an instrument for exploiting the recipient country. Western donors in particular feel threatened by China's foreign aid policy, as an increasing number of developing countries engage in projects with China rather than with traditional donors. [In addition,] as China's economy grows its *structural power* [emphasis added] rises as well, thereby better positioning Beijing to disseminate its ideas and spread its practices of development.[29]

Another topic of interest in terms of China's foreign aid has been how it is implemented in Africa, with some scholars claiming that political leaders of recipient countries use foreign aid inflows to further their own political or personal interests. Others argue that Chinese aid has gotten out of hand and is allocated in some instances to African political leaders' birth regions that are populated by the ethnic groups to which the leaders belong. It is of course a fact that in predominantly agrarian societies colonialism has left two public realms: the civic realm and the primordial realm.[30] While the balance between these public realms, as well as between public and private realms, may differ from country to country depending on the extent of penetration of capitalism and the creation of a middle class and attendant values, the findings of the above research linking foreign aid flows to elites' birth regions are not novel. The dominance of the private over the public realm has been called the patron–client relationship.[31]

The categorization of the private realm and its relations to governance is now increasingly questioned.[32] One scholar argues that only the formation of a strong middle class aware of its historic mission to hold on to the levers of state power can institutionalize the rule of Africa law.[33] Nevertheless, the findings regarding the implementation of foreign assistance in Africa are sobering. As some scholars observed,

> the birthplaces of political leaders receive larger amounts of Chinese aid. This result is strongest for total official financing flows from China, which also include non-concessional loans and grants without development intent, going to regions at the first subnational administrative level (ADM1), such as provinces, states, and governorates. Controlling for country-year and region fixed effects, we find that Chinese official financing to a political leader's birth region nearly triples after that individual assumes power.[34]

Chinese foreign assistance in Africa goes back to the 1960s and was highly ideological at that time. In the initial period, China saw the newly independent nations of Africa as a land of opportunity because the colonial order was decaying and a new order was just being formed. China sought allies and began to assert political leadership, achieving a certain degree of global power.[35] However, despite the achievements of China in asserting its independence on the world stage, realizing national unification and fundamental reordering of state–society relations, very few African nations followed China's leadership due to concerns with the two superpowers, the Soviet Union and the United States.

As discussed in Chapter 1, due to Ethio-U.S. Mutual Defense Agreement of 1953, it was not until the 1970s that China began to assist Ethiopia, and then only modestly. It dispatched a veterinary research demonstration team to undertake pharmaceutical research and lab training in Bahir Dar in northern Ethiopia, where it set up a small plant to produce local herbs and medicines for animal treatment. However, whatever plans the team may have had for an extended stay were cut short by the revolutionary violence that was convulsing Ethiopia; the team had to depart in 1977. But during this time, perhaps impressed by the land reform zeal of the Ethiopian military regime, China financed the 185 miles Woldeya-Woreta Road in northern Ethiopia. As Table 4.1 illustrates, through the 1980s and 1990s China undertook many projects, such as drilling wells for water supplies, building power supply stations to help in rural electrification, and constructing irrigation schemes; these involved and were completed by Chinese corporations. Chinese foreign assistance to Ethiopia since 1991 includes soft loans, grants, technical cooperation, human resource development, and urban planning, making China a key development partner in Ethiopia.

While Western donors remain a major source of foreign assistance to Ethiopia, Chinese development assistance in its various permutations—aid, trade, and investments—has produced tangible results. These include (a) the rehabilitation of Addis Ababa's Bole International Airport, (b) a modern Addis Ababa Ring Road, (c) Gibe and Takeze hydroelectric dams, (d) several industrial parks, (e) the rebuilding of AU headquarters, (f) the building of Ethio-China Polytechnic College in Addis Ababa, and (g) the building of the Addis Ababa-Djibouti Railway.

Ethiopia views Chinese foreign assistance as compatible with its national development objectives for several reasons. The first is, of course, the lack of conditionality and China's principle of noninterference in Ethiopian domestic affairs. In addition, Chinese assistance seems relatively generous in terms of its subsidized interests, but Chinese foreign assistance is heavily tied to the use of Chinese companies and contract workers and the provision of a deeper integration of Chinese aid, trade, and investments. Overall, China's policy of noninterference means its soft power is not used to promote good governance, popular participation, or encouragement of civil society groups that could enhance popular dialogue and deepen democratization.

Table 4.1. Historical Data of Chinese Assistance to Ethiopia (1974–1996)

Name of project	Description of project	Years
Veterinary Research Demonstration Team	Pharmaceutical research and lab training in Bahr Dar. Set up small plant to produce local herbs and medicine for animal treatment.	1974–77
Bamboo Weaving Training Class	Fourteen students learned how to weave bamboo articles (*injera* containers and suitcases).	1974–76
Woreta–Woldeya Road	Northern Ethiopia 293-km road, first infrastructure project financed by China. Financed by zero-sum interest loan. Construction began 1975, completed 1982.	1975–82
Water Supply Projects	Drilled 27 wells in 23 rural towns. Project provided drinking water to 250,000 people.	1972–82
Power Stations	Rural electrification financed by zero-interest loan US$2.3 million, built diesel power plants and distribution lines in six to eight provincial towns.	1972–78
Hare River Irrigation Scheme	In Southern Nations Nationalities Region; financed by China Exim Bank, project begun by CNCPI & EC* 1984. Competed by Jiangxi Corporation, financed by Chinese government zero-interest loan US$3.06 million.	1984–96

Source: Adapted from Brautigam, Deborah, & Tang, Xiaoyang (2012, May). *An overview of Chinese agricultural and rural engagement in Ethiopia* (Discussion Paper 01185). Washington, D.C.: International Food Policy Research Institute.

*China National Complete Plant Import & Export Corporation.

Chinese foreign assistance is channeled through the Joint Ethiopia–China Commission (JECC) established in 1988, which includes agreements for the promotion and protection of investments and provides the two nations with a platform for dialogue about the economy. In the JECC, past and current projects can be reviewed and items of mutual interest worked out. It is a forum in which most development agreements are negotiated.

It is important to note that Ethiopia's five-year Poverty Alleviation and Sustainable Development Program (PASDP) is an important component of its second GTP.[36] The PASDP has six priority areas: agriculture, food security, health, water, education, and infrastructure—the last of which includes power, roads, industry, and cement. To implement these plans, in early 2006, Ethiopia approached the China Export-Import (Exim) Bank for a concessional loan and signed a development cooperation framework with the Chinese Ministry of Foreign Affairs and Commerce. The negotiations between Ethiopia and China were difficult as the latter wanted to use the Angolan model, tying natural resources such as oil to loans as collateral, which necessitated a structure in which Ethiopia's natural resources were used as security, because the model reinforced the strategic objectives of China's African foreign assistance policy, based on the need for collateralizing resources. As noted by one scholar,

> Although Ethiopia has graduated from the Heavily Indebted Poor Countries (HIPC) programme and was cautious . . . the loan had been approved in principle by August 2007 and Ethiopia was expecting a response from the Chinese side on the final details . . . by 2007 [and] EXIM Bank was to finance 85% of the development project while the Ethiopian government was to provide the remaining 15%.[37]

The agreement for the loan was tied to preapproved Chinese companies by the China Exim Bank, with a list provided to the Ethiopian government and cross-checked by its embassy in Beijing. The agreement was signed with the Commercial Bank of Ethiopia and led to the "expansion of the Mugher Cement Enterprise and construction of the Fincha–Amerti–Neshi multi-purpose project . . . a combined value of $276 million."[38]

The situation is similar in Ethiopia's construction sector. Although information is scant on whether the Angolan model was used in securing loans for the development of this booming sector in Ethiopia, Chinese companies have gained tremendous influence, especially in road construction, controlling 50–60% of the sector. While road construction, including the building of the Ring Road in Addis Ababa by the China Road and Bridge Corporation in 2003, is not of the highest quality, the roads have reduced congestion. However, Chinese dominance in the construction sector raises the issue of the importance of Ethiopian entrepreneurs and how to develop the domestic construction industry, which is plagued by an inadequate capital base. In addition, Chinese "tied" foreign assistance that uses Chinese companies and contract workers fosters monopolies that are not competitive, produce inefficiencies, and do not induce technology transfer to Ethiopia.

Thus, the Angola model and/or the automatic use of Chinese companies and workers to complete a project in the manufacturing and construction sectors is an obvious challenge in China–Ethiopia relations. It is, of course, correct to surmise that project-oriented Chinese foreign assistance has raised Ethiopia's negotiation capabilities with traditional donors, as Ethiopia can accept or reject the aid based on its conditions. But at the same time, if Ethiopia wants to enhance the efficiency and competitiveness of development assistance, it must seek and craft a policy that unties Chinese foreign assistance, a policy by which national companies and Ethiopian workers can benefit from the development process.

As things stand, the process of acquiring loans from China's Exim Bank is not transparent, and it is hard to discern whether the loans are designed to prompt economic development and welfare as the main objective. This is because Chinese financial institutions such as the Exim Bank, along with other banks, were set up to facilitate Chinese companies' investments in countries such as Ethiopia. Thus, it is difficult to define Chinese foreign assistance to Ethiopia because it is linked to Chinese trade and investment agreements. For Ethiopia to fully benefit from its relationship with China—that is, to realize the win-win formula—it needs to de-link Chinese investment from foreign assistance. Only in this way can Ethiopia decrease the likelihood of China using its foreign aid to leverage unfair or exploitative trade and investment concessions on existing asymmetrical relations.

Ethiopia, China, and the Horn of Africa

The Horn of Africa countries have made some progress in cooperating on conflict prevention and security and also around regional infrastructure development. They have solid assets on which to base future development—for example, most Horn of Africa countries are rich in natural resources and have renewable and nonrenewable sources of energy, groundwater reserves, great untapped agricultural capacity, and a population that is entrepreneurial, innovative, and increasingly vibrant. The region is likely to undergo substantive change when oil production starts in Kenya, Uganda, and possibly Somalia and Ethiopia. Somaliland has signed production-sharing agreements with foreign firms regarding areas yet to be drilled, and exploration companies report substantial prospects along Somalia's coastline that need to be tested by drilling. Sudan and South Sudan are currently the only oil producers, though almost every state in East Africa is believed to have substantial oil and gas reserves. If well utilized, these resources can contribute tremendously to the development of the region.

However, countries in the Horn of Africa face many challenges, individually and collectively. Peace and security challenges include the presence of conflict-affected and unconsolidated regimes that still face governance crises (Somalia and South Sudan), intracommunal conflicts (i.e., cattle rustling and conflict over water, pasture, and land), tensions between member states (Ethiopia and Eritrea, Djibouti and Eritrea), the proliferation of small arms and light weapons, the growing trend in radical religious movements in the region, rising urban and organized crime. Economic and social challenges in the region include high poverty levels, high levels of income and access inequality, high unemployment (particularly among the youth), and poor infrastructure development and telecommunications. These challenges have greatly impeded the sharing of resources, intraregional trade, and effective utilization of human and material resources.

The Horn of Africa region is affected by four main ongoing conflicts: (a) the fragmentation and now recovery of Somalia and the effects of the military intervention of its neighbors and global actors, (b) the separation of South Sudan from Sudan, (c) the unsolved dispute between Ethiopia and Eritrea, and (d) internal conflict in South Sudan. The reconfiguration of Ethiopia (with Eritrea's independence) and Sudan and the creation of two new states (Eritrea in 1993 and South Sudan in 2011) changed state borders in the Horn of Africa and left two new landlocked countries—Ethiopia and South Sudan—to consider alternative routes to the sea. Ethiopia has been particularly engaged in the effort to find peace in Somalia, where global, regional, and local dynamics sustained a war for decades and brought about the emergence of one of the most aggressive Somalia-based terrorist organizations.

The new government of Somalia was formed in 2004 in Kenya under the auspices of IGAD and with heavy support from both Ethiopia and Kenya. Despite its recognition by some international bodies such as the AU and the UN, the government lacked any meaningful control of Somalia. The Transitional Government was on shaky grounds, and Ethiopia as well as the West had significant concerns about political stability not only in Somalia but also throughout the Horn of Africa. After the attack on American embassies in Kenya and Tanzania by al-Qaeda–affiliated Somali nationals and similar but smaller-scale attacks by Islamists in Ethiopia, both the United States and Ethiopia considered the Islamic Courts—a union of Sharia courts that presented itself as a rival to the Transitional Government—a threat that had to be dealt with. Hence, Ethiopia preemptively invaded Somalia in 2006 with the goal of helping enforce the authority of the Transitional Government of Somalia and lessening the power of the courts. The unfortunate consequence was not only huge devastation in Mogadishu, which had begun to stabilize under the rule of the courts, but also the fragmentation of the courts and the evolution of an offshoot, the Al-Shabaab, a terror organization that has been responsible for many subsequent attacks, including one on the Westgate Mall in Kenya in 2013, in which 65 people were killed.

China, as a permanent member of the UN Security Council, has become involved in African conflicts. Although in the past it adopted the principle of peaceful coexistence, one of the main pillars of the 1955 Bandung Conference, its modernization in the post–Cold War era has necessitated that it be engaged in constructive intervention. Thus, China has taken part in UN peacekeeping operations.[40] Africa is not high in terms of security concerns for China, but its importance to China as a trading partner has grown. In any case, China's policy of constructive intervention has been buttressed by official cooperation between China and Africa in several agreements between 2003 and 2006, culminating in areas of cooperation under the 2009 Sharm El-Sheikh Plan and fleshed out in the Beijing Action Plan 2013–2015 adopted at the Fifth Ministerial Conference of the Forum on China–Africa Cooperation.

China also launched the China–Africa Cooperation Partnership for Peace and Security initiative, which includes financial assistance to the AU Peace and Security Council. This initiative has helped China expand its peacekeeping operations in Africa, an effort that coincides with its commercial and civilian presence on the continent. In 2015, China had more than 2,000 peacekeepers posted around the world. But nearly all are engineers, medical and transport workers, and security guards. China's peacekeeping operation in Africa is a significant shift from its stated policy of noninterference in African conflicts.

Since 1989, China has been involved in peacekeeping operations with the United Nations Transition Assistance Group (UNTAG) in Namibia, and since 1991 China has sent military observers to 15 UN peacekeeping operations in Africa.[41] China plans to be a major player in UN peacekeeping efforts. In 2015, President Xi informed the UN General Assembly it had "decided to lead in setting up a permanent peacekeeping police squad and build a peacekeeping standby force of 8,000 troops."[42] Xi also pledged that China would provide $100 million in military assistance to the AU to support the African Standby Force in boosting its capacity for crisis response. This force came into being after the establishment of the AU Peace and Security Architecture and provides regional standby brigades with the East African Standby Brigade (EASTBRIG), headquartered in Addis Ababa. Thus, Chinese deployment of troops under the UN flag, while modest, demonstrates its aim to strengthen its position within the UN and in its peacekeeping efforts. Its long-term objective may be the buildup of a military presence under UN command, which may eventually open up new possibilities for protecting its citizens and economic assets in Africa.

The relationship between Ethiopia and China has evolved and is based on either economic or security interests or both. For the EU, Ethiopia is an important economic and political ally in its Africa policy and is the largest aid recipient on the continent. EU and Chinese financial flows to Ethiopia are largely complementary and assist the African nation in obtaining resources greatly needed to implement its ambitious development strategy.[43] But more importantly, China is an alternative partner to the Ethiopian government, providing different development strategies.

The United States is also very much engaged with Ethiopia. Although the United States is not building roads, railways, or schools and Americans are not very visible in Ethiopia because of security issues, the United States has provided Ethiopia with much needed assistance for its agricultural growth program, food security, and nutrition as well as in combating HIV/AIDS.[44] In addition, the United States considers Ethiopia an important ally in its War on Terror, countering the influence of al-Qaeda fighters in Somalia and the region. For China, its past involvement with Ethiopia was based on geopolitical values as it needed Ethiopia's support in its quest for African solidarity and alliances against Western imperialism. But China has embarked on a path to great power status, and its traditional ideological policy is being replaced with instruments that facilitate its new aims befitting an emergent power.

China's current aims require relations with both Ethiopia and Djibouti. China is interested in Ethiopia because the nation, with an estimated population of 90 million people, offers a huge market. It is a stable nation in the Horn of Africa, with a large and reputable military force. But more importantly, China's deepening of relations with Ethiopia is also driven by political reasons: Addis Ababa is the headquarters of the AU and the UN Economic Commission for Africa and thus offers China an entrée to the African diplomatic community. Regarding Djibouti, while China's establishment of relations with the nation in many ways is similar to its relations with many African countries, one difference is that Djibouti offers China the means not only to become an important international maritime player at the chokepoint of the narrow strait of Bab el-Mandeb in the Red Sea but also to project its military presence in the Horn of Africa and environs.

Conclusion

This chapter analyzed the strategic elements in the China–Ethiopia relationship. It established that China recognizes Ethiopia as being a strategic state in African diplomacy and one of the pivotal states in the Horn of Africa. Ethiopia fits into China's plan to connect the Addis Ababa–Djibouti Railway into its BRI—discussed in detail in Chapter 5—connecting to South Sudan and the ports of Lamu in Kenya and Bagamoyo in Tanzania; China is building the railway to facilitate economic growth in the region as well as the region's trade with China. The chapter also outlined China's keen interest in regional organizations such as IGAD and efforts to facilitate peace in Somalia and South Sudan, in which it has significant investment.

Second, the chapter discussed Chinese foreign assistance to Ethiopia. It explained that Chinese aid to Africa in the 1960s was highly ideological, based officially on the Eight Principles for Economic Aid and Technical Assistance to Other Countries, and grounded in sovereignty, equality, and mutual respect. Beginning in the 1990s, Chinese aid to Africa became more pragmatic and was related to China's modernizing process, including its "going out" by investing abroad and seeking allies. The discussion established that China's foreign assistance to Ethiopia and other African nations is more appealing to those nations than aid from the West because it does not carry political or economic conditions; this feature has helped China expand its soft power on the continent.

Third, the chapter pointed out that while China has built many infrastructure-related projects in Ethiopia's urban and rural sectors—which coincided with Ethiopia's GTP—it is difficult to untangle Chinese investments, loans, and foreign assistance, and at times loans have been "tied" to resources. It also noted the monopoly of Chinese construction companies, a result of outbidding the few local firms that often lacked capital and technology, and the need for the Ethiopian government to help grow Ethiopian construction companies.

The chapter then described the relationships involving Ethiopia, China, and the Horn of Africa. The chapter pointed out that despite the conventional "knowledge" that the Horn of Africa lacked resources, the region has abundant renewable and nonrenewable resources such as vast ground water reserves, which need only capital and technology to bring them to the surface; great untapped agriculture capacity; and a population that is entrepreneurial, innovative, and vibrant. It noted oil explorations in Somalia and Ethiopia, gas discoveries as well as potential oil discoveries in Ethiopia, and South Sudan's oil production, derailed now by civil war. The chapter also noted the challenges to peace and security in this complex region in which different states were formed that had either indigenous roots or were crafted by different colonial nations with complicated, arbitrary borders.

Finally, the chapter analyzed China's presence in Djibouti, located at the Red Sea. It discussed the reasons for the military base along with the United States, France and soon to be joined by Russia and India in the Red Sea. The chapter noted the security interests of big powers and rising powers in the region. It underscored the importance of the Red Sea as a trade and oil route via the Suez Canal to Europe. It raised the complicated interests of and rivalries among Saudi Arabia, United Arab Emirates, and Egypt, on the one hand, and Qatar, Iran, and Turkey, on the other, who are rivals in the politics of the Red Sea littoral as well as in the Horn of Africa.

CHAPTER 5

China and Ethiopia

Long-term Perspectives

China's presence in Ethiopia is felt every day by ordinary citizens. It is felt in the *Merkato* in Addis Ababa, the largest open-air market in Africa, where traditional goods now made in China are sold. But above all, China's presence is seen in major urban centers where rail, highways, and high-rise buildings are under construction, as well as in rural Ethiopia where water schemes are being developed. Indeed, China has been involved in the transformation of infrastructure in rural Ethiopia and has contributed to most of the dramatic changes in the urban landscape in Addis Ababa. It is perhaps for this reason some scholars, after a multi-country analysis of attitudes, have concluded that China's presence in Ethiopia—and eight other African countries—has been generally positive.[1]

But in some countries, like Ghana and Zambia, Chinese activity has caused tensions and at times conflicts. The conflict between Chinese sojourners and Ghanaian citizens sparked by competition over illegal small-scale mining is well known.[2] In Zambia, there have been clashes between Zambian miners and Chinese companies in the copper belt. But as one scholar observed, such disagreements are linked to "a surge in economic nationalism and new challenges of neo-liberal orthodoxy [rather than] . . . the conceptual resuscitation of colonialism."[3] In South Africa, a combination of a sluggish economy, "a rising tide of xenophobia . . . new malls as well as African traders who have forged their own connections in China, are forcing Chinese traders and business people to consider leaving."[4]

An important but often forgotten aspect of China–Ethiopia relations is the presence of Ethiopians in Guangdong Province of South China, a manufacturing center. The presence of Ethiopians and many other Africans in this province, who arrive there in search of inexpensive goods for sale in their respective homes, is well known.[5] While the fortunes of these traders and entrepreneurs is dependent on the vagaries of the market and the whims of local Chinese officials in providing them visas, more and more are running businesses and manufacturing centers in China.[6] The importance of these African entrepreneurs in Guangdong Province was underscored when the Ethiopian government established a consulate there in 2009—the first African diplomatic center in the area—to serve its citizens as well as others in nearby provinces. The national airline of Ethiopia conducts daily flights to China and often is booked full of African merchants headed to or returning from Guangdong and other destinations in China.

The reverse is also true; according to 2016 estimates, there are 60,000 Chinese in Ethiopia.[7] Although this number does not differentiate sojourners from employees of Chinese companies in Ethiopia, it does indicate an increasing movement of people between the two nations. Thus, Chinese in Ethiopia and Ethiopians in China have become important actors in South–South relations. One little-known aspect of Chinese migration to Ethiopia and the continent at large is the Chinese concept of *fangnu* (mortgage slave) or fixing the mortgage problem (*ba fangdai de wenti jiejue le.*) That is, there is a direct correlation between housing in China and labor migration to Ethiopia. One scholar of this problem explained it as follows:

> The *fangnu* is the child of present-day Chinese society, which is characterized by high social mobility . . . as well as a growing demographic imbalance owing to the one child policy. In this social context, a house [an apartment] is increasingly perceived as a mark of status, especially when competing on for the marriage market . . . [and] the so called *hunfang* (marriage house) become the norm in cities . . . unable to rely on financial support of their kin, temporary migration is a way to cope with this socio-economic pressure when settling in the city.[8]

Thus, while the push factor of Chinese migration to Ethiopia, and other African nations might be the housing factor, as indicated in the Introduction, there have been concerns about the increasing numbers of Chinese in Africa. But some scholars who have done field research in the agri-food sector in Ethiopia and Ghana discount such concerns:

> The realities of Chinese migrants in this sector [does not match] popular media stereotypes of empire building and land grabbing. . . . Far from being a "silent army" promoting larger Chinese state objectives, they operate independently and serve no agenda other than their own.[9]

Relations between nations rather than no relations is inherently good. The relations between Ethiopia and China, be they government to government or people to people, are good for Ethiopia, as are its multilateral relations with the EU and its bilateral relationship with the United States. There are, of course, concerns about Chinse relations with Ethiopia raised by traditional donors such as the United States.[10] This is because China's presence in Ethiopia and other African countries puts competitive pressure on the U.S. and European economic development regimes, but the reality is that Ethiopia now is in a new aid landscape and has entered an age in which it has choices. In addition, China's engagement with Ethiopia sheds light on the gap between U.S. and EU rhetoric and policy practices and puts pressure on traditional donor institutions to reform the development regime.

Nevertheless, there are questions about the degree to which Ethiopia has retained its sovereignty in terms of economic and aid relations with China. But before attempting to address this question, it is important to understand that Ethiopia began relations with donors in the 1950s as a sovereign state; the history of that is treated elsewhere.[11] What is important is that early in the 1990s, Ethiopia implemented its agricultural development–led industrialization strategy, which envisioned the growth of small-scale agriculture as leading industrialization and backward linkages as the main agents of change and development. As mentioned in Chapter 3, this strategy coincided with China's "going out" policy, creating opportunities for both countries to engage with each other. China needed a key ally in Africa and continental investment opportunities in a huge market; Ethiopia needed resources and technology to build its infrastructure, dams, energy, and key capital goods for industrialization. That is, Ethiopia's focus seems to be not so much on juridical sovereignty—it is the oldest independent nation in Africa—but rather economic growth and ability to provision its citizens with basic needs such as education, health, infrastructure and other economic and social goods. China may have a regional vison, that is connecting the East African countries of Ethiopia, Kenya, and Tanzania with Zambia and South Africa by building, in collaboration with the above nations, roads, rail, and ports to facilitate trade with China. This regional vision is to be financed by several Chinese state and private banks including construction companies which have considerable assets.

Ethiopia and China's Belt and Road Initiative

China initiated a major project in 2015, officially named the Silk Road Economic Belt and the 21st Century Maritime Silk Road. The project focuses on two goals. The first is to build six economic cooperation corridors and key maritime pivot points. The second is to strengthen cooperation in infrastructure connection, trade and investment, resource exploration, and finance. This project, originally referred to as the One Belt, One Road Initiative and now known simply as the Belt and Road Initiative (BRI), is not limited to the route of the ancient Silk Road. The objective is to construct a trade and infrastructure network connecting Asia with Europe and Africa.

One pillar of the extensive network in the Horn of Africa is the Addis Ababa–Djibouti Railway, designed to eventually connect the port of Berbera, in the nation of Somaliland, Somalia (at Mogadishu), Kenya (at Lamu), and Tanzania (at Bagamoyo). The plan is to link the central corridor transportation hubs to the TAZARA railway and connect it with other Eastern African countries, including Mozambique, Malawi, Zambia, the Democratic Republic of the Congo, Burundi, Rwanda, Uganda, Comoros, Madagascar, and later Seychelles.

Formally, the BRI emphasizes five areas of cooperation: (a) coordinating development policies, (b) forging networks of infrastructure and facilities, (c) strengthening investment and trade flows, (d) enhancing financial cooperation, and (e) deepening social and cultural exchanges. However, the transformation of Africa requires building continental infrastructure estimated at $100 billion annually, which is beyond the BRI's capacity to generate. Besides, Africa also has an urgent priority: it must address the root causes of migration—poverty, exclusion, marginalization and war—that lead to many African migrants dying in the Mediterranean. Obtaining financing from other sources such as the EU is debatable. The United Kingdom's Brexit will change the EU's policy toward Africa, and receiving resources from the United States under President Trump will be difficult. Another challenge to the BRI is the security gap and failed states. The African Union (AU) must "silence the guns" before the BRI can be fully implemented.

China's BRI is designed to achieve two interconnected goals. First, it is connected to the industrial adjustment of China that is based on export and investment, as well as technology, and industrial development of Africa. Second, it is linked to the strategy of revitalization and development in Africa.[12] In other words, China has reached an apex in its domestic economy, which has been based on infrastructural development, consumption, and services. There is thus the freeing up of resources, in terms of finance as well as human and capital goods, which has been essential to building infrastructure and modernizing China. Thus, according to one scholar, "large state enterprises, such as the China State Construction Engineering Corporation, the China Railway Corporation and the China National Petroleum Corporation, can expect to benefit from the Silk Road initiative."[13]

While the adjustment of China's industrial structure is beyond the scope of this book, one can discern the beginnings of the implementation of the BRI in the Horn and Eastern Africa. It is evident in the transport and other infrastructure connectivity built by the Chinese in Ethiopia and Kenya's standard-gauge Mombasa–Nairobi Railway, which was heavily financed by China's Export-Import (Exim) Bank. China is also involved in building Kenya's Lamu port complex, estimated to cost $24 billion, which is projected to connect South Sudan to Nakodok (northwest Kenya) to Isiolo (central Kenya), and link with Ethiopia's southern frontier town of Moyale, boosting the economic development of the East African region.[14]

The project at Lamu, officially known as the Lamu Port South Sudan Ethiopia Transport (LAPSSET) Corridor, will have 32 berths at completion. The port complex, which is being built by China Communication Construction Company, is important because Kenya will play "a key role in the emerging East Africa oil and gas industry with a new export terminal at Lamu and a crude oil pipeline enabling oil exports to Asia beginning 2017."[15] Ethiopia, Kenya, and South Sudan have been discussing financing options for the LAPSSET project. Farther south in Eastern Africa, China has begun to negotiate building a huge port complex and a special economic zone (SEZ) near Bagamoyo, Tanzania worth at least $10 billion. The port is designed to become, along with Djibouti, Lamu, and Berbera, a transport hub for East Africa along with cities of Djibouti, a transport hub for East Africa.

China is also investing in infrastructure and major developments in Dar es Salaam, Tanzania. The Bagamoyo Agreement is ambitious because it includes a rail connection to Ruvu Station and an extended link with the TAZARA railway, a highway linking the port to the Uhuru Highway that goes to Zambia; construction is now underway.[16] The infrastructure development agreement is financed by China Merchant Holding International and Oman's biggest sovereign wealth fund, the State General Reserve Fund.[17] All of these megaprojects in the Horn and Eastern Africa, planned or under construction, have one objective: to transform agrarian economies through a forward linkage to industry, building robust economies with high wages, leading to the emergence of a middle class that will eventually consume Chinese exports and locally produced goods.

With all its challenges, Chinese credit and investments increase economic activity and facilitate trade growth in the Horn and Eastern Africa region. On the other hand, the BRI is also good for China for several reasons. First, China's infrastructure investment creates some economic growth in the region, but it also confers on China some influence in the regional affairs of Ethiopia, Kenya, and Tanzania. Second, the BRI, through concessionary loans and building of infrastructure in the region, provides short-term employment and also unloads Chinese industrial overcapacity; however, it also impacts state–society relations in terms of ownership of assets in respective East African countries. Thus, while the BRI is beginning to have a major impact in the Horn and Eastern African countries, in the final analysis it serves the long-term strategy of China, boosting its economic leadership in the world and ensuring economic growth for decades to come. But the growth is dependent on the economies of other regions, which eventually will become consumers of Chinese exports. One such country is Ethiopia.

Ethiopia's Development Plan, the BRI, and Regional Integration

Ethiopia is one of the fastest growing economies in the world. Its economic growth, which averaged 10.9% over the past decade, is particularly impressive given that it is not rich in natural resources. It is among the few nations that are on track to achieve most of the Millennium Development Goal targets set by the United Nations. Ethiopia's long-term vision was articulated in its agriculture-led development industrialization policy and its Growth and Transformation Plan (GTP) for 2011–2015. The main goal of this plan was to foster broad and rapid development and increase GDP growth to 11% (see Table 5.1). Ethiopia

Table 5.1. Ethiopia's GDP Growth from 2005 to 2010 (in %)

Sector	Starting (2005)	2006	2007	2008	2009	2010	Average (2006–2010)
Total Growth in GDP	12.6	11.5	11.8	11.2	9.9	10.1	11.0
Agriculture and allied activities	13.5	10.9	9.4	7.5	6.4	6.0	8.0
Industry	9.4	10.2	9.5	10.0	9.9	10.2	10.0
Services	12.8	13.3	15.3	16.0	14.0	14.5	14.6

Source: Federal Democratic Republic of Ethiopia, Ministry of Finance and Economic Development. (2010). *Performance Evaluation of the First Five Years Development Plan (2006–2010) and the Growth and Transformation Planning (GTP) for the Next Five Years (2011–2015)* [A draft document for discussion with the Regional/City administrations translated from Amharic]. Retrieved from https://phe-ethiopia.org/admin/uploads/attachment-404-Growth%20and%20Transformation%20Plan%20Aug%202010%20PPT%20translation%20revised.pdf.

seeks to position itself as Africa's leading manufacturing hub and as an outsourcing alternative to countries such as China, where rising labor costs are driving margin-conscious multinationals to look elsewhere. But Ethiopia will continue to need significant foreign assistance in the short term to continue to grow its economy. It also needs to build the basis for good government, improve the management of bureaucracies, and enhance citizen participation, transparency, and accountability during the development process.

Ethiopia's industrial development strategy addresses four economic subsectors: the textile and garment, meat and leather products, agro-processing, and construction industries. All are agriculture-based and/or labor intensive, and specialized institutes and/or training programs have been created for each one. Small-scale manufacturing enterprises, which constitute a major part of nonfarm employment, require attention because they operate at very low productivity levels. Most are cottage industries and small firms that lack capital as well as technical and managerial skills. The challenge for Ethiopia is how to expand productive formal employment in a way that will fully absorb the currently unemployed or underemployed labor force. The Ethiopian industrial development strategy recognizes the importance of state intervention in challenging and supporting development-oriented firms. The strategy also recognizes the need to build strong relationships with both domestic and foreign investors such as China, as partners in achieving its development plans.

Several tangible institutional changes have been implemented with the aim of achieving the objectives of the GTP. These include civil service reform and the establishment or strengthening of specialized technology institutes for subsector development in leather products, textiles and apparel, the sugar industry, metal, dairy, and meat. Ambitious reforms have been initiated in complementary areas, such as the overhauling of the technical and vocational training system. The Ethiopian industrial development strategy recognizes the role of the private sector as an engine of growth as well as the importance of state intervention, particularly in agriculture.

The focus on agriculture (see Table 5.2) is based on the logic that demand-led industrialization must include a work force that is 85% rural and engaged in agriculture. The hope is that as the productivity of the agricultural workforce increases, it will translate into higher incomes, resulting in demand for inputs from the manufacturing sector. But at present the connection of agriculture to manufacturing is tenuous. According

Table 5.2. Sectoral Distribution of GDP (in %)

Sector	2005	2010
Agriculture and related	47.4	41
Industry	13.6	13
Services	39.0	46
Total	100.0	100

Source: Federal Democratic Republic of Ethiopia, Ministry of Finance and Economic Development. (2010). *Performance Evaluation of the First Five Years Development Plan (2006–2010) and the Growth and Transformation Planning (GTP) for the Next Five Years (2011–2015)* [A draft document for discussion with the Regional/City administrations translated from Amharic]. Retrieved from https://phe-ethiopia.org/admin/uploads/attachment-404-Growth%20and%20Transformation%20Plan%20Aug%202010%20PPT%20translation%20revised.pdf.

to one estimate, manufacturing employed 4.5% of the total workforce in 2013.[18] To mitigate this, the Ethiopian state is investing in rural areas in infrastructure, health, primary education, vocational training centers, and dedicated technology training centers for specific industries (sugar, meat, leather, dairy). It is also increasing the area under irrigation, and several value chain programs are underway.

The second area chosen for selective state intervention is the export sector. Given the limited size of local markets and the need to generate foreign exchange, there is a clear focus on export industries, with some lessons learned from the Asian tigers. Ethiopia's emphasis in this sector is on high-value agriculture (horticulture) and agro-processing industries (leather products). Export industries benefit from favorable land lease rates, soft loans, tax incentives, subsidies for participation in trade fairs and international missions, and other services. In addition, differential interest rates are offered for various products such as horticulture and leather projects, which qualify for soft loans if export targets are agreed upon for individual firms. Devaluation of the birr has helped increase export competitiveness and resolve foreign exchange crises but has also led to increases in the prices of imported inputs critical to development, particularly food items.

The third area in which the Ethiopian state has focused is labor-intensive industries that are more appropriate than capital-intensive ones due to Ethiopia's factor endowment. Ethiopia's industrial development strategy focuses on the agro-processing and garment industries. However, this strategy underlines the fact that low labor productivity seriously constrains export competitiveness in terms of attracting outsourced tasks in global value chains. The beginnings of such endeavors now exist, and Ethiopia's resource base and cheap labor have already attracted Chinese investment and resulted in the establishment of SEZs. So far, two are operational and eight others are planned throughout the country.[19]

The fourth critical venture Ethiopia has undertaken since 1991 is a grand scheme to rebuild its infrastructure. The construction of a modern power and transportation system is part and parcel of Ethiopia's GTP, which envisions—and some of it has already been completed—providing integrated logistics services.[20] This includes the provision of roads and railway infrastructure, air transport, and dry-dock maritime services. The objective of power generation in the energy sector is to create a modern power system that increases capacity fourfold to 10 GW and constructs a 16,000-km road transport system. But the highlight of these schemes was the construction of the 34.24-km Addis Ababa light rail system financed by the Exim Bank of China and built by China Railway Group. The construction of an additional 41-km light rail is planned to be undertaken soon.

In terms of energy and hydropower, Ethiopia is completing the building of the Grand Renaissance Dam 25 miles east of its border with Sudan, which is projected to produce 6,000 MW annually. The dam will be the largest hydroelectric power plant in Africa when completed. The potential impacts of the dam and the methods Ethiopia will use in sharing the waters of the Nile River have been sources of basin-wide cooperation as well as regional controversy.[21] Although China is not entirely financing the construction of the dam, the Chinese Electric Power Equipment and Technology Company, is covering 85% of the cost of the transmission lines; the balance is being financed by the Ethiopian Electric Power Corporation.[22]

In terms of railways, Ethiopia plans to construct a 2,741-km national railway network in five corridors and six routes.[23] A major plank of Ethiopia's railway system is the Addis Ababa–Djibouti Railway, whose service began in 2015. The 750-km track linking Addis Ababa with Djibouti was the first modern electrified railway line in the Horn of Africa. The new railway replaces the 1894 French-built old diesel railroad line that had fallen into disrepair. It is the second transnational railway China has built in Africa; in 1970, China built the TAZARA Railway, which linked Dar es Salaam with Zambia.

It is important to note that when Ethiopia embarked on the Addis Ababa–Djibouti Railway plan, it invited several experts from developed nations, notably Switzerland and Australia, to do a survey. One reported:

> Constructing an electrified railway from the flat desert land around Djibouti right up to the Ethiopian Plateau was an impossible task . . . [but Chinese companies] took the initiative . . . providing geological and hydrological data for the proposed route, collected by technicians.[24]

The project cost of $4 billion was 70% financed by China's Exim Bank and built by two large Chinese state-owned companies: China Civil Engineering Construction Corporation and China Railway Construction Corporation. The Addis Ababa–Djibouti Railway is seen as the start of a trans-African railway project connecting Djibouti to the Atlantic coast; it is expected to buoy relations with China on a continental level.[25] The railway is critical for landlocked Ethiopia, which relies on Djibouti, on the Red Sea coast, as its main gateway, for up to 90% of its imports and exports. But Ethiopia is hedging on the port of Berbera in Somaliland and owns a 19% share with DP World, a Dubai Company; the rest is owned by Somaliland.[26] For China, the completion of the Addis Ababa–Djibouti Railway is

> a symbolic achievement of the Belt and Road Initiative and stands as a landmark project for Sino-African cooperation in building the "three major networks" (railways, roads, regional aviation) to enable industrialization. The railway will be a catalyst for development in Ethiopia and Djibouti.[27]

Ethiopia also has its own design to connect some of its major cities and has rail projects connecting Mekelle in the north, Galafi and Djibouti in the east, Awash in central Ethiopia, Sebeta near Addis Ababa the Ethiopian capital, and Jimma in southwest Ethiopia. The Ethiopia Railway Corporation (ERC) has given 18 Chinese companies permission to design, survey, and supervise construction of the four railway tracks. These railways are envisioned to connect to North Sudan, Central Sudan, and South Sudan. There is also a plan to connect the Addis Ababa-Djibouti Railway to the Lamu corridor and beyond, the main objective being to connect Ethiopia economically to its neighboring countries. While most of the railways will be constructed by China, some such as the Woldeya–Kombolcha–Awash Railway will be financed by a consortium of lenders, including Turkey, Sweden, Denmark, and Switzerland.[28]

In terms of regional integration, the AU officially recognizes the Common Market for East and Southern Africa (COMESA), the East African Community (EAC), and the Intergovernmental Authority for Development (IGAD). Regional economic communities (RECs) are becoming increasingly important in terms of economic development due to the increasing need for coordination among member states to achieve common goals by leveraging each other's resources for security and development. RECs in the region have great potential to contribute to economic development, and they could play an important role with China in facilitating regional approaches to common problems.

In this regard, the EAC, COMESA, and IGAD must be better supported to achieve their core objectives of promoting market integration; developing regional infrastructure with foreign direct investments, including from China; and strengthening stability, predictability, and transparency in regional governance. Despite the active engagement by member states in the COMESA and EAC forums, the lack of adequate infrastructure, including energy; cumbersome customs procedures; and a wide range of formal and informal nontariff barriers (licenses, quotas, embargos, standards, bureaucratic borders, and road checks) continue to hamper interregional trade and integration. Mutual suspicion is also a significant challenge as some countries fear there will be winners and losers in such an integration and do not wish to be on the losing side. A well-devised and structured regional trade and integration policy that distributes gains fairly would be a critical step in enhancing the welfare of all in the region.

A key organization in the Horn of Africa is IGAD, the eight-country organization whose original mandate was to deal with issues relating to drought, famine, environmental degradation, and development. Its role has expanded and incorporates the collective effort within the region to address the multiple conflicts and security dilemmas in the Horn of Africa. IGAD negotiated the current governance structure in Somalia and is presently overseeing the negotiations of the South Sudan parties. These have been challenging conflicts, and the engagement of regional members as parties in those conflicts has complicated efforts to create a sustainable peace. Indeed, regional dynamics and competition between member states often create unresolved tension. IGAD is both a political forum of regional member states—and thus characterized by mutual suspicion, alliance building, and power play—and the regional organization that seeks to develop the institutional capacity to improve peace, security, and development in the region. In addition, IGAD has been at the forefront of dealing with small-scale conflicts, including cattle rustling and conflicts over water and pasture, which take place across the borders of its member states and often create displacements and hundreds of deaths.

Two key challenges to all these institutions are capacity and resources. Often RECS and other regional entities operate with a very small staff, several of them carrying out tasks they are not fully equipped to undertake, and on shoestring budgets; this has led China to contribute some funding to IGAD.[29] To fully contribute to the peace and economic development of the region, these institutions need to develop into well-funded, well-managed, fully capacitated, efficient, and effective regional organizations.

It is obvious from the above discussion that Ethiopia has begun to transform its economy by focusing on agriculture, building infrastructure, and concentrating on energy and hydropower production as building blocks of its development. In terms of employment and transfer of technology and skilled human labor deployed from China, these sectoral developments are good for Ethiopia and the region. While estimates of trade between China and the nations of these two regions of Africa is hard to discern, the BRI connection is set to maximize intraregional trade and facilitate integration already begun through the EAC and COMESA. Ethiopia is not a member of the EAC but soon might join; as the regional military power providing security in the Horn of Africa, it is a member of COMESA.

Thus, Ethiopia will also benefit from regional integration because the BRI will not only enhance the trade of individual nations but will also facilitate trade relations in the Horn and Eastern Africa region, extending down the Swahili coast and across the continent at large. This integration will enable these nations to establish mutually beneficial institutions that could facilitate regional economic growth. As one astute observer wrote,

> The port of Mombasa serves Kenya, Uganda, Rwanda, South Africa and Democratic Republic of the Congo. The Lamu port, which is under construction in Kenya, can serve Kenya,

Ethiopia, South Sudan and Uganda. Similarly, improving the capacity of the Port of Djibouti means improving international trade in the region, including Ethiopia. The port in Dar es Salam has also an important role in facilitating international trade in the region.[30]

Ethiopia is emerging as a regional power, its economy is growing rapidly, it is the region's military power, and its vast hydroelectric potential is beginning to be realized. Its desire to join the EAC is evidenced by its infrastructure and energy agreements with Kenya.[31] It has also entered security and development alliances with South Sudan and will possibly do so in the future with Uganda.

In the past, a big stumbling block for regional integration within the EAC has been the infrastructure deficit, since individual member states are focused on domestic policy and leaders are preoccupied with staying in office. But now the visions of the three main states of the EAC—Kenya, Tanzania, and Uganda—and the increasing stability of Somalia, in conjunction with the rapid development of the Lamu port complex, seem to give greater impetus for regional integration. The Lamu port complex is part of the South Sudan–Ethiopia Transport corridor (LAPSSET) and is being built by China at an estimated cost of $424 billion.[32] Although regional integration and economic growth are part and parcel of the AU's Agenda 2063, a strategic framework for the socioeconomic transformation of the continent over 50 years, their realization is dependent on the provision of peace and security.

The Lamu port and corridor facilities connecting Ethiopia to South Sudan were responses to increased demands on interregional and international trade. Dry cargo throughput at Lamu port will amount to an estimated 13.5 million tons in 2020 and 23.9 million tons in 2030; these estimates are larger than the present figures for Mombasa port.[33] But the main challenges of LAPSSET concern security, particularly in Eastern Equatoria State in South Sudan. While plans are underway to connect Lamu to Isiolo in central Kenya and to Nakodok and then to Juba, the unsolved civil war in South Sudan and risks in the transportation of crude oil to the Lamu port complex in Kenya mean that for now the goal cannot be realized. However, the building of rail lines connecting the three countries of South Sudan, Ethiopia, and Kenya with a standard gauge has either been planned or begun.

Ethiopia, the Horn, and Eastern Africa stand to benefit from the BRI initiative in terms of employment, technology transfer, and the construction of infrastructure as China engages the region with its skilled manpower, high technology, and capital. In short, the connection to the BRI could have substantial impact on the region for two reasons. First, economic integration is beneficial in facilitating trade and investments and working on common problems. Second, BRI can not only facilitate economic integration on the local level but also forge connections between East Africa and neighboring regions. But the BRI in the Horn and Eastern Africa can be realized only if concerned nations in the region invest heavily in building networks of rail and feeder roads and link them to the tentacles of the BRI. But such regional objectives are difficult to realize because of the immediacy of national objectives coupled with the problem of collective action which often tends to produce the "free rider problem" because of asymmetric information.[34] But the BRI in the Horn and Eastern Africa could be very beneficial in regional development. One scholar has observed that

> [the BRI] could partly ease a problem that has bedeviled African development since the end of the colonial era. The lack of coherent trans-border infrastructure networks is the result of incoherent planning by different colonial rulers, resulting in truncated connections that make it extremely expensive to get both raw materials and manufactured goods from one African country to the other.[35]

Thus, building new railways and feeder roads will enable these regions to be fully engaged in international trade, exporting resources and importing goods. In the past, embedded liberalism and globalization had not benefitted Africa due to the technology and digital divide and various imposed economic and political conditions, but now the center of globalization has moved east. The BRI offers a second chance. It offers Africa an opportunity for maintaining, through a combination of diversification, export competitiveness, productivity, and technology upgrades, a strategic edge in global transactions. But there are also risks for Ethiopia, Kenya, and Tanzania from the BRI from China. For the regional countries, the risk is from the modalities of debt.

Table 5.3. Chinese Loan Commitments to Ethiopia by Creditor, 2012–2013

Organization	Signature date	Economic sector	Amount (in US$ million)	Interest rate (%)	Grace period (years)	Maturity (years)
Central government						
Exim Bank China	Mar. 27, 2013	Electric light and power production	292,250,000	2	8	20
	Jun 13, 2013	Rail transport	300,000,000	1.75	5	24
Government of China guaranteed						
China Development Bank	Dec. 19, 2012	Sugar manufacturing	25,000,000	Libor + 2.6	3	10
China Electric Power	Apr. 26, 2013	Electrical distribution	1,002,970,414	3.08	3	15
Exim Bank China	May 15, 2013	Rail transport infrastructure	220,471,000	Libor + 3.0	6	15
	May 15, 2013	Rail transport infrastructure	981,260,000	Libor + 3.0	6	15
	May 15, 2013	Rail transport infrastructure	1,289,029,000	Libor + 3.0	6	15
Non-Chinese government guaranteed						
Huawei	Oct. 1, 2013	Telecommunications	800,000,000	Libor + 1.5	3	15
ZTE	Oct. 10, 2013	Telecommunications	800,000,000	Libor + 1.5	3	15

Source: Cheru, Fantu. (2016). Emerging Southern powers and new forms of South–South cooperation: Ethiopia's strategic engagement with China and India. Third World Quarterly, 37(4), 598.

The top five recipients of Chinese loans in Africa in 2002–2014, by amount, were Angola, the Democratic Republic of the Congo, Ethiopia, Kenya, and Sudan. Resource-backed loans make up 30% of China's total loans in Africa.[36] While trade between China and Africa is dominated by natural resources exported to the former, China views Africa—including Ethiopia—as an export market for consumer goods, electronics, and machinery. China gets the largest share of its imports (64%) from resource-rich South Africa and Angola and 45% of its exports go to two of the most populous nations in Africa: Nigeria and Egypt. But Ethiopia is also gaining ground as an export market. In 2015, Chinese loans totaled $13 billion for Ethiopia, $6.8 billion for Kenya, and $2.34 billion for Tanzania.[37] There are several types of loans and terms of credit, including "tied" loans, which are discussed elsewhere.[38] But as one important scholar noted, referring to Africa in general, "We warn that debt levels are rising, the Chinese are unlikely to cancel these debts, and we express concern that African governments may not be able to absorb the sharply increased pledges made by Chinese leaders in December 2015."[39]

For China, the risk posed by the BRI in the Horn and Eastern Africa regions is political instability. That is, the project could exacerbate existing tensions as one country benefits more than others coupled with the discovery of oil, gas, and other resources. In general, for the Horn and Eastern African regions to benefit from the BRI, the governments of Ethiopia, Kenya, and Tanzania must strengthen their institutions, embedding regulatory institutions with reliable oversight. Otherwise, it will be difficult for the Horn and Eastern African nations to absorb the infusion of development loans and economic and security assistance.

China and Ethiopia: The Long-Term Perspective

The long-term relationship between China and Ethiopia is dependent on three interrelated factors: political stability in Ethiopia, U.S. and EU interest and influence in Ethiopia and among other nations in the Horn of Africa, and the politics of the Red Sea littoral. The issue of long–term political stability in Ethiopia, necessary for economic growth, is complex.

For the most part, Ethiopia's experiment in ethno-national federalism has ensured better peace and security for most of Ethiopia's population. The institutionalization of ethnonational identities and hence ethno-national boundaries is not, in and of itself, either good or bad as long as the process is done in a peaceful and democratic, negotiated way, consistent with human rights for all. Ethiopia's federalism is a work in progress and ethno-national group conflicts cannot be completely eradicated. Nevertheless, in some instances the relationships among ethno-national groups have become progressively more competitive as they assert jurisdictional boundaries and involve government finances.

The challenge is that while Ethiopia's federalism is built on the assumption that every ethno-national group occupies a territorially defined geographic area, in many parts of the country, establishing a neatly homogeneously inhabited territory is very difficult. This has led to several tensions among some subnational units and led to competing claims between Oromia and Somali Regional States as well as ethno-national and interclan competition in Afar and Oromia Regional States over grazing land and water. At times, the difficulty in defining ethno-national groups geographically has also manifested itself in such groups organizing and demanding the recognition of regional-state councils as local state subunits, thereby guaranteeing financial resources for the groups.

Ethnic mobilization is a political reality in Ethiopia, and although at times the competitions have been described as "ethno-national conflicts," they may be the result of rivalry over state resources more often than incompatible ethno-national differences. Ethiopia's ethnolinguistic rearrangement has failed to account for the many Ethiopian farmers who had historically migrated or been forcibly relocated southwards by previous governments because of warfare and/or soil exhaustion in the north, resulting in conflict with local inhabitants. The issue of ethno-national citizenship, and particularly the rights of minorities in majority communities, is very important for peace and stability in Ethiopia. But in practice the rights of ethnic minorities in some regional states have been violated. While these violations of civil rights may not contribute to state fragility, their persistence can reverberate to other regional states, leading to retaliation, unrest, violence, and ultimately to disinvestments. Horizontal inequality based on identity and gender also directly contribute to conflict, and ethnic entrepreneurs often market this issue to their constituents over real or imagined grievances.[40]

An important factor in terms of political stability is the incumbency of the ruling party in Ethiopia, which is a political coalition of regional parties whose relationships are based on degrees of power differences. Nevertheless, the central party controls economic, political, and technical resources. It defines the organization of state structures, and its coexistence with those in its field of operations involves networks of reciprocity that include material benefits, status, protection, and authority, which are exchanged for personal loyalty and obedience. Thus, it is important to ask how the ruling party has been able to maintain its internal cohesion and political order in a political landscape of ethnonational parties in a multinational and multiethnic society. It has done so through elite pacts that depend upon resource distributive capacity at the central level. While a large distribution of resources can strengthen the pact, a lopsided distribution and corruption can lead to dissatisfaction, revolt, and strife. But if the exchange process is seen as mutually beneficial by all elites, the system can maintain itself.[41]

Beginning in 2018, the new leadership, within the ruling party of the EPRDF seems to beat to a different drummer and is leaning towards reforming the federal arrangements established in 1995 and cautiously moving in favor of a presidential system with the nation planning to hold national elections in May–June 2020. While the new leadership has its supporters and detractors—one group favoring federalism and the other a unitary system of government—the important fact remains without political stability, and effective leadership, foreign direct investment and the trajectory of Ethiopia's economic growth and development necessary to propel it to middle income status by 2050 may be stalled. Meanwhile, during the transition process, China-Ethiopia relations has held fast. And thorough 2019, Egypt with the support of its allies in the Middle East, namely Saudi Arabia and the United Arab Emirates—who are major investors in Ethiopia—has been on the diplomatic offensive regarding the completion of Ethiopia's Grand Renaissance Dam which it claims will diminish the Nile water flowing to its delta. The wrangle between Egypt and Ethiopia is being brokered by the US. A second variable to consider as critical in China and Ethiopia's long-term relationship is the politics of the Red Sea littoral—politics among both big and regional powers. The entire Red Sea south from the Suez Canal to the strait of Bab el-Mandeb is a strategic link between the Mediterranean Sea and the Indian Ocean. One source summed up the conundrum posed by this important link as follows:

> The *Bab el-Mandeb Strait* is a chokepoint between the Horn of Africa and the Middle East. . . . Located between Yemen, Djibouti, and Eritrea, it connects the Red Sea with the Gulf of Aden and the Arabian Sea. Most exports from the Persian Gulf that transit the Suez Canal and the SUMED Pipeline (from Saudi Arabia) also pass through *Bab el-Mandeb*.[42]

As a result of the area's strategic location, Aden in Yemen, Djibouti, and Berbera in Somaliland have become arenas where large and small powers—the United States, France, China, Turkey, Iran, Egypt, Qatar, Saudi Arabia, and Japan—project their interests with a variety of objectives, the closure of the strait of Bab el-Mandeb, or the perception of a closure, could have incalculable consequence for the global oil market. Iran and Qatar are exploring bases on Eritrean islands in the Red Sea, Saudi Arabia due to its conflict with Yemen is projecting its power in the area, and Turkey has negotiated with Sudan for a military base in Suakin, south of Port Sudan. The big powers have military bases in Djibouti because of its proximity to restive regions in the Horn of Africa and the Middle East and their need to protect oil routes to the Suez Canal.

There are several reasons China is present in the region. First, it has energy needs, as other big powers do, and 80% of its exports go through the Suez Canal. Second, China has been an active participant in an antipiracy effort off the Somali coast since 2008. Finally, China also wants to assume a greater role as a regional security provider in Africa. As a key member of the UN Security Council, its blue-helmeted troops are in Darfur and Mali as peacekeepers. In addition, China is involved as a mediator, in consultation with and with the support of IGAD, in South Sudan's on-again, off-again peace process. In brief, how events among the big, rising, and regional powers turn out will affect long-term relations between China and Ethiopia.

Another variable to consider in discussing long-term China–Ethiopia relations is the role of big powers in Ethiopia. As discussed elsewhere, Ethiopia is the oldest African ally of the West.[43] In 1951, Ethiopia sent troops as part of an American-led UN force supporting South Korea against the communist North and its ally, China. But after the Cold War ended in 1991, Ethiopia recalibrated its foreign policy with many nations, including China, and China's presence in Ethiopia is very tangible and visible.

It is then important to ask if the presence of China in Ethiopia is a challenge to the development policies of the United States and the European Union. Naturally, some may perceive China's "landing" in Ethiopia as undercutting the U.S. and EU policy of setting material incentives for political reforms. But a balanced view may be that both the United States and the European Union are important development partners of Ethiopia; they provide different economic goods in terms of assistance. While both the European Union and the United States want political reform in Ethiopia through conditionality, China, at least for now, has chosen not to interfere in the domestic affairs of Ethiopia. But this could change in the future as China becomes a leading global power and sees that its interests are well served if it is seen as a "responsible" nation and accepts the human rights norm.

In any case, it is a fact now that China is becoming Africa's biggest trading partner. As some observers have noted,

> U.S. economic activity on the continent remains in the same pattern as it has for over 50 years—focused on energy, finance, and aid. . . . The U.S. can play a tremendous role in Africa's growth over the next 10 years alongside and in collaboration with Chinese actors, but to do so it will have to adapt to today's Africa.[44]

Adapting to the new realities means coping with China's practice of economic relations, a policy of no strings attached and noninterference in the domestic affairs of nations as opposed to the U.S. and EU comprehensive political and policy dialogues and requirements of political and economic reforms.[45] Although the intent of the Western nations may be good, the fact on the ground is that China achieved its economic miracle without democratization and with relative political stability, making donor conditionalities unpalatable to African countries. And different paths to development are now generating debate in EU donor circles about the link between democratic reforms and economic growth in countries in transition.[46]

Therefore, EU donors have attempted to cooperate with China and Africa in a multilateral dialogue to formulate a proactive response to global development. However, persuading China to join the traditional aid system has met with very limited success, and historically China has not taken part in traditional donor rounds.[47] But one thing is clear: the fact that Chinese official flows of trade and investment have been growing in Ethiopia has implications for European development policy. As for Ethiopia, it seems it has devised two separate structures: one for EU donors who usually augment the national budget or are engaged in financing small projects, and another for China, which is involved with megaprojects. However, in the long term, the active presence of China in Ethiopia might prompt the EU to reform its commitment and change the fragmented nature of its aid system.[48]

As for political reforms, Ethiopia had begun to engage in dialogue with both the European Union and the United States and is headed towards political reform. But the road has been difficult and both the United States and the European Union had difficulty implementing their democracy promotion strategy in Ethiopia. After 2005, with the passage of a law governing NGOS, the United States abandoned its support in Ethiopia for civil society groups. But overall a key variable in reducing Ethiopia's vulnerability to political conditionality from the United States and the European Union is China's engagement with the ancient polity.

In 2018, the selection of a new prime minister, Dr. Abyi Ahmed, by the ruling party promised a democratic opening in Ethiopia. Opposition groups from abroad were invited into the country to participate in the political process. There were peace overtures with neighboring Eritrea which now has stalled and the transition to democracy in Ethiopia remains tenuous.

Conclusion

This chapter explored China and Ethiopia's relations in the long term. It briefly described the presence of Chinese in Ethiopia and Ethiopians in China and the increasing movement of people in search of opportunities. It explored China's interest in Ethiopia and Eastern Africa and its BRI. It discussed the building of the Addis Ababa–Djibouti Railway, and described the project as the beginning of a planned trans-Horn and Eastern Africa rail connecting South Sudan, Kenya's Lamu port complex, and Bagamoyo in Tanzania westward to the TAZARA railway and Zambia and then to South Africa. It noted that China's interests in the region, particularly in the Horn of Africa, carry the risk of political instability and that the AU could play a more enhanced role in establishing peace and security in the region. The chapter stressed that while such connectivity is good for Ethiopia's trade with China and other nations and for economic growth, regional integration is critical to transformation of the region, and member states should strengthen such institutions as IGAD, the EAC, and COMESA if the vision is to be realized.

The chapter also noted, briefly, the politics of foreign assistance, the role of the United States and European Union, and of China as a newcomer to the developmental regime. It noted that both the United States and China want Ethiopia to prosper and their differences are only in substance, the former insisting on conditionality, democracy, and human rights, and the latter practicing a policy of noninterference in the domestic politics of Ethiopia. As for the EU aid to Ethiopia, this chapter noted it was highly fragmented and that Chinese foreign assistance to Ethiopia might be beneficial to the European Union in terms of refocusing and restricting its foreign assistance.

The chapter discussed how Ethiopia's development plan fits with China's BRI and enhanced regional integration due to new capital investments being poured into building major infrastructure projects in the region. The chapter briefly discussed Ethiopian's GTP, and how the plan coincided with China's "going out," creating opportunities for Chinese state-owned and privately owned companies to undertake various megaprojects. Finally, in terms of long-term China–Ethiopia relations, the chapter examined the politics of the Horn of Africa and Ethiopia's important role in the region. It noted the presence of the big powers and of China in Djibouti and explored the various motives and interest of regional powers such as Iran, Qatar, and Turkey in the Red Sea littoral. The area is an important route of internal trade, including oil to Europe, a topic on which further research is warranted.

CHAPTER 6

Conclusion

The study has explored political, economic, and security aspects of China–Ethiopia relations. Thus, it is appropriate to ask what can be learned from the Ethiopian case study. As mentioned, China–Ethiopia relations is not wholly based on economic interests but rather political ones and the need for China to utilize "political resources" offered by Ethiopia. Second, and most important, the case study demonstrates Ethiopian agency where elites/leaders had a vison of transforming the country and took the initiative of building relations with China. In other words, Ethiopia, in its quest for rapid development, has a demand for capital and technology. China, which had "stepped out" into the world, became both the supplier and the catalyst in the implementation of Ethiopia's development policy. In other words, Ethiopian agency is demonstrated in its willingness to learn from China's modernization and its use of the current one-party state to achieve its Growth and Transformation Plan (GTP).

Although China has often used terms such as "South–South" to foster solidarity with developing nations, its relations with Ethiopia, while solid, are asymmetric. As for the rhetoric, Chinese leaders admit, despite its GDP, that China is still in the global South but is "a rising developing country rather than a developed one."[1] There seems to be some truth in that because, while China has lifted 800 million people out of poverty, World Bank figures indicate a sixth of its population of 1.3 billion still exists on less than two dollars a day.[2] Ethiopia wants to emulate China's achievements in eradicating poverty and becoming a middle-income nation in the foreseeable future.

The study began by tracing China–Ethiopia relations beginning with the ancien régime of Emperor Haile Selassie. First, it highlighted that China and Ethiopia had similar historical experiences. Although their experiences may differ, both were empires with a feudal past that eventually evolved their own indigenous states. However, the difference between past Ethiopian regimes and the EPRDF government is that it is development oriented. Its GTP has coincided with China's "going out" policy, which on the surface seems an expression of China's global ambitions.

But China's "going out" is more than that and is rooted in China's domestic politics as well as its political economy in shaping its bigger role in foreign economic policy. Some factors driving the new policy, besides China's massive foreign reserves, may be the challenges posed by the old industrial growth model and the evolving relationship between private and state enterprises, including financial institutions, as China embarks on a global Belt and Road Initiative and African investments. In Ethiopia, such investments have helped boost economic growth with the provisioning of basic infrastructure, dams, energy, and so forth. The Ethiopian government sees China as a model for certain economic policies, such as those for agriculture and rural development as well as poverty alleviation. The downside, however, may be that in the future economic slowdown and financial market instability in China could cause Ethiopia to lose its momentum.

Ethiopia and China agree policy of noninterference in the domestic affairs of nations. But such a stand has its detractors in Ethiopia, from NGOs to external actors and domestic interests to civil society groups. Ethiopia also supports China on the Taiwan issue, as do many African nations.

In terms of regional relations, such as between Ethiopia and Eritrea, China is cautious. However, in the 1998–2000 Ethiopian–Eritrean War, China was a major supplier of arms to the Ethiopian government. Ethiopia's importance in the restive Horn of Africa region was underlined by the presence of a Chinese military attaché at its embassy in Addis Ababa—the first in sub-Saharan Africa, indicating China's military footprint along with its economic interest in the Horn and Eastern Africa. In terms of China–Ethiopia economic relations, an entry sector was the construction industry, which historically and for the most part was an enclave of Italians under the imperial era as well as a state enterprise under the military regime; it was not innovative and the industry has not matured. Beginning in the 1990s, when the Ethiopian state began to undertake massive construction of its infrastructure, it was China that provided the service as national firms were either marginal or elbowed out due to underbidding by the more experienced Chinese firms, which often brought their own experts. In any case, these firms were part and parcel of Chinese economic assistance as they got preferential treatment in Ethiopia projects due to loan conditionalities. But the Ethiopian government, cognizant of the weakness of the Ethiopian construction industry, has now begun to award contracts to Ethiopian firms for road construction and some irrigation projects.

It is in the manufacturing sector that China is making inroads in Ethiopia. This sector historically has been marginal, but it is improving. Ethiopia is still moving through the early stages of economic development, and manufacturing is essential to sustaining long-term growth and poverty alleviation. There are many challenges in this sector. First is limited access to credit and land, as an investor must grasp not only national laws but regional state laws as well. Second is unreliable energy; although this may change soon with the completion of the Grand Renaissance Dam, it is still difficult for Ethiopian entrepreneurs to start a business. Finally, Ethiopia's tax system is cumbersome and customs complicated, and trade-related regulations increase the cost of doing business and thus often discourage foreign investors.

But despite some hurdles, Chinese companies in Ethiopia are thriving. There are several industrial zones in Ethiopia at various stages of development, some owned by Chinese companies. In terms of investments, most Chinese-licensed projects are in Addis Ababa, and in Oromia Regional State, mainly due to the infrastructural link to Djibouti and beyond. Chinese companies are engaged in the textile and shoe industries but have also branched out into railroad building and are engaged in partnership with the Ethiopian government in the provisioning of electric power and telecommunications. The Chinese company Huajian, located near Addis Ababa, is now the largest shoe manufacturer in Ethiopia. While there have been concerns raised by scholars regarding its impact on the nascent Ethiopian shoe industry, Huajian's products are for export elsewhere. Huajian was attracted to Ethiopia because of its comparative advantage in terms of low wages, productivity, and natural resources—it is home to the largest number of cattle in Africa.

China and Ethiopia have also stated that their partnership is strategic, with China providing finance and technology and Ethiopia working with China in regional connectivity—transportation networks, telecommunications links as well as electricity. This is in addition to cooperation in the fields of agriculture, mining, and energy. However, there are many actors cooperating with China and Ethiopia, and not all of the investment and loans come from Beijing. Simultaneously, there are multiple Chinese actors, such as state institutions, private companies, and, at times, important entrepreneurs seemingly working at cross purposes, at times creating tensions between political interests and commercial markets. In brief, not all Chinese entities in Ethiopia work for the Chinese state.

A second reason why Ethiopia is considered a strategic partner by China is because it is a key player in regional organizations that China wants to influence. One such entity in the Horn of Africa is the Intergovernmental Authority for Development (IGAD). In 2002 and again 2012, IGAD embarked on finding solutions to the South Sudanese conflicts, culminating in successful conclusion of the Comprehensive Peace Agreement (CPA). But the civil war in South Sudan continues in one form or another. In any case, China treads carefully and its diplomatic effort seems designed to work within the overall peace process of IGAD, which is the first order of business for trade and investments in the region.

In terms of Chinese foreign assistance to Ethiopia, the study underlined that it is a newcomer to the development regime dominated by the West, and is one of many emerging donors that are beginning to change the name of the game. In the past, China's foreign assistance to Africa was based on ideological principles of the Maoist era with strong anti-imperialist rhetoric. But it is now much more pragmatic and is based on securing resources, such as raw materials, necessary to modernize China. Second, Chinese foreign assistance is also politically motivated and is used to cultivate friendly nations, such as Ethiopia, that are big players in African politics, as it aspires to global power. And finally, the motive of China's foreign assistance is the extension of soft power Chinese ideals and culture, eschewing policies imposed by traditional donor nations, such as interference in domestic affairs, and this resonates with many African leaders, including Ethiopia.

Historically China's foreign assistance to Ethiopia, beginning in the early 1970s, was in visible and practical undertakings—veterinary; research; training in bamboo weaving; road, water supply, and power station projects, and irrigation schemes. But now foreign assistance is channeled through the Joint Ethiopia–China Commission (JECC) established in 1988, a forum where most development projects are negotiated and agreed upon. But overall, little is known about China's foreign assistance because it involves many Chinese actors, the Export-Import Bank, and the Chinese Ministry of Foreign Affairs, and at times development projects involving loans are often collateralized with resources. Thus, Chinese foreign assistance in Ethiopia and in Africa, as well as its implementation, is a topic on which further research is warranted.

In terms of China in the Horn of Africa and the pivotal role played by Ethiopia in the region, the research highlighted that although peace and stability have been elusive, the expert conclusion that the region is bereft of resources is premature and unwanted. The Horn of Africa has immense resources in terms of untapped underground water, renewable and nonrenewable energy, great untapped agricultural capacity, and an entrepreneurial population. A British company has discovered oil in Ethiopia with estimated potential of two billion barrels, and a Chinese company has discovered vast natural gas reserves. Oil has also been discovered in Kenya, and Somalia has attractive oil and gas prospects.

The Horn of Africa, particularly Djibouti, is becoming a contested area in which big and emerging powers, as well as other nations such as India, are attempting to contain China. Russia also has indicated an interest in the region. While in the past China's navy has been active in the region—it captured Somali pirates in the Indian Ocean—in 2017. By all accounts, as its interests in the Horn of Africa—Ethiopia, North and South Sudan, and Somalia—grows, it may feel entirely entitled to protect its people and investments, leading perhaps to a more interventionist policy.

In addition, as a permanent member of the UN Security Council, China has taken part in UN peacekeeping operations in African conflicts, including in Darfur and Mali. China's involvement is not benign as Africa's importance as a trading partner is growing. This was underlined in 2015 with the China–Africa Cooperation Partnership for Peace and Security, which includes financial assistance to the African Union. The African Union Peace and Security Architecture (AUPSC) works also with the East Africa Standby Brigade headquartered in Addis Ababa. The United States, a traditional ally of Ethiopia, is very much present in the country and is involved in many types of projects, such as combating HIV/AIDS as well as enhancing agricultural productivity and, of course, educational projects. But for security reasons, it is not as visible as China, which is building roads, bridges, and other infrastructure. For a while it had a low-profile facility in Arba Minch in Southern Ethiopia from which it was sending out drones in its war against terror, particularly in Somalia, but the facility has moved elsewhere in the Horn of Africa region.

Ethiopia is governed by a political coalition of regional parties whose relationship is based on degrees of power differences. For now, the political party controls political, economic, and technical resources. It defines the organization of state structures, and its coexistence with its field of operations involves networks of reciprocity that include material benefits, status, protection, and authority, which are exchanged for personal loyalty and obedience. The political order is based on the principal of autonomy and self-determination of nationalities. The challenge which faces the Ethiopian political order is that of deepening inclusive processes and strengthening institutions of political—but particularly economic—governance. The lack of strong institutions, that, among other things, govern the market in Ethiopia has produced crony capitalism and corruption, leading to the 2017–2018 political unrest.

Although Chinese companies are famous for taking risks that Western companies shun and investing in nations that are in turmoil, in terms of the long term, China's investment and continued presence in Ethiopia will be based on political stability in Ethiopia and the Horn of Africa. The Chinese presence in Ethiopia is not resented by ordinary citizens, who consider them for the most part to be hardworking individuals. There are, of course, on occasions nationalist sentiments about low wages paid by Chinese companies, particularly in the industrial parks. But this does not compare to the open resentment shown to cut flower farms and their European investors because of chemicals used in the growing process, which has affected many Ethiopian workers, particularly women. It is well known that a developing nation such as Ethiopia lacks capital and technology to fulfill its GTP. There are also important pressing issues such as food security to a rapidly growing population estimated in 2019 to be 108 million. The recent unrest triggered by Ethiopian youth demonstrates rising expectations for political and economic goods in the age of the Internet and mass media, where citizens witness daily how citizens in developed nations live.

The Chinese presence in Ethiopia—for that matter, in Africa—also raises another significant question. China is now involved in the Belt and Road Initiative (BRI). While this is planned to connect China to Tajikistan, Iran, Turkey, Russia, and eventually the Netherlands, it is also planned to connect India (Kolkata) to Kenya (Lamu), Djibouti, and Egypt, then north to Greece and finally to Italy. While this massive initiative is a daunting task, estimated to cost $4 trillion, it will naturally require security alliances with nations to protect such investments and where such alliances are not available, particularly in its African leg, will it require military bases? In East Africa, the BRI is planned to connect Djibouti and the Addis Ababa–Djibouti Railway to Lamu (Kenya) and Bagamoyo (Tanzania), and then to the TAZARA railway in order to reach copper-rich Zambia and South Africa. The BRI in Eastern Africa is projected to grow the economies of the nations in the Horn of Africa and Eastern Africa by contributing regional development via international trade with China.

Meanwhile, geopolitical competition is intensifying in the region, and China is expanding its influence in the Horn of Africa. Recently, there has been a rapprochement between Ethiopia and Eritrea, a development that is bound to accelerate this influence. Eritrea is emerging from its isolation, after numerous sanctions by the UN, and it will seek to have strategic partnership with other states, such as China, that will not balk at its authoritarianism. Russia also is not standing by idle and has shown interest in the Horn of Africa and Red Sea littoral. Russian delegates recently visited Eritrea and agreed to the construction of a naval logistics center as part of a broader long-term Russian effort to establish a strategic military position on the Red Sea and the Gulf of Aden. Russia is also interested in building a military base in Somaliland. These different bases on the Red Sea are bound to affect Djibouti's revenue from landlocked Ethiopia and will likely drive it toward closer ties with China. As for the United States, its concern about China in Africa was recently unveiled by John Bolton, former National Security Advisor to President Donald Trump, who indicated the United States would pour more resources into and pay greater attention to Africa, "casting it as a crucial battleground in the global economic contest between the United States and China."[3] But the reality is that the United States cannot unilaterally transfer billions of dollars into Africa as investment or otherwise, as does China, because of internal political constraints.

Some other important players in the Greater Horn of Africa region are Saudi Arabia and the Gulf States (Kuwait, Qatar, United

Arab Emirates), which are involved in trade and investment. To date, these states have invested approximately $13 billion between 2000 and 2017 in sectors such as agriculture, manufacturing, and construction, which are key to providing the working capital required for deepening cooperation and in the process providing a degree of economic stability in the region. Such largess is driven by political consideration, to limit Iranian influence, but is devoid of a developed long-term strategy. In addition, there is also the danger that some Gulf funding deepens various existing divisions within Horn of Africa's ethno-national groups and has the potential to destabilize the region.[4]

Finally, some observations are warranted regarding the literature that has emerged that attempts to foist dependency theory on China–Africa relations. It is true, of course, that there are countries in Africa, including Ethiopia, that need Chinese investments and technology in order to undertake development projects. From this angle, China–Africa relations do resemble associated development—that is, Africa's resources in exchange for China's financial investments and technology. But to extrapolate from this an outdated theory of the 1960s that sees African leaders as pawns subject to the demands of the Chinese dragon, which is benefiting at the expense of Africa, is quite a stretch. Indeed one prominent scholar of the global south argues the jury is still out on such assumption.[5]

The fact is, almost two decades after the inauguration of the Forum on China–Africa Cooperation, the relationship has not, overall, been harmful to either Ethiopia or Africa. In this era of globalization, dependency theory which presents African nations as pawns, instead of willing partners, does not advance knowledge. As in many countries, including developed ones, there is the issue of rent and corruption in Africa. But to simply assert that African leaders are stooges of the Asian dragon instead of self-interested rational actors attempting to maximize deals in the national interest (for the most part) is groundless. As for Ethiopia, its economic growth over the last decade also has to do, besides careful planning, with massive Chinese investments. However, while its balance of trade with China for now is negative, the overall balance of trade of Africa with China does not always favor this emerging Asian power. Finally, the issue of the complexity and lack of transparency of Chinese loans to Ethiopia—and by extension to all African nations—is a cause for concern. While one cannot generalize about China–Africa economic relations, the phenomenon of loans "tied" to either resources or to using Chinese companies, instead of African, on a project or the so-called "Angolan Model" needs to be explored and warrants further research.

Notes

Introduction

1. Mohan, Giles, & Lampert, Ben. (2013). Negotiating China: Reinserting African agency into China–Africa relations. *African Affairs*, *112*(446), 92.

2. Mohan, Giles, & Lampert, Ben. (2013). Negotiating China: Reinstating African agency into China–Africa relations. *African Affairs*, *112*(446), 92–110.

3. See Carmody, Padraig, Hampway, Geoffrey, & Sakala, Enock. (2012). Globalization and the rise of the state? Chinese geo-governance in Zambia. *New Political Economy*, *17*(2), 209–229.

4. Alden, Chris, & Large, Daniel. (2011). China's exceptionalism and the challenges of delivering difference in Africa. *Journal of Contemporary China*, *20*(68), 21–38.

5. Zenawi, Meles. (n.d.). *African development: Dead ends and new beginnings*. Unpublished manuscript. Retrieved from http://www.meleszenawi.com/african-development-dead-ends-and-new-biginnings-by-meles-zenawi/.

6. Federal Democratic Republic of Ethiopia, Ministry of Finance and Economic Development. (2010). *Growth and transformation plan 2010/11–2014/15. Vol. I: Main text*. Addis Ababa: Author. Retrieved from http://extwprlegs1.fao.org/docs/pdf/eth144893.pdf.

7. Akombo, Allan. (2016, March 27). Oil and gas Africa: Disputes simmer over exploration rights in eastern Africa. *AFK Insider*. Retrieved from http://afkinsider.com/88551/oil-gas-africa-disputes-simmer-exploration-rights-eastern-africa/.

8. Sun, Degang. (2015, March 11). China's soft military presence in the Middle East. Retrieved from Middle East Institute website: http://www.mei.edu/content/map/china%E2%80%99s-soft-military-presence-middle-east.

9. Tesfaye, Aaron. (2016). China, Ethiopia and the West. In Chris Alden, Abiodun Alao, Chun Zhang, & Laura Barber (Eds.), *China and Africa: Building peace and security cooperation on the continent* (pp. 269–287). New York, NY: Palgrave Macmillan.

10. Fick, Maggie. (2018, May 1). Harboring ambitions: Gulf States scramble for Somalia. *Reuters.* Retrieved from https://www.reuters.com/article/us-somalia-gulf-analysis/harboring-ambitions-gulf-states-scramble-for-somalia-idUSKBN1I23B4.

11. Sheldon-Duplaix, Alexandre. (2016, March 25). China's "imminent issue": Djibouti and overseas military interests (Commentary). European Council on Foreign Relations. Retrieved from https://www.ecfr.eu/article/commentary_chinas_imminent_issue_djibouti_and_overseas_interests4069.

12. Ethiopia. (n.d.). *Economist Intelligence Unit.* Retrieved from http://country.eiu.com/Ethiopia.

13. Cabestan, Jean-Pierre. (2012). China and Ethiopia: Authoritarian affinities and economic cooperation. *China Perspectives, 4,* 53–62.

14. Taylor, Ian. (2006). *China and Africa: Engagement and compromise.* New York, NY: Routledge.

15. Alden, Chris, & Alves, Ana Cristina. (2008). History and identity in the construction of China's Africa policy. *Review of African Political Economy, 115,* 47.

16. See Monson, Jamie. (2013). Remembering work on the Tazara Railway in Africa and China, 1965–2011: When "new men" grow old. *African Studies Review, 56*(1), 45–64.

17. Taylor, Ian. (1998). China's foreign policy towards Africa in the 1990s. *Journal of Modern African Studies, 36*(3), 444.

18. Legum, Colin (Ed.). (1987). *Africa contemporary record: Annual survey and documents, Vol. 18, 1985–1986.* Teaneck, NJ: Holmes and Meier.

19. Snow, Philip. (1995). China and Africa: Consensus and camouflage. In Thomas W. Robinson & David Shambaugh (Eds.), *Chinese foreign policy: Theory and practice* (pp. 283–321). New York, NY: Oxford University Press.

20. Wang, Yuan-kang. (2010). China's response to the unipolar world. *Journal of Asian and African Studies, 45*(5), 554–567. doi:10.1177/0021909610373898.

21. Armstrong, David. (1994). Chinese perspectives on the new world order. *Journal of East Asian Affairs, 8*(2), 454–481.

22. Forum on China–Africa Cooperation. (2009, October 21). China has cancelled 150 mature debts of 32 African countries. Retrieved from http://www.focac.org/eng/ltda/dscbzjhy/FA32009/t623384.htm.

23. Clapham, Christopher. (1999). Sovereignty and the Third World state. *Political Studies, 47*(3), 522–537.

24. Li, Xiaojun. (2017). Does conditionality still work? China's development assistance and democracy in Africa. *China Political Science Review, 2,* 206.

25. Urbina-Ferretjans, Marian, & Surender, Rebecca. (2013). Social policy in the context of new global actors: How far is China's developmental model in Africa impacting traditional donors? *Global Social Policy, 13*(2), 261.

26. Nye, Joseph. (2007). Notes for a soft-power research agenda. In Felix Berenskoetter & Michael J. Williams (Eds.), *Power in World Politics* (pp. 162–172). New York, NY: Routledge.

27. See Li, Mingjiang (Ed.). (2009). *Soft power: China's emerging strategy in international politics*. Plymouth, KY: Lexington Books.

28. Mulupi, Dinfin. (2013, December 2). China's investment in Africa is positive. *How We Made It in Africa*. Retrieved from http://www.howwemadeitinafrica.com/chinas-investment-in-africa-is-positive-says-investment-advisor/33013/.

29. Alden, Chris. (2007). *China in Africa: Partner, competitor or hegemon?* New York, NY: Zed Books.

30. French, Howard. (2015). *China's new continent: How a million migrants are building a new empire in Africa*. New York, NY: Vintage.

31. Brautigam, Deborah. (2011). *The dragon's gift: The real story of China in Africa*. New York, NY: Oxford University Press.

32. Marton, Peter, & Matura, Tamara. The "voracious dragon," the "scramble," and the "honey pot": Conceptions of conflict over Africa's natural resources. *Journal of Contemporary African Studies, 29*(2), 155–167.

33. Wang, Jian-Ye. (2007, October). *What drives China's growing role in Africa?* (Working Paper WP/07/211). Washington, DC: International Monetary Fund. Retrieved from https://www.imf.org/external/pubs/ft/wp/2007/wp07211.pdf.

34. United States International Trade Commission. (2009). *Sub-Saharan Africa: Effects of infrastructure conditions on export competitiveness, third annual report* (Investigation No. 332-477, USITC Publication 4071). Retrieved from https://www.usitc.gov/publications/332/pub4071.pdf.

35. Gramlich, Edward. (1994). Infrastructure investment: A review essay. *Journal of Economic Literature, 32*, 1176–1196; Straub, Stephanie. (2008). *Infrastructure and growth in developing countries: Recent advances and research challenges* (Policy Research Working Paper 4460). Washington, DC: World Bank.

36. Rebol, Max. (2010). China aid to Africa: Filling the gap the others left. *Alternatives: Turkish Journal of International Relations, 9*(2), 43.

37. Gill, Bates, & Reilly, James. (2007). The tenuous hold of China Inc. in Africa. *Washington Quarterly, 30*(3), 37–52.

38. Ofodile, Uche. (2009). Trade, aid and human rights: China's Africa policy in perspective. *Journal of International Commercial Law and Technology, 4*(2), 89.

39. Alden, Chris, & Large, Daniel. (2011). China's exceptionalism and the challenges of delivering difference in Africa. *Journal of Contemporary China, 20*(68), 21–38.

40. Mohan, Giles, & Lampert, Ben. (2013). Negotiating China: Reinserting African agency into China–Africa relations. *African Affairs, 112*(446), 92.

41. Wang, Jian-Ye. (2007, October). *What Drives China's Growing Role in Africa?* (Working Paper WP/07/211). Washington, DC: International Monetary Fund. Retrieved from https://www.imf.org/external/pubs/ft/wp/2007/wp07211.pdf.

42. Bandung Conference, Asia–Africa 1955. (n.d.). In *Encyclopedia Britannica*. Retrieved from https://www.britannica.com/event/Bandung-Conference.

43. Munemo, Jonathan. (2015). Examining the imports of capital goods from China as a channel for technology transfer and growth in sub-Saharan Africa. *Journal of African Business*, 14(2), 106–116.

44. Ademola, Titiloye O., Bankole, Abiodun S., & Odewuyi, Adeolu O. (2009). China–Africa trade relations: Insights from AERC scoping studies. *European Journal of Development Research*, 21(4), 485–505.

45. Diaw, Diadie, & Lessoua, Albert. (2013). Natural resource exports, diversification and economic growth of CEMAC countries: On the impact of trade with China. *African Development Review*, 25(2), 189–202.

46. Ajakaiye, Olusanya, & Kaplinsky, Raphael. (2009). China in Africa: A relationship in transition. *European Journal of Development Research*, 21(4), 479–484.

47. Drauwe, Paul, Houssa, Romain, & Picillo, Giulia. (2012). African trade dynamics: Is China a different partner? *Journal of Chinese Economic and Business Studies*, 10(1), 15–54.

48. Drogendijk, Rian, & Blomkvist, Katarina. Drivers and motives for Chinese outward foreign direct investment in Africa. *Journal of African Business*, 14(2), 75–84.

49. Alden, Chris, & Alves, Ana Cristian. (2008). History and identity in the construction of China's Africa policy. *Review of African Political Economy*, 35(115), 43–58.

50. Fishman, Ted. (2005). *China, Inc.: The rise of the next superpower challenges America and the world*. London: Simon and Schuster.

51. See Carmody, Padraig, Hampway, Geoffrey, & Sakala, Enock. (2012). Globalization and the rise of the state? Chinese geogovernance in Zambia. *New Political Economy*, 17(2), 209–229.

52. Alden, Chris, & Large, Dan. (2011). China's exceptionalism and the challenges of delivering difference in Africa. *Journal of Contemporary China*, 20(68), 21–38.

53. Mohan, Giles, & Lampert, Ben. (2013). Negotiating China: Reinserting African agency into China–Africa relations. *African Affairs*, 112(446), 92.

54. Moody, Andrew, & Chao, Wang. (2014, April 11–17). China "stepped into the breach," *China Daily Africa*. Retrieved from http://africa.chinadaily.com.cn/weekly/2014-04/11/content_17426606.htm.

Chapter 1

1. Anshan, Li. (2005). African studies in China in the twentieth century: A historiographical survey. *African Studies Review*, 48(1), 59–87.

2. Metaferia, Getachew. (2009). *Ethiopia and the United States: History, diplomacy, and analysis*. New York, NY: Algora.

3. Ruggie, John Gerard. (1974). Contingencies, constraints, and collective security: Perspectives on UN involvement in international disputes. *International Organization, 28*(3), 493–520.

4. Varhola, Michael J. (2000). *Fire and ice: The Korean War, 1950–1953*. Boston, MA: Da Capo Press, 134.

5. Stueck, William. (1995). *The Korean War: An international history*. Princeton, NJ: Princeton University Press.

6. Adem, Seifudein. (2012). China and Ethiopia: Diplomacy and economic Sino-optimism. *Africa Studies Review, 55*(1), 44.

7. Clarke, J. Calvitt, III. (2007, March 14). Foreign Minister Heruy's mission to Japan in 1931: Ethiopia's effort to find a non-Western model for modernization. *Selected Annual Proceedings of the Florida Conference of Historians* (pp. 17–18). Miami Beach, Florida.

8. Zewde, Bahru. (2002). *Pioneer of changes in Ethiopia: Reformist intellectuals of early twentieth century*. Columbus, OH: Ohio University Press.

9. Venkataraman, M., & Gamora, Gedion. (2009). An analysis of China–Ethiopia relations during the Cold War. *China Report, 45*(1), 11.

10. Setiawan, H. (2005). Learning from history: The Bandung spirit. In D. Khudori (Ed.), *Rethinking solidarity in global society: The challenges of globalisation for social and solidarity movements* (pp. 20–28). Yogyakarta, Gadjah Mada University, Indonesia.

11. Acharya, Amitav. (2014). Who are the norm makers? The Asian–African Conference in Bandung and the evolution of norms. *Global Governance, 20*, 415.

12. Wondam, Paik. (2016). The 60th anniversary of the Bandung Conference and Asia. *Journal of Inter-Asian Cultural Studies, 17*, 149.

13. Nehru, Jawaharlal. (1994). *The discovery of India*. New Delhi: Jawaharlal Nehru Memorial Fund.

14. Siu, Helen F., & McGovern, Mike. (2017). China–Africa encounters: Historical legacies and contemporary realities. *Annual Review of Anthropology, 46*, 341.

15. Lefebvre, Jeffrey A. (1993). The United States and Egypt: Confrontation and accommodation in northeast Africa, 1956–60. *Middle Eastern Studies, 29*(2), 325; see also Abruish, Said. (2004). *Nasser, the last Arab*. New York, NY: St. Martin's Press.

16. Royal Institute of International Affairs. (1942). The agreement with Ethiopia. *Bulletin of International News, 19*(4), 138–140. Retrieved from http://www.jstor.org/stable/25643208.

17. Adem, Seifudein. (2012). Imperial Ethiopia's relations with Maoist China. *African and East Asian Affairs, 1*, 31–53.

18. Vestal, Theodore M. (2009). The Lion of Judah at Camelot: U.S. foreign policy toward Ethiopia as reflected in the second visit of Emperor Haile Selassie to the United States. *International Journal of Ethiopian Studies, 4*(1/2), 135–152.

19. Scalapino, Robert A. (1964). Sino-Soviet competition in Africa. *Foreign Affairs, 42*(4), 640–654.

20. Goldstein, Lyle J. (2001). Return to Zhenbao Island: Who started shooting and why it matters. *China Quarterly, 168,* 985–997.

21. Kissinger, Henry. (1979). *The White House years.* Boston, MA: Little, Brown.

22. Lyons, Roy. (1978). The USSR, China and the Horn of Africa. *Review of African Political Economy, 5*(12), 5–30.

23. Tarke, Gebru. (2009). *The Ethiopian Revolution.* New Haven, CT: Yale University Press.

24. Sheik-Abdi, Abdi. (1977). Somali nationalism: Its origins and future. *Journal of Modern African Studies, 15*(4), 657–665; see also Laitin, David. (1979). The War in the Ogaden: Implications for Siyaad's role in Somali history. *Journal of Modern African Studies, 17*(1), 95–115.

25. Natsios, Andrew S. (2012). China in Sudan: The challenges of non-interference in a failed state. *Georgetown Journal of International Affairs, 13*(2), 62.

26. Tekle, Amare. (1989). The determinants of the foreign policy of revolutionary Ethiopia. *Journal of Modern African Studies, 27*(3), 479–502.

27. Taylor, Ian. (2006). *China and Africa: Engagement and compromise.* London: Routledge.

28. Wang, Yuan-kang. (2010). China's response to the unipolar world: The strategic logic of peaceful development. *Journal of African and Asian Studies, 45*(5), 554–567.

29. See Tesfaye, Aaron. (2012). *Political power and ethnic federalism: The struggle for democracy in Ethiopia.* Lanham, MD: University Press of America.

30. Ayalew, Sosina. (1994). A synopsis of the foreign policy of the Transitional Government of Ethiopia (TGE) since the adoption of the Charter in July 1991. *EthioScope, 1,* 1–2.

31. Salidjanova, Nargiza. (2011). *Going out: An overview of China's outward foreign direct investment.* Retrieved from U.S.–China Economic & Security Review Commission website: https://www.uscc.gov/sites/default/files/Research/GoingOut.pdf.

32. Federal Democratic Republic of Ethiopia, Ministry of Finance and Economic Development. (2010). *Growth and transformation plan 2010/11–2014/15. Vol. I: Main text.* Addis Ababa: Author. Retrieved from http://extwprlegs1.fao.org/docs/pdf/eth144893.pdf.

33. Alemu, Dawit, & Scoones, Ian. (2013). Negotiating new relationships: How the Ethiopian state is involving China and Brazil in agriculture and rural development. *IDS Bulletin, 44*(4), 91–100.

34. Grimm, Sven. (2012). *The Forum on China–Africa Cooperation (FOCAC): Political rationale and functioning* (Working paper). Stellenbosch, Centre for Chinese Studies, Stellenbosch University, South Africa.

35. Taylor, Ian. (2012) *The Forum on China–Africa Cooperation (FOCAC)*. New York, NY: Routledge.

36. Forum on China–Africa Cooperation. (2003, December 16). *The Forum on China–Africa Cooperation—Addis Ababa Action Plan (2004–2006)*. Second Ministerial Conference of the FOCAC. Retrieved from http://www.fmprc.gov.cn/zflt/eng/zyzl/hywj/t157710.htm.

37. Federal Democratic Republic of Ethiopia, Ministry of Finance and Economic Development. (2015). *Growth and transformation plan, 2010/11–2014/15. Vol. II: Policy matrix*. Addis Ababa: Author.

38. Menyah, Kojo, & Wolde-Rufael, Yemane. (2013). Government expenditure and economic growth: The Ethiopian experience 1950–2007. *Journal of Development Areas, 47*(1), 263–280.

39. Furie, Elsje. (2015). China's example for Meles' Ethiopia: When development models land. *Journal of Modern African Studies, 53*(3), 295.

40. Ramo, J. (2004, May 8). China has discovered its own economic consensus. Retrieved from Foreign Policy Centre website: https://fpc.org.uk/wp-content/uploads/2006/09/240-1.pdf.

41. Bekele, Sehen, & Regassa, Tsegaye. (2012). *Democratizing in a developmental state: The case of Ethiopia: Issues, challenges, prospects* (UNDP Development Brief: Ethiopia No. 1/2012). Retrieved from United Nations Development Programme website: https://www.et.undp.org/content/dam/ethiopia/docs/Democratization%20in%20a%20Developmental%20State.pdf.

42. See World Bank. (2012). *China: World Bank country survey 2012*. Washington, DC: Author.

43. King, Kenneth. (2011). China's cooperation with Ethiopia with a focus on human resources. *Organization for Social Science Research in Eastern and South Africa Bulletin, 3*, 95–100.

44. Embassy of the People's Republic of China in the Federal Democratic Republic of Ethiopia. (2014). *Confucius Institute inaugurated in Addis Ababa University*. Retrieved from http://et.china-embassy.org/eng/sgxx/t1227008.htm.

45. Eversheds Southerland. (2012, April 18). *Oil & gas in the Horn of Africa—the opportunities and risks*. Retrieved from http://www.eversheds.com/global/en/what/articles/index.page?ArticleID=en/Oil-Gas-in-the-Horn-of-Africa_the-opportunities-and-risks.

Chapter 2

1. Van Donge, Jan Kees, Henley, David, & Lewis, Peter. (2012). Tracking development in Southeast Asia and sub-Saharan Africa: The primacy of policy. *Development Policy Review, 30*(1), 1–13.

2. Lehman, Howard P. (2008, March 26–29). *The Asian economic model and Africa: Japanese developmental lessons for Africa*. Paper presented at the Annual International Studies Association, San Francisco, CA.

3. World Bank. (2015, November 23). *With continued rapid growth, Ethiopia is poised to become a middle income country by 2025*. Retrieved from http://www.worldbank.org/en/country/ethiopia/publication/ethiopia-great-run-growth-acceleration-how-to-pace-it.

4. Zhu, Ling, Forum on China–Africa Cooperation. (2006). *China Africa Policy*. Part IV, 2(10). Xinhua News Agency. Retrieved from http://www.gov.cn/misc/2006-01/12/content_156490.htm.

5. Zhu, Ling, Forum on China–Africa Cooperation. (2006). *China Africa Policy*. Part II, 2(10). Xinhua News Agency. Retrieved from http://www.gov.cn/misc/2006-01/12/content_156490.htm.

6. Mesfin, Mahlet. (2011, July 25). Ethiopia: Chinese firm eyes gas export from Calub through Berbera. *Addis Fortune*. Retrieved from http://allafrica.com/stories/201107270752.html.

7. Hutchinson, Sharon E. (2001). A curse from God? Religious and political dimensions of the post-1991 rise of ethnic violence in South Sudan. *Journal of Modern African Studies*, 39(2), 307–331.

8. See Young, John. Ethiopia's western frontier: Gambella and Benishangul in transition. *Journal of Modern African Studies*, 37(2), 321–346.

9. Maasho, Aaron. (2016, July 26). South Sudan delays shutdown of oil pipelines to Ethiopia. *Reuters*. Retrieved from https://www.reuters.com/article/us-sudan-southssudan-pipeline/sudan-delays-shutdown-of-oil-pipelines-ethiopia-idUSBRE96P0JV20130726.

10. Eisenman, Joshua, & Kurlantzick, Joshua. (2006). China's Africa strategy. *Current History*. 105(691), 219–224.

11. Embassy of the People's Republic of China in the Federal Democratic Republic of Ethiopia. (2016, November 11). China, Ethiopia agree to augment military cooperation. Retrieved from http://et.china-embassy.org/eng/zagx/t1419796.htm.

12. See Tesfaye, Aaron. (2009). *The political economy of the Nile waters regime in the twentieth century*. New York, NY: Edwin Mellen Press.

13. Davidson, William. (2013, October 21). Egypt, Ethiopia and Sudan mull new probe Nile dam impact. *Bloomberg News*. Retrieved from https://www.bloomberg.com/news/articles/2013-10-21/egypt-ethiopia-and-sudan-mull-new-probe-nile-dam-impact.

14. Berhane, Daniel. (2013, April 26). China provides $1 billion for Renaissance Dam transmissions lines. *Horn Affairs*. Retrieved from https://hornaffairs.com/2013/04/26/nile-china-finance-billion-dollar-renaissance-dam/.

15. World Bank. (2008, July 10). New financiers are narrowing Africa's infrastructure deficit [Press release]. Retrieved from https://www.worldbank.org/en/news/press-release/2008/07/10/new-financiers-narrowing-africas-infrastructure-deficit.

16. Broadman, Harry. (2007). *Africa's Silk Road: China and India's new economic frontier*. Washington, DC: World Bank.

17. Federal Democratic Republic of Ethiopia, Ministry of Finance and Economic Cooperation. (2012). *China plans to double its development assistance to Ethiopia*. Addis Ababa: Author.

18. Federal Democratic Republic of Ethiopia, Ministry of Foreign Affairs, Asia Australasia and the Middle East General Directorate. (2016, September). *An overview of the bilateral relations between the Federal Democratic Republic of Ethiopia and the People's Republic of China*. Addis Ababa: Author. Retrieved from https://www.saiia.org.za/wp-content/uploads/2008/05/Zemene_Ethiopia.pdf.

19. Shinn, David. (2014, June 11). Ethiopia and China: When two former empires connected. *International Policy Digest*. Retrieved from https://intpolicydigest.org/2014/06/11/ethiopia-and-china-when-two-former-empires-connected/.

20. Verhoeven, Harry. (2015, April). Africa's new hegemon: Behind Ethiopia's power plays. *Foreign Affairs*. Retrieved from https://www.foreignaffairs.com/articles/ethiopia/2015-04-12/africas-next-hegemon.

21. Hofstedt, Todd A. (2009). China in Africa: An AFRICOM response. *Naval War College Review*, 62(3), 96. Retrieved from https://apps.dtic.mil/dtic/tr/fulltext/u2/a519315.pdf.

22. Shinn, David, & Eisenman, Joshua. (2008) "Responding to China in Africa," *American Foreign Policy Council*. Retrieved https://www.afpc.org/publications/policy-papers/responding-to-china-in-africa.

23. Ethiopia, Somaliland and China to sign trilateral deals. (2011, August 14). *Ezega Press*. Retrieved from https://www.ezega.com/News/NewsDetails?Page=heads&NewsID=3015.

24. Jones, Mark T. (2014, July 18). Port challenges in East Africa afford a golden opportunity for Berbera. Retrieved from https://somaliland1991.wordpress.com/2014/07/page/2/.

25. Lee, John. (2015, April 23). China comes to Djibouti: Why Washington should be worried. *Foreign Affairs*. Retrieved from https://www.foreignaffairs.com/articles/east-africa/2015-04-23/china-comes-djibouti.

26. Jiang, Anquan, & Zhang, Jianbo. (2013, March 11). Djibouti welcomes China to build a military base. *Global Times*. Retrieved from http://www.chinaafricaproject.com/djibouti-welcomes-china-to-build-a-military-base-translation.

27. Perlez, Jane, & Buckley, Chris. (2015, November 26). China retools its military with a first overseas outpost in Djibouti. *The New York Times*. Retrieved from https://www.nytimes.com/2015/11/27/world/asia/china-military-presence-djibouti-africa.html.

28. Brooks, Aaron. Djibouti and China to build global trade routes. *East Africa Monitor*. Retrieved from https://eastafricamonitor.com/djibouti-china-ink-plans-build-global-trade-routes/.

29. Boden, Christopher. (2015, November 26). China in talks with Djibouti on establishing logistics base. *Associated Press.* Retrieved from http://english.alarabiya.net/en/News/world/2015/11/26/China-in-talks-with-Djibouti-on-establishing-logistics-base.html.

30. Lena Partzsch, Laura Kemper. (February 2019). Cotton certification in Ethiopia: Can an increasing demand for certified textiles create a "fashion revolution"? *Geoforum,* 99, 111–119. Retrieved from: https://www.sciencedirect.com/science/article/pii/S0016718518303543?via%3Dihub, https://doi.org/10.1016/j.geoforum.2018.11.017. Also see, Special Correspondent, "Ethiopia Invites Investments from Textile Industry," *The Hindu,* July 22, 2017. Retrieved from: https://www.thehindu.com/news/cities/Coimbatore/ethiopia-invites-investments-from-textile-industry/article19329733.ece.

31. Ethiopia draws Asian manufacturing interests. (2014, August 4). *VOA News.* Retrieved from http://www.voanews.com/content/ethiopia-drawing-asia-manufacturing-interest/1970953.html.

32. Liang, Shangang. (2015, June 5). Interview: Ethiopia keen to bolster cooperation with China in manufacturing sector, Ethiopian President Mulatu Teshome. Xinhua News Agency.

33. Information/data obtained from field research in northern Ethiopia, February 2011 and June 2013.

34. McKenna, Edward. (2012, October 4). Ethiopia charts a Chinese course. *Inter Press Service.* Retrieved from http://www.ipsnews.net/2012/10/ethiopia-charts-a-chinese-course/.

35. Tesfaye, Aaron. (2017). *State and economic development in Africa: The case of Ethiopia.* New York, NY: Palgrave Macmillan.

36. Dittgen, Romain, & Demisse, Abel Abate. (2017, January). *Own ways of doing: National pride, power and China's political calculus in Ethiopia* (Occasional Paper 249). South Africa Institute of International Affairs. doi:10.13140/RG.2.2.23077.91368.

37. Richard Lough, "Ethiopia pushes retail door ajar to foreigner," Reuters, May 26, 2014. Retrieved from https://www.reuters.com/article/ethiopia-retail/ethiopia-pushes-retail-door-ajar-to-foreigners-idUSL6N0O81SL20140526.

38. Li, Anshan. (2016). Technology transfer in China–Africa relation: Myth or reality. *Transnational Corporation Review,* 8(3), 190.

39. Breeze, Victoria, & Moore, Nathan. (2017, June 27). China tops US and UK as destination for Anglophone African students. *The Conversation.* Retrieved from http://theconversation.com/china-tops-us-and-uk-as-destination-for-anglophone-african-students-78967.

40. Yohannes, Robel. (2017, June 21). Ethiopia, China to strengthen strategic partnership. *Ethiopian Herald.* Retrieved from https://allafrica.com/stories/201611240916.html.

Chapter 3

1. American Enterprise Institute. (2017). China global investment tracker [data set]. Retrieved from https://www.aei.org/china-global-investment-tracker/.

2. Federal Democratic Republic of Ethiopia, Investment Commission. (2015). *Chinese investments in Ethiopia*. Addis Ababa: Author.

3. World Bank. (2012). *Chinese FDI in Ethiopia: A survey*. Retrieved from http://documents.worldbank.org/curated/en/151961468038140377/Chinese-FDI-in-Ethiopia-a-World-Bank-survey.

4. Federal Democratic Republic of Ethiopia, Investment Commission. Chinese Investment in Ethiopia (2017). Addis Ababa: Author.

5. Tilahun Taddese Haile, personal communication, August 17, 2016.

6. Tan, Xiaomei, Zhao, Yingzhen, Polycarp, Clifford, & Bai, Jianwan. (2013). *China's overseas investments in the wind and solar industries: Trends and drivers* (Working paper). Washington, DC: World Resources Institute. Retrieved from http://pdf.wri.org/chinas_overseas_investments_in_wind_and_solar_trends_and_drivers.pdf.

7. Conrad, B., Fernandez, M., & Houshyani, B. (2010). *Towards an energizing partnership? Exploring China's role as catalyst of renewable energy development in Africa*. Washington DC: World Wildlife Fund.

8. International Energy Agency. (2014). *Africa energy outlook: A focus on energy prospects in sub-Saharan Africa* (World Energy Outlook Special Report). Retrieved from https://www.iea.org/publications/freepublications/publication/WEO2014_AfricaEnergyOutlook.pdf.

9. Ethiopia and China sign $1 billion power deal. (2013, April 26). Energy Daily. Retrieved from http://www.energy-daily.com/reports/Ethiopia_and_China_sign_1_billion_power_deal_999.html.

10. Kiganda, Anthony. (2016, August 11). Chinese firm begins constructing luxury apartments in Ethiopia. *Construction Review Online*. Retrieved from https://constructionreviewonline.com/2016/08/chinese-firm-begins-constructing-luxury-apartments-in-ethiopia/.

11. Aidoo, Richard, & Hess, Steve. Non-interference 2.0: China's evolving foreign policy towards a changing Africa. *Journal of Current Chinese Affairs*, 44(1), 107–139.

12. Dittgen, Romain, & Demisse, Abel Abate. (2017, January). *Own ways of doing: National pride, power and China's political calculus in Ethiopia* (Occasional Paper 249). South Africa Institute of International Affairs. doi:10.13140/RG.2.2.23077.91368.

13. Alemu, Dawit, & Scoones, Ian. (2013). Negotiating new relationships: How the Ethiopian state is involving China and Brazil in agriculture and rural development. *IDS Bulletin*, 44(4), 91–93.

14. Chakrabarty, Malancha. (2016). Ethiopia–China economic relations: A classic win-win situation? *World Review of Political Economy, 7*(2), 226–248.

15. Atkins, Lucas, Brautigam, Deborah, Chen, Yunnan, & Hwang, Jyhjong. (2017). *Challenges of and opportunities from the commodity price slump* (CARI Economic Bulletin #1). Washington, DC: China Africa Research Initiative. Retrieved from https://static1.squarespace.com/static/5652847de4b033f56d2bdc29/t/59f85883ec212d5a70e9624c/1509447812591/bulletin+v5.pdf.

16. Gill, Bates, & Reilly, James. (2007). The tenuous hold of China Inc. in Africa. *Washington Quarterly, 30*(3), 37–52.

17. Martel, Francis. (2018, March 7). Tillerson: China's "predatory loan practices and corrupt deals" threaten Africa. *Breitbart News*. Retrieved from http://www.breitbart.com/national-security/2018/03/07/tillerson-chinas-predatory-loan-practices-corrupt-deals-threaten-africa/.

18. Rimmer, Douglas. (1990). External debt and structural adjustment in tropical Africa. *African Affairs, 89*(355), 283–291.

19. Geda, Alemayehu. (2008). *AERC Scoping study on the Chinese relation with sub-Saharan Africa: The case of Ethiopia* (Working paper). Nairobi, Kenya: African Economic Research Consortium. Retrieved from https://www.africaportal.org/publications/aerc-scoping-study-on-the-chinese-relation-with-sub-saharan-africa-the-case-of-ethiopia/.

20. Tull, Dennis M. (2006). China's engagement in Africa: Preliminary scoping of African case studies: Angola, Ethiopia, Gabon, Uganda, South Africa, Zambia. *Journal of Modern African Studies, 44*(3), 459–479.

21. World Bank. (2012). *Chinese FDI in Ethiopia: A survey*. Retrieved from http://documents.worldbank.org/curated/en/151961468038140377/Chinese-FDI-in-Ethiopia-a-World-Bank-survey.

22. Gebre-Egziabher, Tegegne. (2009). The development impact of Asian drivers on Ethiopia with special emphasis on small-scale footwear producers. *World Economy, 232*(11), 1613–1637. doi:10.1111/j.1467-9701.2009.01252.x. Retrieved from http://www.tips.org.za/files/forum/2006/papers/TheDevelopmentalimpactofChinaandIndiaonEthiopia.pdf.

23. Geda, Alemayehu. (2008). *AERC Scoping study on the Chinese relation with sub-Saharan Africa: The case of Ethiopia* (Working paper). Nairobi, Kenya: African Economic Research Consortium. Retrieved from https://www.africaportal.org/publications/aerc-scoping-study-on-the-chinese-relation-with-sub-saharan-africa-the-case-of-ethiopia/.

24. Dinh, Hinh T., Palmade, Vincent, Chandra, Vandana, & Cossar, Frances. (2013). *Light manufacturing in Africa: Targeted policies to enhance private investment and create jobs*. Washington, DC: World Bank.

25. Brautigam, Deborah, & Tang, Xiaoyang. (2011). African Shenzhen: China's special economic zones in Africa. *Journal of Modern African Studies, 49*(1), 27–54.

26. Davison, William. (2013, March 8). Ethiopia to open first industrial zone to bolster economy. *Bloomberg News*. Retrieved from https://www.bloomberg.com/news/articles/2013-03-18/ethiopia-to-open-first-industrial-zone-to-boost-economic-growth.

27. Cheru, Fantu. (2016). Emerging Southern powers and new forms of South–South cooperation: Ethiopia's strategic engagement with China and India. *Third World Quarterly*, 37(4), 598.

28. Chinese firm to build new industrial park in Ethiopia. (2017, October 6). New China. Retrieved from http://www.xinhuanet.com//english/2017-06/10/c_136355619.htm.

29. Naidu, S., Corkin, L., & Herman, H. (2009). China's re-emerging relations with Africa. *Politikon*, 36(10), 87–115.

30. Gebru, Bereket. (2017, December 8) Ethiopia: the rising hub of textile manufacturing. *Walta Information Service*. Retrieved from http://www.waltainfo.com/index.php/FeaturedArticles/detail?cid=35365&locale=en.

31. Farquharson, Michael. (2017, April 19) Chinese infrastructure investment in Ethiopia. *Borgen Magazine*. Retrieved from https://www.borgenmagazine.com/chinese-infrastructure-investment-in-ethiopia/.

32. Davison, William. (2013, May 3). Ethiopia courts BRICS for rail projects to spur economic growth. *Bloomberg News*. Retrieved from https://www.bloomberg.com/news/articles/2013-05-01/ethiopia-courts-brics-for-rail-projects-to-spur-economic-growth.

33. Knorringa, Peter, & Pegler, Irene. (2006). *Social capital for industrial development: Operationalizing the concept*. Vienna: United Nations Industrial Development Organization.

34. Federal Democratic Republic of Ethiopia, Ministry of Finance and Economic Development. (2015). *Growth and transformation plan, 2010/11–2014/15. Vol. II: Policy matrix*. Addis Ababa: Author.

35. Gebre-Egzaber, Tegegne. Impacts of Chinese imports and coping strategies of local producers: The case of small-scale foot wear enterprise in Ethiopia. *Journal of Modern African Studies*, 45(4), 614–679.

36. Tekleberhan, M. (2012, October 16) Hujian receives additional land grant in Ethiopia. Retrieved from https://www.2merkato.com/news/manufacturing/1692-hujian-receives-additional-land-grant-in-ethiopia.

37. Haugen, Heidi Ostabo. (2011). Chinese exports to Africa: Competition, complementarity and cooperation between micro-level actors. *Forum for Development Studies*, 38(2), 165.

38. Ethiopia's revised *Investment Code of 1996* reserves investment in broadcasting, air transport services, travel agency services, forwarding and shipping agencies, retail trade and brokerage, and wholesale trade (excluding supply of petroleum) only for Ethiopian citizens. See U.S. Department of State. (2015). Ethiopia: Investment climate statement 2015. Retrieved from https://www.state.gov/documents/organization/241767.pdf.

39. Donahue, Bill. (2018, March 2). China is turning Ethiopia into a giant fashion factory. *The New York Times*. Retrieved from https://www.bloomberg.com/news/features/2018-03-02/china-is-turning-ethiopia-into-a-giant-fast-fashion-factory.

40. Preuss, Simon. (2017, February 14). Chinese textile and apparel firms intensify investments in Ethiopia. *FashionUnited*. Retrieved from https://fashionunited.com/news/business/chinese-textile-and-apparel-firms-intensify-investments-in-ethiopia/2017021414682.

41. Jobson, Elissa. (2013, February 13). Ethiopia achieves development target of reducing child mortality rate. *The Guardian*. Retrieved from https://www.theguardian.com/global-development/2013/sep/13/ethiopia-achieves-development-target-child-mortality.

42. Ademola, Oyejide T., Bankole, Abiodun S., & Adewuyi, Adeolu O. (2009). China–Africa trade relations: Insights from AERC scoping studies. *European Journal of Development Research, 21*(4), 485–505; Bamon, Ernest. (2006). *Evaluating Asian drivers impacts on sub-Saharan Africa oil and gas industries: A methodological framework* (Paper). Nairobi: African Economic Research Consortium.

43. Renard, Mary-Françoise. (2011). *China's trade and FDI in Africa* (Working Paper No. 126). Tunis: African Development Bank.

44. See Thakur, Monika. (2009). *Building on progress? Chinese engagement in Ethiopia* (Occasional Paper No. 38). Johannesburg: South African Institute of International Affairs.

45. Chakrabarty, Malancha. (2016). Ethiopia–China economic relations: A classic win-win situation? *World Review of Political Economy, 7*(2), 229.

46. Hatfield, R., & Davies, J. (2006). *Global review of the economics of pastoralism* (Research report prepared for the World Initiative for Sustainable Pastoralism). Nairobi: IUCN.

47. Tesfaye, Aaron. (2017). *State and economic development in Africa: The case of Ethiopia*. New York, NY: Palgrave Macmillan.

48. Ethiopian imports, 2006–2017. (2017). *Trading Economics*. Retrieved from https://tradingeconomics.com/ethiopia/imports.

49. Ethiopian imports, 2006–2017. Retrieved from https://tradingeconomics.com/ethiopia/imports.

50. Bräutigam, Deborah. (2011). Ethiopia's partnership with China. *The Guardian*. Retrieved from https://www.theguardian.com/global-development/poverty-matters/2011/dec/30/china-ethiopia-business-opportunities.

51. Chakrabarty, Malancha. (2016). Ethiopia–China economic relations: A classic win-win situation? *World Review of Political Economy, 7*(2), 229.

52. Venkataraman, Manickam, & Gofie, Solomon. (2015). The dynamics of China–Ethiopia trade relations: Economic capacity, balance of trade and trade regimes. *Bandung Journal of the Global South, 2*(8), 9. doi:10.1186/s40728-014-0007-1.

Chapter 4

1. Eisenman, Joshua, & Kurlantzick, Joshua. (2006). China's Africa strategy. *Current History*, 105(691), 219. See also Sun, Yun. (2014, April). *Africa in China's foreign policy*. Washington, DC: Brookings Institution.

2. Vafeiads, Michael. (2017, March 1). China "buying out" Africa: Top five destinations of Chinese money. *Christian Science Monitor*. Retrieved from https://www.csmonitor.com/World/2012/0301/China-buying-out-Africa-Top-5-destinations-of-Chinese-money/Angola.

3. Jones, Tim. (2018, February 17). China pledges $2bn for development goals and says it will write off debts. *The Guardian*. Retrieved from https://www.theguardian.com/global-development/2015/sep/27/china-pledges-2bn-for-development-goals-and-says-it-will-write-off-debts.

4. See also China offers Africa billions in aid, debt forgiveness. (2009, November 8). *Newser*. Retrieved from http://www.newser.com/story/73563/china-offers-africa-billions-in-aid-debt-forgiveness.html.

5. Ferdjani, Hannane. (2012). *African students in China: An exploration of increasing numbers and their motivations in Beijing*. Center for Chinese Studies, Stellenbosch University, South Africa. Retrieved from http://citeseerx.ist.psu.edu/viewdoc/download?doi=10.1.1.470.8611&rep=rep1&type=pdf.

6. Abota, Arka. (2006). *Ethiopia's foreign policy under Emperor Haile Selassie I: An appraisal* (Unpublished master's thesis). Addis Ababa University, Ethiopia.

7. See Schraeder, Peter J. (1996). *United States foreign policy towards Africa: Incrementalism, crisis and change*. Cambridge, United Kingdom: Cambridge University Press.

8. Tekle, Amare. (1989). The determinants of the foreign policy of revolutionary Ethiopia. *Journal of Modern African Studies*, 27(3), 479–502.

9. Tesfaye, Aaron. (2018). China, Ethiopia and the West. In Chris Alden, Abiodun Alao, Chun Zhang, & Laura Barber (Eds.), *China and Africa: Building peace and security cooperation on the continent* (pp. 269–288). New York, NY: Palgrave Macmillan.

10. Ethiopian News Agency. (2017, June 21). Ethiopia, China to strengthen strategic partnership. Retrieved from http://www.ena.gov.et/en/index.php/economy/item/3371-ethiopia-china-to-strengthen-strategic-partnership.

11. Wang, Yi, & Ghebreyesus, Tedros Adhanom. (2014, January 12). China–Ethiopia relations: An excellent model for South–South cooperation. Ministry of Foreign Affairs, People's Republic of China. Retrieved from http://www.fmprc.gov.cn/mfa_eng/zxxx_662805/t1215597.shtml.

12. Wolff, Peter. (2015). *China's "Belt and Road" Initiative—Challenges and opportunities* (Report prepared for the 2016 Annual Meeting of the Asian Development Bank). Berlin: German Development Institute.

13. Ethiopian Airlines. (2018, February 9). *Ethiopian wins the first Cargo Transportation Award in China* [Press release]. Addis Ababa: Author.

14. Gill, Bates, & Reilly, James. (2007). The tenuous hold of China Inc. in Africa. *Washington Quarterly, 30*(3), 37–52.

15. Gu, Jing, Zhang, Chuanhong, Vaz, Alcides, & Mukwereza, Langton. (2016). Chinese state capitalism? Rethinking the role of the state and business in Chinese development cooperation in Africa. *World Development, 81*, 24–34. doi:10.1016/j.worlddev.2016.01.001.

16. See Hackenesch, Christine. (2011, November). *Competing for development? The European Union and China in Ethiopia* (Discussion paper). Center for Chinese Studies, University of Stellenbosch, South Africa.

17. See Tesfaye, Aaron. (2017). *State and economic development in Africa: The case of Ethiopia*. New York, NY: Palgrave Macmillan.

18. Shinn, David. (2014, June 11). Ethiopia and China: When two former empires connected. *International Policy Digest*. Retrieved from https://intpolicydigest.org/2014/06/11/ethiopia-and-china-when-two-former-empires-connected/.

19. Eisenman, Joshua, & Kurlantzick, Joshua. (2006). China's Africa strategy. *Current History, 105*(691), 219.

20. Intergovernmental Authority on Development. (2011, November 21). *Cooperation with China*. Retrieved from http://igad.int/index.php?option=com_content&view=article&id=370:cooperation-with-china&catid=46:executive-secretary&Itemid=123.

21. Healey, Sally. (2011). Seeking peace and security in the Horn of Africa: The contribution of Intergovernmental Authority on Development. *International Affairs, 87*(1), 105–120.

22. Zhou, Hang. (2014). Testing the limits: China's expanding role in the South Sudanese Civil War. *China Brief, 14*(19). Retrieved from https://jamestown.org/program/testing-the-limits-chinas-expanding-role-in-the-south-sudanese-civil-war/.

23. Genyi, George Akwaya. (2015). South Sudan: Resolving conflicts in Africa—A test case for China. *Conflict Studies Quarterly, 13*, 17–28.

24. People's Republic of China, Office of the State Council. (2014, July 10). *China's foreign aid (2014)* (White paper). Beijing: Author. Retrieved from http://english.gov.cn/archive/white_paper/2014/08/23/content_281474982986592.htm.

25. Zhou, Enlai. (1964, January 15). *The Chinese government's eight principles for economic aid and technical assistance to other countries* (Selected diplomatic papers of Zhou Enlai). Washington, DC: History and Public Policy Program, Woodrow Wilson International Center for Scholars. Retrieved from http://digitalarchive.wilsoncenter.org/document/121560.pdf?v=7abac3e22dfa18df4a30915a4a7b1700.

26. People's Republic of China, Office of the State Council. (2014, July 10). *China's foreign aid (2014)* (White paper). Beijing: Author. Retrieved from http://english.gov.cn/archive/white_paper/2014/08/23/content_281474982986592.htm.

27. Sun, Yun. (2014, February 7). *China aid to Africa: A monster or a messiah?* Washington, DC: Brookings Institution. Retrieved from https://www.brookings.edu/opinions/chinas-aid-to-africa-monster-or-messiah/.

28. Cheng, Zhanghxi, & Taylor, Ian. (2017). *China's aid to Africa: Does friendship really matter?* London: Routledge.

29. Lengauer, Sara. (2011) China's foreign aid policy: Motive and method. *Culture Mandala: The Bulletin of the Centre for East-West Cultural & Economic Studies*, 9(2), 36. Retrieved from http://www.international-relations.com/CM2011/PRC-Foreign-Aid-2011.pdf.

30. Ekeh, Peter P. (1975). Colonialism and the two publics in Africa: A theoretical statement. *Comparative Studies in Society and History*, 17(1), 91–112.

31. Berman, Bruce J. (1998). Ethnicity, patronage and the African state: The politics of uncivil nationalism. *African Affairs*, 97(388), 305–341.

32. Pitcher, Anne, Moran, Mary H., & Johnston, Michael. (2009). Rethinking patrimonialism and neopatrimonialism in Africa. *African Studies Review*, 52(1), 125–156.

33. Fatton, Robert, Jr. (1988). Bringing the ruling class back in. *Comparative Politics*, 20(3), 253–264.

34. Dreher, Axel, Fuchs, Abel, Hodler, Roland, Parks, Bradley, Raschky, Paul, & Tierney, Michael J. (2014, November). *Aid on demand: African leaders and the geography of China's foreign assistance* (Working Paper No. 3), 5. Retrieved from http://docs.aiddata.org/ad4/files/inline/wp3_-_revised_working_paper_series_dreher_et_al_2016_october.pdf.

35. Lee, Joseph Tse-Hei. (2008, March). China's Third World policy from the Maoist era to the present (Occasional Paper No. 3). *Global Asia Journal*, 1–53.

36. Federal Democratic Republic of Ethiopia, Ministry of Finance and Economic Development. (2015). *Growth and transformation plan, 2010/11–2014/15. Vol. II: Policy matrix*. Addis Ababa: Author.

37. Davies, Martyn, Edinger, Hannah, Tay, Nastasya, & Nadu, Sanusha. (2008, February). *How China delivers developmental assistance to Africa*. Center for Chinese Studies, University of Stellenbosch, South Africa.

38. Davies, Martyn, Edinger, Hannah, Tay, Nastasya, & Nadu, Sanusha. (2008, February). *How China delivers developmental assistance to Africa*. Center for Chinese Studies, University of Stellenbosch, South Africa.

39. Lee, John. (2015, April 23). China comes to Djibouti: Why Washington should be worried. *Foreign Affairs*. Retrieved from https://www.foreignaffairs.com/articles/east-africa/2015-04-23/china-comes-djibouti.

40. He, Yin. (2007). *China's changing policy on UN peacekeeping operations*. Stockholm: Institute for Security and Development Policy.

41. Mathews, Kay. (2013). China and UN peacekeeping operations in Africa. In Gebrehiwot Berhe & Hongwu Liu (Eds.), *China–Africa relations: Governance, peace and security* (pp. 55–73). Addis Ababa: Addis Ababa University Press.

42. Martina, Michael, & Brunnstrom, David. (2015, September 28). China's Xi says to commit 8,000 troops for U.N. peacekeeping force. *Reuters*. Retrieved from http://news.yahoo.com/chinas-xi-says-commit-8-000-troops-u-160032557.html.

43. See Moller, Lars Christian. (2015). *Ethiopia's great run: The growth acceleration and how to pace it* (Working paper). Washington, DC: World Bank Group.

44. United States Agency for International Development. (2017). *Agriculture and food security*. Retrieved from https://2012-2017.usaid.gov/ethiopia/agriculture-and-food-security.

Chapter 5

1. Sautman, Barry, & Yan, Hairong. (2009). African perspectives on China–Africa links. *China Quarterly, 199*, 728–759.

2. Hilson, Gayin, Hilson, Abigail, & Adu-Darko, Eunice. (2014). Chinese participation in Ghana's informal gold mining economy: Drivers, implication and clarifications. *Journal of Rural Studies, 34*, 291–303.

3. Negri, Rohi. (2008). Beyond the Chinese scramble: The political economy of anti-China sentiment in Zambia. *African Geography Review, 27*(1), 41–63.

4. Kuo, Lily. (2017, April 30). Chinese migrants have changed the face of South Africa. Now they're leaving. *Quartz*. Retrieved from https://qz.com/940619/chinese-traders-changed-south-africa-now-theyre-leaving/.

5. Castillo, Roberto. (2014). Feeling at home in the "Chocolate City": an exploration of place-making practices and structures of belonging amongst Africans in Guangzhou. *Inter-Asia Cultural Studies, 15*(2), 235–257.

6. Yebo, Yepoka. (2013, May 13). African traders flocked to Guangzhou for cheap goods but are staying to run manufacturing operations. *Quartz*. Retrieved from http://qz.com/81642/african-traders-flocked-to-guangzhou-for-the-cheap-goods-but-are-staying-to-run-manufacturing-operations/.

7. China empowers a million Ethiopians: Ambassador. (2016, January 26). *African News Agency*. Retrieved from https://www.enca.com/money/china-empowers-million-ethiopians-ambassador.

8. Driessen, Miriam. (2015, February). Migrating for the bank: Housing and Chinese labor migration in Ethiopia. *China Quarterly, 221*, 144.

9. Cook, S., Lu, J., Tugendhat, H., & Alemu, D. (2016). Chinese migrants in Africa: Facts and fiction from the agri-food sector in Ethiopia and Ghana. *World Development, 81*, 61.

10. Maasho, Aaron. (2018, March 8). Africa should avoid forfeiting sovereignty to China over loans: Tillerson. *Reuters*. Retrieved from https://www.reuters.com/article/us-usa-africa/africa-should-avoid-forfeiting-sovereignty-to-china-over-loans-tillerson-idUSKCN1GK114.

11. See Furtado, Xavier, & Smith, W. James. (2009). Ethiopia retaining sovereignty in aid relations. In Lindsay Whitefield (Ed.), *The politics of aid: African strategies to dealing with donors* (pp. 131–155). London: Oxford University Press.

12. Nuo, Dai. (2009). *The adjustment of China's industrial structure after 1978* (Unpublished master's thesis). University of Oslo, Norway.

13. Murphy, Padraig. (2016, March 24). *The Silk Road, XXI century: "One belt one road."* Retrieved from Institute of International and European Affairs website: https://www.iiea.com/publication/the-silk-road-xxi-century-one-belt-one-road/.

14. Chinese-built Lamu port on course to transform Kenya, E. Africa. (2015, July 13). *New China*. Retrieved from http://eng.chinamil.com.cn/news-channels/2015-07/13/content_6584295.htm.

15. Mwangi, George. (2014, April 3). Chinese firm signs $478.9 million Kenya Lamu port deal. *The Wall Street Journal*. Retrieved from https://blogs.wsj.com/frontiers/2014/08/03/chinese-firm-signs-478-9-million-kenya-lamu-port-deal/.

16. Minnie, Tom. (2014, October 30). Tanzania's $10 bn China-funded port will start in 2015. *African Capital Markets*. Retrieved from http://www.africancapitalmarketsnews.com/2506/tanzanias-10bn-china-funded-port-will-start-in-2015/.

17. Ng'Wanakilala, Fumbu. (2014, October 27). China says construction of China-funded port to start in 2015. *Reuters*. Retrieved from https://www.reuters.com/article/tanzania-port/tanzania-says-construction-of-china-funded-port-to-start-in-2015-idUSL5N0SM1QT20141027.

18. Oqubay, Arkebe. (2018, June). *The structure and performance of the Ethiopian manufacturing sector* (Working Paper Series No. 299). African Development Bank, 4. Retrieved from https://www.tralac.org/images/docs/13204/the-structure-and-performance-of-the-ethiopian-manufacturing-sector-afdb-wps-299-june-2018.pdf.

19. Zhang, X., Taxera, D., Zou, C., Wang, Z., Zhao, J., Gebremenfas, E. A., & Dhavle, (2018). *Industrial park development in Ethiopia: Case study report* (Inclusive and Sustainable Industrial Development Working Paper 21/2018). Vienna, Austria: UN Industrial Development Organization.Retrieved from https://www.unido.org/api/opentext/documents/download/10694802/unido-file-10694802.

20. Federal Democratic Republic of Ethiopia, National Planning Commission. (2016). *Growth and transformation plan II (GTPII) (2015/16–2019/20). Vol. 1: Main text*. Addis Ababa: Author. Retrieved from https://europa.eu/capacity4dev/resilience_ethiopia/document/growth-and-transformation-plan-ii-gtp-ii-201516-201920.

21. Tesfaye, Aaron. (2012). Environmental security, regime building and international law in the Nile basin. *Canadian Journal of African Studies, 46*(2), 271–287. doi:10.1080/00083968.2012.702087.

22. Berhane, Daniel. (2013, April 26). China provides $1 billion for Renaissance Dam transmissions lines. *Horn Affairs*. Retrieved from http://daniel berhane.com/2013/04/26/nile-china-finance-billion-dollar-renaissance-dam/.

23. These corridors are Mekele–Hara Gebeya (268 km), Hara Gebeya–Assayta (229 km), Asayta–Tajura Port (210 km), Awash–Hara Gebeya (389 km), Addis Ababa/Sebeta–Ejaji–Jimma–Bedele–Tepi–Dima (740 km).

24. Lu, Rucai. (2017, February 28). Enhancing connectivity in East Africa: The Addis Ababa–Djibouti Railway. *China Today*. Retrieved from http://www.chinatoday.com.cn/english/spc/2017-02/28/content_739335.htm.

25. Zhou, Laura. (2017, January 10). All aboard for Africa's heartland, on a train built by China. *South China Morning Post*. Retrieved from http://www.koreatimes.co.kr/www/world/2019/02/672_221830.html.

26. Manek, Nizar. (2017, June 8). Ethiopia eyes role in DP World–managed port in Somaliland. *Bloomberg*. Retrieved from https://www.bloomberg.com/news/articles/2017-06-08/landlocked-ethiopia-eyes-role-in-dp-world-managed-somali-port.

27. Lu, Rucai. (2017, February 28). Enhancing connectivity in East Africa: The Addis Ababa–Djibouti Railway. *China Today*. Retrieved from http://www.chinatoday.com.cn/english/spc/2017-02/28/content_739335.htm.

28. Molinari, Michele, & Gunzinger, Noah. (2015, June 3). Ethiopia turns big plans into reality. *International Railway Journal*. Retrieved from http://www.chinatoday.com.cn/english/spc/2017-02/28/content_739335.htm.

29. Intergovernmental Authority for Development. (2018, March 21). *Recently China contributed $100,000 to support operational cost of IGAD. Cooperation with China*. Retrieved from https://igad.int/executive-secretary/370-cooperation-with-china.

30. Mulualem, Melaku. (2017, January–March). OBOR: What is there for Africa? Discourse: Debating African Issues. *Dissent*, 137–138.

31. Oluoch, Fred. (2016, June 25). Kenya, Ethiopia in rail and pipeline deals. *The East African*. Retrieved from http://www.theeastafrican.co.ke/news/Kenya-and-Ethiopia-in-rail-pipeline-deals-/2558-3267116-jshm6kz/index.html.

32. Chinese-built Lamu port on course to transform Kenya, E. Africa. (2015, July 13). *New China*. Retrieved from http://eng.chinamil.com.cn/news-channels/2015-07/13/content_6584295.htm.

33. Brown, Adrian J. (2015, December 17). *LAPSSET: The history and politics of an eastern African megaproject*. Nairobi, Kenya: Rift Valley Institute.

34. Olson, Mancour, Jr. (1971). *The logic of collective action: Public goods and the theory of groups*. Cambridge, MA: Harvard University Press.

35. Van Staden, Cobus. (2017). One belt one road and East Africa: Beyond Chinese influence. *China Brief*, 17(14), 2. Retrieved from https://jamestown.org/program/one-belt-one-road-east-africa-beyond-chinese-influence/.

36. Bräutigam, Debora, & Hwang, Jyhjong. (2016, April). *Eastern promises new data on Chinese loans in Africa: 2000–2014* (Working Paper No. 4). China–Africa Research Initiative, School of Advanced International Studies, Johns

Hopkins University, Washington, DC. Retrieved from https://static1.square space.com/static/5652847de4b033f56d2bdc29/t/58ac91ede6f2e1f64a20d11a/ 1487704559189/eastern+promises+v4.pdf.

37. China–Africa Research Initiative. (2019). *Chinese loans to Africa: Loan Data Base*. School of Advanced International Studies, Johns Hopkins University, Washington, DC. Retrieved from http://www.sais-cari.org/data-chinese-loans-and-aid-to-africa.

38. Brautigam, Deborah, & Gallagher, Kevin. (2014). Bartering globalization: China's commodity-backed finance in Africa and Latin America. *Global Policy, 5*(3), 342–346.

39. Brautigam, Debora, & Hwang, Jyhjong. (2016, April). *Eastern promises new data on Chinese loans in Africa: 2000–2014* (Working Paper No. 4). China–Africa Research Initiative, School of Advanced International Studies, Johns Hopkins University, Washington, DC. Retrieved from https://static1.squarespace.com/static/5652847de4b033f56d2bdc29/t/58ac91ede6f2e1f64a20d11a/1487704559189/eastern+promises+v4.pdf.

40. Gudrun Østby. (2005, January 5–7). *Horizontal inequalities and civil conflict*. Paper presented at the 13th Annual National Political Science Conference, Hurdalsjøen, Norway. Retrieved from http://citeseerx.ist.psu.edu/viewdoc/download?doi=10.1.1.163.6506&rep=rep1&type=pdf.

41. See Mehler, Andreas. (2009). Peace and power sharing in Africa: A not so obvious relationship. *African Affairs, 108*(432), 453–473.

42. United States Energy Information Administration. (2017, August 4). *Three important oil trade chokepoints are located around the Arabian Peninsula*. Retrieved from https://www.eia.gov/todayinenergy/detail.php?id=32352.

43. Tesfaye, Aaron. (2017). Ethiopia, China and the West. In Chris Alden, A. Alao, C. Zhang, & L. Barber (Eds.), *China and Africa: Building peace and security cooperation on the continent* (pp. 269–288). New York, NY: Palgrave Macmillan.

44. Jayaram, Kartik, Kassiri, Omid, & Sun, Irene Yuan. (2017, June). The closest look yet of Chinese engagement in Africa. *McKinsey Report*. Retrieved from https://www.mckinsey.com/featured-insights/middle-east-and-africa/the-closest-look-yet-at-chinese-economic-engagement-in-africa.

45. Hai, Helen, & Cohen, Aaron. (2017, October 18). China is Africa's biggest economic partner, but what role for the United States? *Forbes*, 1.

46. Hackenesch, Christine. (2013). Aid donor meets strategic partner? The European Union and China's relations with Ethiopia. *Journal of Current Chinese Affairs, 42*, 15.

47. Wissenbach, Uwe. (2009). The EU's response to China's Africa safari: Can triangular cooperation match needs? *European Journal of Development Research, 21*(16), 662–674.

48. Hackenesch, Christine. (2015.) Not as bad as it seems: EU and US democracy promotion faces China in Africa. *Democratization, 22*(3), 419–437.

Chapter 6

1. Qiu, J. (2019, April 26). Why is China still a developing country? *Beijing Review*. Retrieved from http://www.bjreview.com/Opinion/201904/t20190426_800166194.html.

2. Fish, Isaac S. (2014, September 25). Is China still a developing country? *Foreign Policy*. Retrieved from https://foreignpolicy.com/2014/09/25/is-china-still-a-developing-country/.

3. Landler, Mark, & Wong, Edward. (2018, December 13). Bolton outlines a strategy for Africa that's really about countering China. *The New York Times*. Retrieved from https://www.nytimes.com/2018/12/13/us/politics/john-bolton-africa-china.html.

4. Meester, Jos, van De Berg, Willem, & Verhoven, Harry. (2018, April). *Riyal politik: The political economy of Gulf investments in the Horn of Africa*. Retrieved from Clingendael Institute website: https://www.clingendael.org/sites/default/files/2018-04/riyal-politik.pdf.

5. Bellow, Waldon. (2019, February 10.) *China: An imperial power in the image of the West?* Retrieved from Focus on the Global South website: https://focusweb.org/wp-content/uploads/2019/10/A4_ChinaAnImperialPower_WEB.pdf.

Bibliography

Abota, A. (2006). *Ethiopia's foreign policy under Emperor Haile Selassie I: An appraisal* (Unpublished master's thesis). Addis Ababa University, Ethiopia.
Acharya, A. (2014). Who are the norm makers? The Asian–African conference in Bandung and the evolution of norms. *Global Governance, 20*, 415.
Adem, S. (2012). China and Ethiopia: Diplomacy and economic Sino-optimism. *Africa Studies Review, 55*(1), 44.
Adem, S. (2012). Imperial Ethiopia's relations with Maoist China. *African and East Asian Affairs, 1*, 31–53.
Ademola, T. O., Bankole, A. S., & Odewuyi, A. O. (2009). China–Africa trade relations: Insights from AERC scoping studies. *European Journal of Development Research, 21*(4), 485–505.
Aidoo, R., & Hess, S. (2015). Non-interference 2.0: China's evolving foreign policy towards a changing Africa. *Journal of Current Chinese Affairs, 44*(1), 107–139.
Ajakaiye, O., & Kaplinsky, R. (2009). China in Africa: A relationship in transition. *European Journal of Development Research, 21*(4), 479–484.
Akombo, A. (2015, March 27). Oil and gas Africa: Disputes simmer over exploration rights in eastern Africa. *AFK Insider*. Retrieved from http://afkinsider.com/88551/oil-gas-africa-disputes-simmer-exploration-rights-eastern-africa/.
Alden, C. (2007). *China in Africa: Partner, competitor or hegemon?* New York, NY: Zed Books.
Alden, C., & Alves, A. C. (2008). History and identity in the construction of China's Africa policy. *Review of African Political Economy, 115*, 43–58.
Alden, C., & Large, D. (2011). China's exceptionalism and the challenges of delivering difference in Africa. *Journal of Contemporary China, 20*(68), 21–38.
Alemu, D., & Scoones, I. (2013). Negotiating new relationships: How the Ethiopian state is involving China and Brazil in agriculture and rural development. *IDS Bulletin, 44*(4), 91–100.
American Enterprise Institute. (2017). *China global investment tracker* [Data set]. Retrieved from https://www.aei.org/china-global-investment-tracker/.

Armstrong, D. (1994). Chinese perspectives on the new world order. *Journal of East Asian Affairs*, 8(2), 454–481.

Atkins, L., Brautigam, D., Chen, Y., & Hwang, J. (2017). *Challenges of and opportunities from the commodity price slump* (CARI Economic Bulletin #1). Washington, DC: China Africa Research Initiative. Retrieved from https://static1.squarespace.com/static/5652847de4b033f56d2bdc29/t/59f-85883ec212d5a70e9624c/1509447812591/bulletin+v5.pdf.

Ayalew, S. (1994). A synopsis of the foreign policy of the Transitional Government of Ethiopia (TGE) since the adoption of the Charter in July 1991. *EthioScope*, 1, 1–2.

Bamon, E. (2006). *Evaluating Asian drivers impacts on sub-Saharan Africa oil and gas industries: A methodological framework* (Paper). Nairobi: African Economic Research Consortium.

Bandung Conference, Asia–Africa 1955. (n.d.). In *Encyclopedia Britannica*. Retrieved from https://www.britannica.com/event/Bandung-Conference.

Bekele, S., & Regassa, T. (2012). *Democratizing in a developmental state: The case of Ethiopia: Issues, challenges, prospects* (UNDP Development Brief: Ethiopia No. 1/2012). Retrieved from United Nations Development Programme website: https://www.et.undp.org/content/dam/ethiopia/docs/Democratization%20in%20a%20Developmental%20State.pdf.

Bellow, W. (2019, February 10). *China: An imperial power in the image of the West?* Retrieved from Focus on the Global South website: https://focusweb.org/wp-content/uploads/2019/10/A4_ChinaAnImperialPower_WEB.pdf.

Berhane, D. (2013, April 26). China provides $1 billion for Renaissance Dam transmissions lines. *Horn Affairs*. Retrieved from https://hornaffairs.com/2013/04/26/nile-china-finance-billion-dollar-renaissance-dam/.

Berman, B. J. (1998). Ethnicity, patronage and the African state: The politics of uncivil nationalism. *African Affairs*, 97(388), 305–341.

Boden, C. (2015, November 26). China in talks with Djibouti on establishing logistics base. *Associated Press*. Retrieved from http://english.alarabiya.net/en/News/world/2015/11/26/China-in-talks-with-Djibouti-on-establishing-logistics-base.html.

Bräutigam, D. (2011). *The dragon's gift: The real story of China in Africa*. New York, NY: Oxford University Press.

Bräutigam, D. (2011, December 30). Ethiopia's partnership with China. *The Guardian*. Retrieved from https://www.theguardian.com/global-development/poverty-matters/2011/dec/30/china-ethiopia-business-opportunities.

Bräutigam, D., & Gallagher, K. (2014). Bartering globalization: China's commodity-backed finance in Africa and Latin America. *Global Policy*, 5(3), 342–346.

Bräutigam, D., & Hwang, J. (2016, April). *Eastern promises new data on Chinese loans in Africa: 2000–2014* (Working Paper No. 4). China–Africa Research Initiative, School of Advanced International Studies, Johns Hopkins University, Washington, DC. Retrieved from https://static1.squarespace.com/static/5652847de4b033f56d2bdc29/t/58ac91ede6f2e-1f64a20d11a/1487704559189/eastern+promises+v4.pdf.

Bräutigam, D., & Tang, X. (2011). African Shenzhen: China's special economic zones in Africa. *Journal of Modern African Studies*, 49(1), 27–54.

Breeze, V., & Moore, N. (2017, June 27). China tops US and UK as destination for anglophone African students. *The Conversation*. Retrieved from http://theconversation.com/china-tops-us-and-uk-as-destination-for-anglophone-african-students-78967.

Broadman, H. (2007). *Africa's Silk Road: China and India's new economic frontier*. Washington, DC: World Bank.

Brooks, A. (2016, June 28). Djibouti and China to build global trade routes. *East Africa Monitor*. Retrieved from https://eastafricamonitor.com/djibouti-china-ink-plans-build-global-trade-routes/.

Brown, A. J. (2015, December 17). *LAPSSET: The history and politics of an eastern African megaproject*. Nairobi, Kenya: Rift Valley Institute.

Cabestan, J.-P. (2012). China and Ethiopia: Authoritarian affinities and economic cooperation. *China Perspectives*, 2012(4), 53–62. Retrieved from http://journals.openedition.org/chinaperspectives/6041.

Castillo, R. (2014). Feeling at home in the "Chocolate City": An exploration of place-making practices and structures of belonging amongst Africans in Guangzhou. *Inter-Asia Cultural Studies*, 15(2), 235–257.

Chakrabarty, Malancha. (2016). Ethiopia–China economic relations: A classic win-win situation? *World Review of Political Economy*, 7(2), 226–248.

Cheng, Z., & Taylor, Ian. (2017). *China's aid to Africa: Does friendship really matter?* London: Routledge.

Cheru, Fantu. (2016). Emerging Southern powers and new forms of South–South cooperation: Ethiopia's strategic engagement with China and India. *Third World Quarterly*, 37(4), 592–610.

China empowers a million Ethiopians: Ambassador. (2016, January 26). *African News Agency*. Retrieved from https://www.enca.com/money/china-empowers-million-ethiopians-ambassador.

Chinese firm to build new industrial park in Ethiopia. (2017, October 6). *New China*. Retrieved from http://www.xinhuanet.com//english/2017-06/10/c_136355619.htm.

Chinese-built Lamu port on course to transform Kenya, E. Africa. (2015, July 13). *New China*. Retrieved from http://eng.chinamil.com.cn/news-channels/2015-07/13/content_6584295.htm.

Clapham, C. (1999). Sovereignty and the third world state. *Political Studies, 47*(3), 522–537.

Clarke, J. C., III. (2007, March 14). Foreign Minister Heruy's mission to Japan in 1931: Ethiopia's effort to find a non-Western model for modernization (pp. 17–18). In *Selected Annual Proceedings of the Florida Conference of Historians* (pp. 17–18). Miami Beach, FL.

Conrad, B., Fernandez, M., & Houshyani, B. (2010). *Towards an energizing partnership? Exploring China's role as catalyst of renewable energy development in Africa*. Washington, DC: World Wildlife Fund.

Cook, S., Lu, J., Tugendhat, H., & Alemu, D. (2016). Chinese migrants in Africa: Facts and fiction from the agri-food sector in Ethiopia and Ghana. *World Development, 81*, 61–70.

Cooperation with China. (2018, March 21). Retrieved from https://igad.int/executive-secretary/370-cooperation-with-china.

Data: Chinese loans to Africa. (2019). China–Africa Research Initiative, School of Advanced International Studies, Johns Hopkins University, Washington, DC. Retrieved from http://www.sais-cari.org/data-chinese-loans-to-africa.

Davies, M., Edinger, H., Tay, N., & Nadu, S. (2008, February). *How China delivers developmental assistance to Africa*. Center for Chinese Studies, University of Stellenbosch, South Africa.

Davidson, W. (2013, October 21). Egypt, Ethiopia and Sudan mull new probe Nile dam impact. *Bloomberg News*. Retrieved from https://www.bloomberg.com/news/articles/2013-10-21/egypt-ethiopia-and-sudan-mull-new-probe-nile-dam-impact.

Davison, W. (2013, March 8). Ethiopia to open first industrial zone to bolster economy. *Bloomberg News*. Retrieved from https://www.bloomberg.com/news/articles/2013-03-18/ethiopia-to-open-first-industrial-zone-to-boost-economic-growth.

Diaw, D., & Lessoua, A. (2013). Natural resource exports, diversification and economic growth of CEMAC countries: On the impact of trade with China. *African Development Review, 25*(2), 189–202.

Dinh, H. T., Palmade, V., Chandra, V., & Cossar, F. (2013). *Light manufacturing in Africa: Targeted policies to enhance private investment and create jobs*. Washington, DC: World Bank.

Dittgen, R., & Demisse, A. A. (2017, January). *Own ways of doing: National pride, power and China's political calculus in Ethiopia* (Occasional Paper 249). Johannesburg, South Africa Institute of International Affairs. doi:10.13140/RG.2.2.23077.91368.

Donahue, B. (2018, March 2). China is turning Ethiopia into a giant fashion factory. *The New York Times*. Retrieved from https://www.bloomberg.com/news/features/2018-03-02/china-is-turning-ethiopia-into-a-giant-fast-fashion-factory.

Bibliography 153

Drauwe, P., Houssa, R., & Picillo, Giuli. (2012). African trade dynamics: Is China a different partner? *Journal of Chinese Economic and Business Studies*, *10*(1), 15–54.

Dreher, A., Fuchs, A., Hodler, R., Parks, B., Raschky, P., & Tierney, M. J. (2014, November). *Aid on demand: African leaders and the geography of China's foreign assistance* (Working Paper No. 3). Retrieved from http://docs.aiddata.org/ad4/files/inline/wp3_-_revised_working_paper_series_dreher_et_al_2016_october.pdf.

Driessen, M. (2015, February). Migrating for the bank: Housing and Chinese labor migration in Ethiopia. *China Quarterly*, *221*, 144.

Eisenman, J., & Kurlantzick, J. (2006). China's Africa strategy. *Current History*, *105*(691), 219–224.

Ekeh, P. P. (1975). Colonialism and the two publics in Africa: A theoretical statement. *Comparative Studies in Society and History*, *17*(1), 91–112.

Embassy of the People's Republic of China in the Federal Democratic Republic of Ethiopia. (2014). *Confucius Institute inaugurated in Addis Ababa University*. Retrieved from http://et.china-embassy.org/eng/sgxx/t1227008.htm.

Embassy of the People's Republic of China in the Federal Democratic Republic of Ethiopia. (2016, November 11). *China, Ethiopia agree to augment military cooperation*. Retrieved from http://et.china-embassy.org/eng/zagx/t1419796.htm.

Ethiopia. (n.d.). *Economist Intelligence Unit*. Retrieved from http://country.eiu.com/Ethiopia.

Ethiopia and China sign $1 billion power deal. (2013, April 26). *Energy Daily*. Retrieved from http://www.energy-daily.com/reports/Ethiopia_and_China_sign_1_billion_power_deal_999.html.

Ethiopia, China to strengthen strategic partnership. (2017, June 21). *Xinhua*. Retrieved from http://www.xinhuanet.com//english/2017-06/22/c_136386698.htm.

Ethiopia draws Asian manufacturing interests. (2014, August 4). *VOA News*. Retrieved from http://www.voanews.com/content/ethiopia-drawing-asia-manufacturing-interest/1970953.html.

Ethiopia, Somaliland and China to sign trilateral deals. (2011, August 14). *Ezega Press*. Retrieved from https://www.ezega.com/News/NewsDetails?Page=heads&NewsID=3015.

Ethiopian Airlines. (2018, February 9). *Ethiopian wins the first Cargo Transportation Award in China* [Press release]. Addis Ababa: Author.

Ethiopian imports, 2006–2017. (2017). *Trading Economics*. Retrieved from https://tradingeconomics.com/ethiopia/imports.

Eversheds Southerland. (2012, April 18). *Oil & gas in the Horn of Africa—the opportunities and risks*. Retrieved from http://www.eversheds.com/global/

en/what/articles/index.page?ArticleID=en/Oil-Gas-in-the-Horn-of-Africa_the-opportunities-and-risks.

Farquharson, M. (2017, April 19). Chinese infrastructure investment in Ethiopia. *Borgen Magazine.* Retrieved from https://www.borgenmagazine.com/chinese-infrastructure-investment-in-ethiopia/.

Fatton, R. (1988). Bringing the ruling class back in. *Comparative Politics, 20*(3), 253–264.

Federal Democratic Republic of Ethiopia, Investment Commission. (2015). *Chinese investments in Ethiopia.* Addis Ababa: Author.

Federal Democratic Republic of Ethiopia, Investment Commission. (2017). *Chinese investments in Ethiopia.* Addis Ababa: Author.

Federal Democratic Republic of Ethiopia, Ministry of Finance and Economic Cooperation. (2012). *China plans to double its development assistance to Ethiopia.* Addis Ababa: Author.

Federal Democratic Republic of Ethiopia, Ministry of Finance and Economic Development. (2010). *Growth and transformation plan 2010/11–2014/15. Vol. 1: Main text.* Addis Ababa: Author. Retrieved from http://extwprlegs1.fao.org/docs/pdf/eth144893.pdf.

Federal Democratic Republic of Ethiopia, Ministry of Finance and Economic Development. (2015). *Growth and transformation plan, 2010/11–2014/15. Vol. II: Policy matrix.* Addis Ababa: Author.

Federal Democratic Republic of Ethiopia, Ministry of Foreign Affairs, Asia Australasia and the Middle East General Directorate. (2016, September). *An overview of the bilateral relations between the Federal Democratic Republic of Ethiopia and the People's Republic of China.* Addis Ababa: Author. Retrieved from https://www.saiia.org.za/wp-content/uploads/2008/05/Zemene_Ethiopia.pdf.

Federal Democratic Republic of Ethiopia, National Planning Commission. (2016). *Growth and transformation plan II (GTPII) (2015/16–2019/20). Vol. 1: Main text.* Addis Ababa: Author. Retrieved from https://europa.eu/capacity4dev/resilience_ethiopia/document/growth-and-transformation-plan-ii-gtp-ii-201516-201920.

Ferdjani, H. (2012). *African students in China: An exploration of increasing numbers and their motivations in Beijing.* Center for Chinese Studies, Stellenbosch University, South Africa. Retrieved from http://citeseerx.ist.psu.edu/viewdoc/download?doi=10.1.1.470.8611&rep=rep1&type=pdf.

Fick, M. (2018, May 1). Harboring ambitions: Gulf states scramble for Somalia. *Reuters.* Retrieved from https://www.reuters.com/article/us-somalia-gulf-analysis/harboring-ambitions-gulf-states-scramble-for-somalia-idUSKBN1I23B4.

Fish, I. S. (2014, September 25). Is China still a developing country? *Foreign Policy.* Retrieved from https://foreignpolicy.com/2014/09/25/is-china-still-a-developing-country/.

Fishman, T. (2005). *China, Inc.: The rise of the next superpower challenges America and the world*. London: Simon and Schuster.
Forum on China–Africa Cooperation. (2003, December 16). *The Forum on China–Africa Cooperation—Addis Ababa Action Plan (2004–2006)*. Second Ministerial Conference of the FOCAC. Retrieved from http://www.fmprc.gov.cn/zflt/eng/zyzl/hywj/t157710.htm.
Forum on China–Africa Cooperation. (2006). *China's Africa policy*. Retrieved from http://www.gov.cn/misc/2006-01/12/content_156490.htm.
Forum on China–Africa Cooperation. (2009, October 21). *China has cancelled 150 mature debts of 32 African countries*. Retrieved from https://www.focac.org/eng/ljhy_1/dscbzjhy/FA32009/t623384.htm.
French, H. (2015). *China's new continent: How a million migrants are building a new empire in Africa*. New York, NY: Vintage.
Furie, E. (2015). China's example for Meles' Ethiopia: When development models land. *Journal of Modern African Studies, 53*(3), 289–316. doi:10.1017/S0022278X15000397.
Furtado, Xavier, & Smith, W. James. (2009). Ethiopia retaining sovereignty in aid relations. In Lindsay Whitefield (Ed.), *The politics of aid: African strategies to dealing with donors* (pp. 131–155). London: Oxford University Press.
Gebre-Egziaber, T. (2007). Impacts of Chinese imports and coping strategies of local producers: The case of small-scale foot wear enterprise in Ethiopia. *Journal of Modern African Studies, 45*(4), 614–679.
Gebre-Egziabher, T. (2009). The development impact of Asian drivers on Ethiopia with special emphasis on small-scale footwear producers. *World Economy, 232*(11), 1613–1637. doi:10.1111/j.1467-9701.2009.01252.x.
Gebru, B. (2017, December 8). Ethiopia: the rising hub of textile manufacturing. *Walta Information Service*. Retrieved from http://www.waltainfo.com/index.php/FeaturedArticles/detail?cid=35365&locale=en.
Geda, Alemayehu. (2008). *AERC scoping study on Chinese relations with sub-Sahara Africa: The case of Ethiopia* (Working paper). Nairobi, Kenya: African Economic Research Consortium. Retrieved from https://www.africaportal.org/publications/aerc-scoping-study-on-the-chinese-relation-with-sub-saharan-africa-the-case-of-ethiopia/.
Genyi, G. A. (2015). South Sudan: Resolving conflicts in Africa: A test case for China. *Conflict Studies Quarterly, 13*, 17–28.
Gill, B., & Reilly, J. (2007). The tenuous hold of China Inc. in Africa. *Washington Quarterly, 30*(3), 37–52.
Goldstein, L. J. (2001). Return to Zhenbao Island: Who started shooting and why it matters. *China Quarterly, 168*, 985–997.
Gramlich, E. (1994). Infrastructure investment: A review essay. *Journal of Economic Literature, 32*, 1176–1196.

Grimm, S. (2012). *The Forum on China–Africa Cooperation (FOCAC): Political rationale and functioning* (Working paper). Stellenbosch Centre for Chinese Studies, Stellenbosch University, South Africa.

Gu, J., Zhang, C., Vaz, A., & Mukwereza, L. (2016). Chinese state capitalism? Rethinking the role of the state and business in Chinese development cooperation in Africa. *World Development, 81,* 24–34. doi:10.1016/j.worlddev.2016.01.001.

Hackenesch, C. (2013). Aid donor meets strategic partner? The European Union and China's relations with Ethiopia. *Journal of Current Chinese Affairs, 42,* 15.

Hackenesch, C. (2015). Not as bad as it seems: EU and US democracy promotion faces China in Africa. *Democratization, 22*(3), 419–437.

Hai, H., & Cohen, A. (2017, October 18). China is Africa's biggest economic partner, but what role for the United States? *Forbes, 1.* Retrieved from https://www.forbes.com/sites/realspin/2017/10/18/china-is-africas-biggest-economic-partner-but-what-role-for-the-united-states/#4fad2d467f43.

Hatfield, R., & Davies, J. (2006). *Global review of the economics of pastoralism* (Research report prepared for the World Initiative for Sustainable Pastoralism). Nairobi, Kenya: International Union for Conservation of Nature.

Haugen, H. O. (2011). Chinese exports to Africa: Competition, complementarity and cooperation between micro-level actors. *Forum for Development Studies, 38*(2), 165.

He, Y. (2007). *China's changing policy on UN peacekeeping operations.* Stockholm: Institute for Security and Development Policy. Retrieved from http://isdp.eu/content/uploads/publications/2007_he_chinas-changing-policy.pdf.

Healey, S. (2011). Seeking peace and security in the Horn of Africa: The contribution of Intergovernmental Authority on Development. *International Affairs, 87*(1), 105–120.

Hilson, G., Hilson, A., & Adu-Darko, E. (2014). Chinese participation in Ghana's informal gold mining economy: Drivers, implication and clarifications. *Journal of Rural Studies, 34,* 291–303.

Hofstedt, T. A. (2009). China in Africa: An AFRICOM response. *Naval War College Review, 62*(3), 78–100. Retrieved from https://apps.dtic.mil/dtic/tr/fulltext/u2/a519315.pdf.

Hutchinson, S. E. (2001). A curse from God? Religious and political dimensions of the post-1991 rise of ethnic violence in South Sudan. *Journal of Modern African Studies, 39*(2), 307–331.

Intergovernmental Authority on Development. (2011, November 21). *Cooperation with China.* Retrieved from http://igad.int/index.php?option=com_content&view=article&id=370:cooperation-with-china&catid=46:executive-secretary&Itemid=123.

International Energy Agency. (2014). *Africa energy outlook: A focus on energy prospects in sub-Saharan Africa* (World Energy Outlook Special Report).

Retrieved from https://www.iea.org/publications/freepublications/publication/WEO2014_AfricaEnergyOutlook.pdf.

Jayaram, K., Kassiri, O., & Sun, I. Y. (2017, June). The closest look yet of Chinese engagement in Africa. *McKinsey Report*. Retrieved from https://www.mckinsey.com/featured-insights/middle-east-and-africa/the-closest-look-yet-at-chinese-economic-engagement-in-africa.

Jiang, A., & Zhang, J. (2013, March 11). Djibouti welcomes China to build a military base. *Global Times*. Retrieved from http://www.chinaafricaproject.com/djibouti-welcomes-china-to-build-a-military-base-translation.

Jobson, E. (2013, February 13). Ethiopia achieves development target of reducing child mortality rate. *The Guardian*. Retrieved from https://www.theguardian.com/global-development/2013/sep/13/ethiopia-achieves-development-target-child-mortality.

Jones, M. T. (2014, July 18). Port challenges in East Africa afford a golden opportunity for Berbera. Retrieved from https://somaliland1991.wordpress.com/2014/07/page/2/.

Jones, T. (2018, February 17). China pledges $2bn for development goals and says it will write off debts. *The Guardian*. Retrieved from https://www.theguardian.com/global-development/2015/sep/27/china-pledges-2bn-for-development-goals-and-says-it-will-write-off-debts.

Kiganda, A. (2016, August 11). Chinese firm begins constructing luxury apartments in Ethiopia. *Construction Review Online*. Retrieved from https://constructionreviewonline.com/2016/08/chinese-firm-begins-constructing-luxury-apartments-in-ethiopia/.

King, K. (2011). China's cooperation with Ethiopia with a focus on human resources. *Organization for Social Science Research in Eastern and South Africa Bulletin*, 3, 95–100.

Kissinger, H. (1979). *The White House years*. Boston, MA: Little, Brown.

Knorringa, P., & Pegler, I. (2006). *Social capital for industrial development: Operationalizing the concept*. Vienna: United Nations Industrial Development Organization.

Kuo, L. (2017, April 30). Chinese migrants have changed the face of South Africa. Now they're leaving. *Quartz*. Retrieved from https://qz.com/940619/chinese-traders-changed-south-africa-now-theyre-leaving/.

Landler, M., & Wong, E. (2018, December 13). Bolton outlines a strategy for Africa that's really about countering China. *The New York Times*. Retrieved from https://www.nytimes.com/2018/12/13/us/politics/john-bolton-africa-china.html.

Lee, J. (2015, April 23). China comes to Djibouti: Why Washington should be worried. *Foreign Affairs*. Retrieved from https://www.foreignaffairs.com/articles/east-africa/2015-04-23/china-comes-djibouti.

Lee, J. T.-H. (2008, March). China's Third World policy from the Maoist era to the present (Occasional Paper No. 3). *Global Asia Journal*, 1–53.

Lefebvre, J. A. (1993). The United States and Egypt: Confrontation and accommodation in northeast Africa, 1956–60. *Middle Eastern Studies*, 29(2), 321–338.

Legum, C. (Ed.). (1987). *Africa contemporary record: Annual survey and documents, Vol. 18, 1985–1986*. Teaneck, NJ: Holmes and Meier.

Lehman, H. P. (2008, March 26–29). *The Asian economic model and Africa: Japanese developmental lessons for Africa*. Paper presented at the Annual International Studies Association, San Francisco, CA.

Lengauer, S. (2011) China's foreign aid policy: Motive and method. *Culture Mandala: The Bulletin of the Centre for East-West Cultural & Economic Studies*, 9(2), 35–81. Retrieved from http://www.international-relations.com/CM2011/PRC-Foreign-Aid-2011.pdf.

Lian, Shanggang, (2015, June 5). Ethiopia keen to bolster cooperation with China in manufacturing sector: President. *China Daily*. Retrieved from http://www.chinadaily.com.cn/business/2015-06/06/content_20927430.htm.

Li, A. (2016). Technology transfer in China–Africa relation: Myth or reality. *Transnational Corporation Review*, 8(3), 183–195. doi:10.1080/19186444.2016.1233718.

Li, A. (2005). African studies in China in the twentieth century: A historiographical survey. *African Studies Review*, 48(1), 62–63.

Li, X. (2017). Does conditionality still work? China's development assistance and democracy in Africa. *China Political Science Review*, 2, 206.

Lu, Rucai. (2017, February 28). Enhancing connectivity in East Africa: The Addis Ababa–Djibouti Railway. *China Today*. Retrieved from http://www.chinatoday.com.cn/english/spc/2017-02/28/content_739335.htm.

Lyons, R. (1978). The USSR, China and the Horn of Africa. *Review of African Political Economy*, 5(12), 5–30.

Maasho, A. (2016, July 26). South Sudan delays shutdown of oil pipelines to Ethiopia. *Reuters*. Retrieved from https://www.reuters.com/article/us-sudan-southssudan-pipeline/sudan-delays-shutdown-of-oil-pipelines-ethiopia-idUSBRE96P0JV20130726.

Maasho, A. (2018, March 8). Africa should avoid forfeiting sovereignty to China over loans: Tillerson. *Reuters*. Retrieved from https://www.reuters.com/article/us-usa-africa/africa-should-avoid-forfeiting-sovereignty-to-china-over-loans-tillerson-idUSKCN1GK114.

Manek, N. (2017, June 8). Ethiopia eyes role in DP World–managed port in Somaliland. *Bloomberg*. Retrieved from https://www.bloomberg.com/news/articles/2017-06-08/landlocked-ethiopia-eyes-role-in-dp-world-managed-somali-port.

Martel, F. (2018, March 7). Tillerson: China's "predatory loan practices and corrupt deals" threaten Africa. *Breitbart News*. Retrieved from https://www.breitbart.com/national-security/2018/03/07/tillerson-chinas-predatory-loan-practices-corrupt-deals-threaten-africa/.

Martina, M., & Brunnstrom, D. (2015, September 28). China's Xi says to commit 8,000 troops for U.N. peacekeeping force. *Reuters.* Retrieved from http://news.yahoo.com/chinas-xi-says-commit-8-000-troops-u-160032557.html.

Marton, P., & Matura, T. (2011). The "voracious dragon," the "scramble," and the "honey pot": Conceptions of conflict over Africa's natural resources. *Journal of Contemporary African Studies, 29*(2), 155–167. doi:10.1080/02589001.2011.555191.

Mathews, Kay. (2013). China and UN peacekeeping operations in Africa. In G. Berhe & H. Liu (Eds.), *China–Africa relations: Governance, peace and security* (pp. 55–73). Addis Ababa: Addis Ababa University Press.

McKenna, E. (2012, October 4). Ethiopia charts a Chinese course. *Inter Press Service.* Retrieved from http://www.ipsnews.net/2012/10/ethiopia-charts-a-chinese-course/.

Meester, J., van De Berg, W., & Verhoven, H. (2018, April). *Riyal politik: The political economy of Gulf investments in the Horn of Africa.* Retrieved from Clingendael Institute website: https://www.clingendael.org/sites/default/files/2018-04/riyal-politik.pdf.

Menyah, K., & Wolde-Rufael, Y. (2013). Government expenditure and economic growth: The Ethiopian experience 1950–2007. *Journal of Development Areas, 47*(1), 263–280.

Mesfin, M. (2011, July 25). Ethiopia: Chinese firm eyes gas export from Calub through Berbera. *Addis Fortune.* Retrieved from http://allafrica.com/stories/201107270752.html.

Metaferia, G. (2009). *Ethiopia and the United States: History, diplomacy, and analysis.* New York, NY: Algora.

Minnie, T. (2014, October 30). Tanzania's $10 bn China-funded port will start in 2015. *African Capital Markets.* Retrieved from http://www.africancapitalmarketsnews.com/2506/tanzanias-10bn-china-funded-port-will-start-in-2015/.

Mohan, G., & Lampert, B. (2013). Negotiating China: Reinserting African agency into China–Africa relations. *African Affairs, 112*(446), 92–110.

Morant, S. (2015, June 3). Ethiopia turns big plans into reality. *International Railway Journal.* Retrieved from https://www.railjournal.com/in_depth/ethiopia-turns-big-plans-into-reality.

Moody, A., & Chao, W. (2014). China "stepped into the breach." *China Daily Africa.* Retrieved from http://africa.chinadaily.com.cn/weekly/2014-04/11/content_17426606.htm.

Mulualem, M. (2017, January–March). OBOR: What is there for Africa? Discourse: Debating African Issues. *Dissent,* 137–138.

Mulupi, D. (2013, December 2). China's investment in Africa is positive. *How We Made It in Africa.* Retrieved from http://www.howwemadeitinafrica.com/chinas-investment-in-africa-is-positive-says-investment-advisor/33013/.

Munemo, J. (2015). Examining the imports of capital goods from China as a channel for technology transfer and growth in sub-Saharan Africa. *Journal of African Business*, *14*(2), 106–116.

Murphy, P. (2016, March 24). *The Silk Road, XXI century: "One belt one road."* Retrieved from Institute of International and European Affairs website: https://www.iiea.com/publication/the-silk-road-xxi-century-one-belt-one-road/.

Mwangi, G. (2014, April 3). Chinese firm signs $478.9 million Kenya Lamu port deal. *The Wall Street Journal*. Retrieved from https://blogs.wsj.com/frontiers/2014/08/03/chinese-firm-signs-478-9-million-kenya-lamu-port-deal/.

Naidu, S., Corkin, L., & Herman, H. (2009). China's re-emerging relations with Africa. *Politikon*, *36*(10), 87–115.

Natsios, A. S. (2012). China in Sudan: The challenges of non-interference in a failed state. *Georgetown Journal of International Affairs*, *13*(2), 62.

Negri, R. (2008). Beyond the Chinese scramble: The political economy of anti-China sentiment in Zambia. *African Geography Review*, *27*(1), 41–63.

Nehru, J. (1994). *The discovery of India*. New Delhi: Jawaharlal Nehru Memorial Fund.

Ng'Wanakilala, F. (2014, October 27). China says construction of China-funded port to start in 2015. *Reuters*. Retrieved from https://www.reuters.com/article/tanzania-port/tanzania-says-construction-of-china-funded-port-to-start-in-2015-idUSL5N0SM1QT20141027.

Nuo, D. (2009). *The adjustment of China's industrial structure after 1978* (Unpublished master's thesis). University of Oslo, Norway.

Nye, J. (2007). Notes for a soft-power research agenda. In F. Berenskoetter & M. J. Williams (Eds.), *Power in world politics* (pp. 162–172). New York, NY: Routledge.

Ofodile, U. (2009). Trade, aid and human rights: China's Africa policy in perspective. *Journal of International Commercial Law and Technology*, *4*(2), 89.

Olson, M., Jr. (1971). *The logic of collective action: Public goods and the theory of groups*. Cambridge, MA: Harvard University Press.

Oluoch, F. (2016, June 25). Kenya, Ethiopia in rail and pipeline deals. *The East African*. Retrieved from http://www.theeastafrican.co.ke/news/Kenya-and-Ethiopia-in-rail-pipeline-deals-/2558-3267116-jshm6kz/index.html.

Oqubay, A. (2018, June). *The structure and performance of the Ethiopian manufacturing sector*. (Working Paper Series No. 299). African Development Bank. Retrieved from https://www.tralac.org/images/docs/13204/the-structure-and-performance-of-the-ethiopian-manufacturing-sector-afdb-wps-299-june-2018.pdf.

Østby, G. (2005, January 5–7). *Horizontal inequalities and civil conflict*. Paper presented at the 13th Annual National Political Science Conference, Hurdalsjøen, Norway. Retrieved from http://citeseerx.ist.psu.edu/viewdoc/download?doi=10.1.1.163.6506&rep=rep1&type=pdf.

People's Republic of China, Office of the State Council. (2014, July 10). *China's foreign aid (2014)* (White paper). Beijing: Author. Retrieved from http://english.gov.cn/archive/white_paper/2014/08/23/content_281474982986592.htm.

Perlez, J., & Buckley, C. (2015, November 26). China retools its military with a first overseas outpost in Djibouti. *The New York Times*. Retrieved from https://www.nytimes.com/2015/11/27/world/asia/china-military-presence-djibouti-africa.html.

Pitcher, A., Moran, M. H., & Johnston, M. (2009). Rethinking patrimonialism and neopatrimonialism in Africa. *African Studies Review, 52*(1), 125–156.

Preuss, S. (2017, February 14). Chinese textile and apparel firms intensify investments in Ethiopia. *FashionUnited*. Retrieved from https://fashionunited.com/news/business/chinese-textile-and-apparel-firms-intensify-investments-in-ethiopia/2017021414682.

Qiu, J. (2019, April 26). Why is China still a developing country? *Beijing Review*. Retrieved from http://www.bjreview.com/Opinion/201904/t20190426_800166194.html.

Ramo, J. (2004, May 8). China has discovered its own economic consensus. Retrieved from Foreign Policy Centre website: https://fpc.org.uk/wp-content/uploads/2006/09/240-1.pdf.

Rebol, M. (2010). China aid to Africa: Filling the gap the others left. *Alternatives: Turkish Journal of International Relations, 9*(2), 43.

Renard, M.-F. (2011). *China's trade and FDI in Africa* (Working Paper No. 126). Tunis: African Development Bank.

Rian, D., & Blomkvist, K. (2013). Drivers and motives for Chinese outward foreign direct investment in Africa. *Journal of African Business, 14*(2), 75–84. doi:10.1080/15228916.2013.804320.

Rimmer, D. (1990). External debt and structural adjustment in tropical Africa. *African Affairs, 89*(355), 283–291.

Royal Institute of International Affairs. (1942). The agreement with Ethiopia. *Bulletin of International News, 19*(4), 138–140. Retrieved from http://www.jstor.org/stable/25643208.

Ruggie, J. G. (1974). Contingencies, constraints, and collective security: Perspectives on UN involvement in international disputes. *International Organization, 28*(3), 493–520.

Salidjanova, Nargiza. (2011). *Going out: An overview of China's outward foreign direct investment* (Research report). Retrieved from U.S.–China Economic & Security Review Commission website: https://www.uscc.gov/sites/default/files/Research/GoingOut.pdf.

Sautman, B., & Yan, H. (2009). African perspectives on China–Africa links. *China Quarterly, 199*, 728–759.

Scalapino, R. A. (1964). Sino-Soviet competition in Africa. *Foreign Affairs*, 42(4), 640–654.

Setiawan, H. (2005). Learning from history: The Bandung spirit. In D. Khudori (Ed.), *Rethinking solidarity in global society: The challenges of globalisation for social and solidarity movements* (pp. 20–28). Yogyakarta, Gadjah Mada University, Indonesia.

Sheik-Abdi, A. (1977). Somali nationalism: Its origins and future. *Journal of Modern African Studies*, 15(4), 657–665.

Sheldon-Duplaix, A. (2016, March 25). China's "imminent issue": Djibouti and overseas military interests (Commentary). European Council on Foreign Relations. Retrieved from https://www.ecfr.eu/article/commentary_chinas_imminent_issue_djibouti_and_overseas_interests4069.

Shinn, D. (2014, June 11). Ethiopia and China: When two former empires connected. *International Policy Digest*. Retrieved from https://intpolicydigest.org/2014/06/11/ethiopia-and-china-when-two-former-empires-connected/.

Shinn, D., & Eisenman, J. (2008). *Responding to China in Africa*. Retrieved from American Foreign Policy Council website: https://www.afpc.org/uploads/documents/ChinaAfrica.pdf.

Siu, H. F., & McGovern, M. (2017). China–Africa encounters: Historical legacies and contemporary realities. *Annual Review of Anthropology*, 46, 337–355. doi:10.1146/annurev-anthro-102116-041531.

Snow, P. (1995). China and Africa: Consensus and camouflage. In T. W. Robinson & D. Shambaugh (Eds.), *Chinese foreign policy: Theory and practice* (pp. 283–321). New York, NY: Oxford University Press.

Straub, S. (2008). *Infrastructure and growth in developing countries: Recent advances and research challenges* (Policy Research Working Paper 4460). Washington, DC: World Bank.

Stueck, William. (1995). *The Korean War: An international history*. Princeton, NJ: Princeton University Press.

Sun, D. (2015, March 11). China's soft military presence in the Middle East. Retrieved from Middle East Institute website: http://www.mei.edu/content/map/china%E2%80%99s-soft-military-presence-middle-east.

Sun, Y. (2014, February 7). China aid to Africa: A monster or a messiah? *Brookings Institution*. Retrieved from https://www.brookings.edu/opinions/chinas-aid-to-africa-monster-or-messiah/.

Tan, X., Zhao, Y., Polycarp, C., & Bai, J. (2013). *China's overseas investments in the wind and solar industries: Trends and drivers* (Working paper). Washington, DC: World Resources Institute. Retrieved from http://pdf.wri.org/chinas_overseas_investments_in_wind_and_solar_trends_and_drivers.pdf.

Tarke, G. (2009). *The Ethiopian Revolution*. New Haven, CT: Yale University Press.

Taylor, I. (1998). China's foreign policy towards Africa in the 1990s. *Journal of Modern African Studies*, 36(3), 444.

Taylor, I. (2006). *China and Africa: Engagement and compromise.* New York, NY: Routledge.

Taylor, I. (2012). *The Forum on China–Africa Cooperation (FOCAC).* New York, NY: Routledge.

Tekle, A. (1989). The determinants of the foreign policy of revolutionary Ethiopia. *Journal of Modern African Studies, 27*(3), 479–502.

Tekleberhan, M. (2012, October 16). Hujian receives additional land grant in Ethiopia. *2Merkato.* Retrieved from https://www.2merkato.com/news/manufacturing/1692-hujian-receives-additional-land-grant-in-ethiopia.

Tesfaye, A. (2009). *The political economy of the Nile waters regime in the twentieth century.* New York, NY: Edwin Mellen Press.

Tesfaye, A. (2012). Environmental security, regime building and international law in the Nile basin. *Canadian Journal of African Studies, 46*(2), 271–287. doi:10.1080/00083968.2012.702087.

Tesfaye, A. (2017). *State and economic development in Africa: The case of Ethiopia.* New York, NY: Palgrave Macmillan.

Tesfaye, A. (2018). Ethiopia, China and the West. In C. Alden, A. Alao, C. Zhang, & L. Barber (Eds.), *China and Africa: Building peace and security cooperation on the continent* (pp. 269–288). New York, NY: Palgrave Macmillan.

Tull, D. M. (2006). China's engagement in Africa: Preliminary scoping of African case studies: Angola, Ethiopia, Gabon, Uganda, South Africa, Zambia. *Journal of Modern African Studies, 44*(3), 459–479.

United States Agency for International Development. (2017). *Agriculture and food security.* Retrieved from https://2012-2017.usaid.gov/ethiopia/agriculture-and-food-security.

United States Energy Information Administration. (2017, August 4). *Three important oil trade chokepoints are located around the Arabian Peninsula.* Retrieved from https://www.eia.gov/todayinenergy/detail.php?id=32352.

United States International Trade Commission. (2009). *Sub-Saharan Africa: Effects of infrastructure conditions on export competitiveness, third annual report* (Investigation No. 332-477, USITC Publication 4071). Retrieved from https://www.usitc.gov/publications/332/pub4071.pdf.

Urbina-Ferretjans, M., & Surender, R. (2013). Social policy in the context of new global actors: How far is China's developmental model in Africa impacting traditional donors? *Global Social Policy, 13*(2), 261.

Vafeiads, M. (2017, March 1). China "buying out" Africa: Top five destinations of Chinese money. *Christian Science Monitor.* Retrieved from https://www.csmonitor.com/World/2012/0301/China-buying-out-Africa-Top-5-destinations-of-Chinese-money/Angola.

Van Donge, J. K., Henley, D., & Lewis, P. (2012). Tracking development in Southeast Asia and sub-Saharan Africa: The primacy of policy. *Development Policy Review, 30*(1), 1–13. doi.org/10.1111/j.1467-7679.2012.00563.x.

Van Staden, C. (2017). One belt one road and East Africa: Beyond Chinese influence. *China Brief*, *17*(14). Retrieved from https://jamestown.org/program/one-belt-one-road-east-africa-beyond-chinese-influence/.

Varhola, M. J. (2000). *Fire and ice: The Korean War, 1950–1953*. Boston, MA: Da Capo Press.

Venkataraman, M., & Gamora, G. (2009). An analysis of China–Ethiopia relations during the Cold War. *China Report*, *45*(1), 11.

Venkataraman, M., & Gofie, S. (2015). The dynamics of China–Ethiopia trade relations: Economic capacity, balance of trade and trade regimes. *Bandung Journal of the Global South*, *2*(8), 9. doi:10.1186/s40728-014-0007-1.

Verhoeven, H. (2015, April). Africa's new hegemon: Behind Ethiopia's power plays. *Foreign Affairs*. Retrieved from https://www.foreignaffairs.com/articles/ethiopia/2015-04-12/africas-next-hegemon.

Vestal, T. M. (2009). The Lion of Judah at Camelot: U.S. foreign policy toward Ethiopia as reflected in the second visit of Emperor Haile Selassie to the United States. *International Journal of Ethiopian Studies*, *4*(1/2), 135–152.

Wang, J.-Y. (2007, October). *What drives China's growing role in Africa?* (Working Paper WP/07/211). Washington, DC: International Monetary Fund. Retrieved from https://www.imf.org/external/pubs/ft/wp/2007/wp07211.pdf.

Wang, Y., & Ghebreyesus, T. A. (2014, January 12). *China–Ethiopia relations: An excellent model for South–South cooperation*. Beijing: Ministry of Foreign Affairs, People's Republic of China. Retrieved from http://www.fmprc.gov.cn/mfa_eng/zxxx_662805/t1215597.shtml.

Wang, Y.-K. (2010). China's response to the unipolar world. *Journal of Asian and African Studies*, *45*(5), 554–567. doi:10.1177/0021909610373898.

Wissenbach, U. (2009). The EU's response to China's Africa safari: Can triangular cooperation match needs? *European Journal of Development Research*, *21*(16), 662–674.

Wolff, P. (2015). *China's "Belt and Road" initiative—Challenges and opportunities* (Report prepared for the 2016 Annual Meeting of the Asian Development Bank). Berlin: German Development Institute.

Wondam, P. (2016). The 60th anniversary of the Bandung Conference and Asia. *Journal of Inter-Asian Cultural Studies*, *17*, 148–157. doi:10.1080/14649373.2016.1150246.

World Bank. (2008, July 10). *New financiers are narrowing Africa's infrastructure deficit* [Press release]. Retrieved from https://www.worldbank.org/en/news/press-release/2008/07/10/new-financiers-narrowing-africas-infrastructure-deficit.

World Bank. (2012). *Chinese FDI in Ethiopia: A survey*. Retrieved from http://documents.worldbank.org/curated/en/151961468038140377/Chinese-FDI-in-Ethiopia-a-World-Bank-survey.

World Bank. (2015, November 23). *With continued rapid growth, Ethiopia is poised to become a middle income country by 2025*. Retrieved from http://www.worldbank.org/en/country/ethiopia/publication/ethiopia-great-run-growth-acceleration-how-to-pace-it.

Yebo, Y. (2013, May 13). African traders flocked to Guangzhou for cheap goods but are staying to run manufacturing operations. *Quartz*. Retrieved from http://qz.com/81642/african-traders-flocked-to-guangzhou-for-the-cheap-goods-but-are-staying-to-run-manufacturing-operations/.

Yohannes, R. (2017, June 21). Ethiopia, China to strengthen strategic partnership. *Ethiopian Herald*. Retrieved from https://allafrica.com/stories/201611240916.html.

Zenawi, M. (n.d.). *African development: Dead ends and new beginnings*. Unpublished manuscript. Retrieved from http://www.meleszenawi.com/african-development-dead-ends-and-new-biginnings-by-meles-zenawi/.

Zewde, B. (2002). *Pioneer of changes in Ethiopia: Reformist intellectuals of early twentieth century*. Columbus, OH: Ohio University Press.

Zhang, X., Taxera, D., Zou, C., Wang, Z., Zhao, J., Gebremenfas, E. A., & Dhavle, J. (2018). *Industrial park development in Ethiopia: Case study report* (Inclusive and Sustainable Industrial Development Working Paper 21/2018). Vienna, Austria: UN Industrial Development Organization. Retrieved from https://www.unido.org/api/opentext/documents/download/10694802/unido-file-10694802.

Zhou, E. (1964, January 15). *The Chinese government's eight principles for economic aid and technical assistance to other countries* (Selected diplomatic papers of Zhou Enlai). Washington, DC: History and Public Policy Program, Woodrow Wilson International Center for Scholars. Retrieved from http://digitalarchive.wilsoncenter.org/document/121560.pdf?v=7abac3e22dfa18df4a30915a4a7b1700.

Zhou, H. (2014). Testing the limits: China's expanding role in the South Sudanese Civil War. *China Brief*, *14*(19). Retrieved from https://jamestown.org/program/testing-the-limits-chinas-expanding-role-in-the-south-sudanese-civil-war/.

Zhu, L. Forum on China–Africa Cooperation. (2006). *China Africa Policy*. Part IV, 2(10). Xinhua News Agency. Retrieved from http://www.gov.cn/misc/2006-01/12/content_156490.htm.

Zhu, L. Forum on China–Africa Cooperation. (2006). *China Africa Policy*. Part II, 2(10). Xinhua News Agency. Retrieved from http://www.gov.cn/misc/2006-01/12/content_156490.htm.

Index

AASNP. *See* Addis Ababa School Net Project
Accra Summit, 20
Adama, 55–56
Addis Ababa, 4, 34–35, 52, 60
Addis Ababa-Djibouti Railway, 16, 48–49, 52, 60–62, 82, 89, 96, 102–103, 114
Addis Ababa Light Rail System, 102
Addis Ababa Ring Road, 47, 82, 85
Addis Ababa School Net Project (AASNP), 48
Aden, 112
Afar, 110
Africa-China relations, 7–14, 87. *See also* Ethiopia-China relations
African Standby Force, 4, 88
African Union (AU), 1, 28, 33–37, 49, 77–78, 87–89, 96, 104–106, 121. *See also* Organization of African Unity
African Union Peace and Security Architecture (AUPSC), 121
Afro-Asian Solidarity Conference, 20
agency, African, 1–2, 12–14, 117
Agenda 2063, African Union, 106
Agreement of Economic, Technical, Scientific and Trade Cooperation, 47

agriculture-led industrialization, 2–3, 27–29, 34–38, 45–48, 55, 68, 77, 95, 100–101
agro-processing, 68, 101
Ahmed, Abyi, 114
airports, 48, 76, 82
Akaki, 64
Algerian Liberation Front (ALF), 20
al-Qaeda, 89
Al-Shabaab, 87
Angola, 84, 109, 125
anti-piracy operations, 6
Anuak militants, 36
apparel industry, 65–66, 100
Aptidon, Hassan Gouled, 42
Arba Minch, 122
Ashgoda, 55
Asmara, 22
associated development, 124
Aswan Dam, 21
asymmetric relationships, 6, 14, 85, 117
AU. *See* African Union
AUPSC. *See* African Union Peace and Security Architecture
authoritarianism, 7
autonomy, of nationalities, 122
Awash, 103
Ayka Assis Industrial Park, 63

Index

Aysha, 56

Bab el-Mandeb Strait, 5, 15, 31, 42, 111–112
Bagamoyo, 89, 96–98
Bahir Dar, 82
Baiyun International Airport, 76
balance of trade, 68–71, 69, 124
Bandung Peace Conference, 12–13, 19, 20, 31, 35, 74
Bank BNP Paribas, 55
banking policy, 11–12
Barre, Siad, 24
Beijing Action Plan, 87
Beijing Consensus, 29
Beijing Declaration, 10
Belt and Road Initiative (BRI), 16, 75, 89, 96–109, 114–115, 118, 123
Berbera, 35, 41–42, 49, 96, 103, 112
bilateral relations, 1, 6, 34, 70
birr (Ethiopian currency), 68–69
birth regions, of political leaders, 81
Blue Nile River, 36, 56
Bole International Airport, 82
Bole Lemi Industrial Zone, 62
Bolton, John, 123
Bonga, 25
Brazil, 37
Brexit, 96
BRI. *See* Belt and Road Initiative
BRIC nations, 37
Britain. *See* Great Britain

Camp Lemonnier, 6–7, 42
Castro, Fidel, 24
centralization, of national policy, 43–44
Chamber of Commerce, Chinese, 54
Chiang Kai-shek, 19
China: African students in, 48; Cultural Revolution, 47; as developing country, 117; development financing, 9, 38; development model, 9–10, 47, 49–50; economic relations with, 113; Ethiopian entrepreneurs in, 93–94; Horn of Africa presence of, 7, 123; industrial adjustment of, 97; multiple actors, 120; one-China policy, 10, 28–30, 35, 38–39; as positive presence, 93; regional vision of, 95–96; residents in Ethiopia, 94; Revolution, 17–18, 43; rift with Soviet Union, 22; similarities to Ethiopia, 17; tensions caused by, 93; United Nations membership, 20–23, 32; United States as rival to, 40, 82. *See also* Africa-China relations; Ethiopia-China relations
China-Africa Cooperation Partnership for Peace and Security, 87, 121
China Agriculture Development Bank, 11
China Civil Engineering Construction Corporation (CCECC), 64, 103
China Communication Construction Company, 97
China-Djibouti Economic and Trade Seminar, 42
China Electric Power Equipment and Technology, 56
China-Ethiopia light rail, 60
China Export-Import (Exim) Bank, 11, 13, 55–56, 62, 69, 84–85, 97, 102–103, 121
China Merchant Holdings, 43, 98
China Overseas Engineering Group (COEG), 60
China Railway Construction Corporation, 103
China Railway Group, 60, 64, 102

China Road, 25
China Road and Bridge Corporation, 85
"China's African Policy" (white paper), 10
Chinese Development Bank, 11
Chinese Electric Power Equipment and Technology Company, 37, 102
Chinese Overseas Special Economic Zones (COSEZ), 62. *See also* special economic zones (SEZs)
Chinese PetroTrans, 41
Chinese Young Volunteers Serving Africa program, 30
civic realm, 81
civil service reform, 100
civil society, 114
climate change, 55
COEG. *See* China Overseas Engineering Group
coexistence, peaceful, 87
coffee exports, 67–68
Cold War, 15, 18–22, 26, 30–32, 74, 112
collateral, natural resources as, 84
collective security, 18
colonialism, 14, 37
COMESA. *See* Common Market for East and Southern Africa
Commercial Bank of Ethiopia, 84
Commission for Africa, United Nations, 4
Common Market for East and Southern Africa (COMESA), 104–105
communications industry, 59–60
communism, international leadership of, 22
Communist Party, Chinese, 39
Comprehensive Peace Agreement (CPA), 120

conflicts: ongoing, 41, 86, 104; prevention of, 85–86; regional, 7
Confucius Institute, 30, 73, 79
Congo, 22, 109
connectivity, regional, 75, 120
construction industry, 54–58, 84–85, 118–119
containment, of Soviet Union, 18
contemporary relations, Ethiopia-China, 33–50
cooperation: development, 84; economic, 34; military, 4–5, 27–30, 36, 77–78, 118; multilayered, 6, 76; security, 85–86
corruption, 122–124
COSEZ. *See* Chinese Overseas Special Economic Zones
counterterrorism, 7
CPA. *See* Comprehensive Peace Agreement
crony capitalism, 122
Cuba, 23–25
Cultural Revolution, Chinese, 47
currency, Ethiopian, 68–69

Damansky Island, 22
Dar es Salaam, 97–98, 106
Darfur, 112, 121
Debre Zeit/Bishoftu, 59
debt: cancellation of, 47, 73; modalities of, 107–109; Third World crisis, 57
decentralization, 44
democratic reforms, 113–114
Deng Xiaoping, 8, 17, 25, 33, 44, 77
dependency theory, 14, 31, 124
development: Angolan model of, 84, 125; Asian model of, 29, 33–34; associated, 124; Chinese model of, 9–10, 47, 49–50; cooperation frameworks, 84; financing, 38; Japanese model of, 19; objectives

development (continued)
of, 46; projects, 82–83, 83; state-led, 43–44, 46
diplomacy: Chinese interest in Ethiopia, 34–40; economic, 33; establishment of relations, 21–23; multilateral, 9–10; objectives of, 4
Dire Dawa, 41, 60
distribution of resources, 111
diversification, economic, 13
Djibouti, 5–7, 15, 31, 42, 78, 89–90, 103, 112, 121–123
donors, traditional, 2, 16, 80, 95, 113, 120
DP World, 103
drones, 7
Dukem, 63

East African Community (EAC), 78, 105–106
East African Standby Brigade (EASTBRIG), 88
East Asian Tigers, 44–45
EASTBRIG. See East African Standby Brigade
Eastern Africa, 107
Eastern Industrial Zone, 63–65
economic challenges, 86
Economic Commission for Africa, UN, 1, 35, 89
economic cooperation, 34
economic growth, 6–7, 40, 44, 51–52, 66, 98–100, 99, 124
economic integration, 107
economic reform, 77
economic relations, 51–71, 113
educational exchanges, 30
education-related projects, 48
efficiency seeking, 55
Egypt, 5, 20–24, 36–37, 91, 109–111
Eight Principles for Economic Aid and Technical Assistance to Other Countries, 79, 90

EIPDC. See Ethiopia's Industrial Parks Development Corporation
elections, 27, 111
elites: access to, 2; birth regions of, 81; pacts between, 111
employment, expansion of, 100
energy: bottlenecks, 11; development, 28, 37; power generation, 102; reliability of, 119; renewable, 55–56; security, 41
entrepreneurs, African, 65, 94
EPRDF. See Ethiopian People's Revolutionary Democratic Front
EPRP. See Ethiopian People's Revolutionary Party
ERC. See Ethiopia Railway Corporation
Eritrea, 5–7, 24–26, 32, 41, 86, 114, 118, 123
Eritrean Liberation Front, 21–24, 31
Eritrean People's Liberation Front, 23–25, 32
ETC. See Ethiopian Telecommunication Corporation
Ethio-China Polytechnic College, 82
Ethio-Chinese Friendship Road system, 58
Ethiopia: case study of, 117; exports, 67–68; imperial period, 18–23; investment in, 55–66, 58, 59; migration to, 94; rural, 51–52; similarities to China, 17; Somali invasion of, 23–24; urban poor, 46
Ethiopia-China relations, 1–3, 16, 33–50
Ethiopian Airlines, 44, 76
Ethiopian Electric Power Corporation, 37, 55, 102
Ethiopian-Eritrean War, 118
Ethiopian Investment Commission, 66
Ethiopian People's Revolutionary Democratic Front (EPRDF), 2–3, 25–33, 39, 111, 118

Ethiopian People's Revolutionary Party (EPRP), 24
Ethiopian Revolution, 74
Ethiopian Telecommunication Corporation (ETC), 59–60
Ethiopia Railway Corporation (ERC), 103
Ethiopia's Industrial Parks Development Corporation (EIPDC), 62
Ethiopia-U.S. relations, 7, 17, 95, 114, 121–122. *See also* Mutual Defense Agreement, Ethiopia-U.S.
ethno-national federalism, 109–110
European Union (EU), 77, 88, 96, 112–115
Exim Bank. *See* China Export-Import Bank
exploitative trade, 85
exports: buyers' credit, 69; China to Africa, 66–67; Ethiopian, 67–71; Ethiopia to China, 67; livestock, 68; markets for, 11, 28, 89; of oil, 67; selective state intervention, 101; of sesame seeds, 68

failed states, 96
Fan Changlong, 36
fascism, 19
federalism, 109–110
Fincha-Amerti-Neshi multi-purpose project, 84
five principles of peaceful coexistence, 8, 13
floriculture, 68
FOCAC. *See* Forum on China-Africa Cooperation
food assistance, 25
food security, 122
footwear. *See* shoe industry
foreign assistance, 16, 57–58, 79–85, 90, 120–121

foreign direct investment, 26, 29–30, 46, 52–54
Forum on China-Africa Cooperation (FOCAC), 3, 6, 10, 28, 34, 52, 64, 77, 87, 124
Forum on China-Africa Cooperation and Addis Ababa Action Plan 2004–2006, 28
Four Modernizations, 33
Fourth Agreement of Economic and Trade Cooperation, 26
France, 6, 42, 55, 90
free rider problem, 107
free trade arrangements, 11
French Development Bank, 55
friendship, use of term, 80

Galafi, 103
garment industry. *See* apparel industry
gas development, 4, 41, 49, 54–55, 90, 97, 121
GCL POLY Petroleum Investment, 41
GDP. *See* gross domestic product
Genale Dawa III, 56
George Shoes Industrial Park, 63
Germany, 55
Gezira Scheme, 36
Ghana, 93–95
Gibe II Dam, 56, 82
globalization, 14, 107, 124
"going out" policy, 2, 26, 55, 70, 90, 95, 115, 118
government-owned enterprises, 59
Grand Renaissance Dam, 5, 36–37, 56, 102, 111, 119
grants, 46–47, 58
Great Britain, 37
Greater Somalia, 22–24, 32
great powers, 6, 15, 90–91, 112, 115
green energy, 55–56
green revolution, 33
gross domestic product (GDP), 51–52, 66, 98–100, 99, 101

growth, economic, 6–7, 40, 44, 51–52, 66, 98–100, 124
Growth and Transformation Plan (GTP), 2–3, 15, 27–29, 52, 56–57, 77, 98–102, 115–122
Guangdong Province, 93–94
Guelleh, Ismail Omar, 42
Gulf of Aden, 43, 123

Hargeisa, 35
Hawassa Industrial Park, 62
Heavily Indebted Poor Countries (HPIC) program, 84
hierarchy of interests, 3
Horn of Africa region, 3–6, 36, 40, 52, 73–78, 85–90, 107, 118–124
housing, 94
HPIC. *See* Heavily Indebted Poor Countries program
Huajian Group, 58–59, 65, 119
Huawei Technology Company, 48, 60
Hujian Industrial Park, 63
Hu Jintao, 8, 26
human resource development, 48
human rights, 8, 13, 19, 39, 110, 113
Human Rights Commission, United Nations, 39
Hutchison Port Holdings, 42
hydroelectric dams, 36–37, 55, 56, 82, 102

ideology, foreign policy and, 8, 26, 31, 120
IGAD. *See* Intergovernmental Authority for Development
imperialism, 8, 20
imperial period, 18–23
imports: Africa to China, 67; Chinese, 64, 66–67; tariffs on, 70
incentives, economic, 29, 56, 66, 101
incumbency, of ruling party, 110–111
independence, African, 8, 22

India, 5, 7, 20, 37, 90, 121
industrial aid, 12
industrialization, 19, 33. *See also* agriculture-led industrialization
industrial parks, 62–63, *63*
industrial zones. *See* special economic zones (SEZs)
inequality, horizontal, 110
infrastructure, 38, 44–46, 54, 64, 85–86, 93–98, 102, 106–107
instability, political, 109
integration, regional, 98–109, 104–106, 114–115
Intergovernmental Authority for Development (IGAD), 1, 4, 35, 78, 87–89, 104, 112, 120
internationalism, 28
International Monetary Fund, 2
Internet, 122
intervention, constructive, 87, 121
investment: in Ethiopia, 57–66, *58*, *59*; foreign assistance and, 85; foreign direct, 26–30, 46, 52–54; licensed Chinese projects, *53*, *61*; protection of, 52–54; by United States, 123
Iran, 91, 112
Isiolo, 97, 106
Islamic Courts, 87

Japan, 6, 19
JECC. *See* Joint Ethiopia-China Commission
Jiangsu Sunshine Group, 66
Jiang Zemin, 3, 8–10, 25–26, 32–34, 77
Jimma, 103
Ji Peiding, 42
Joint Ethiopia-China Commission (JECC), 26, 32, 52, 84, 121
Joint Ministerial Commission, Ethiopia-China, 34

Juba, 106

Kagnew Station, 18, 22
Kenya, 4, 41, 87–89, 96–97, 105–106, 121
Konare, Alpha Oumar, 28
Korean War, 8, 18, 31, 112
Kuwait, 123

labor: low cost, 45, 54, 100–102; migration, 94; outsourcing, 66, 100; productivity, 102
labor-intensive industries, 54, 101–102
Lamu Port South Sudan Ethiopia Transport (LAPSSET) Corridor, 89, 96–97, 103–106
land: leasing, 45; nationalization, 23; reform, 74; state ownership of, 44, 46
landlocked countries, 86–87
LAPSSET. *See* Lamu Port South Sudan Ethiopia Transport Corridor
leather industry, 65, 68, 100, 101
Leather Industry Technology Institute, 65
Lee Kuan Yew, 34
liberalization, of trade, 11, 13
light rail, 60
Liu Shaoqi, 21
livestock development, 55, 68
loans: Chinese commitments to Ethiopia, 66, 108; collateral for, 84; interest-free, 47, 58; low-interest, 8, 51; mutual benefit loans, 69; predatory, 57; process of acquiring, 85; resource-backed, 109; tied, 10, 90, 109, 125; transparency of, 124
long-term perspectives, 93–115
lost decade, 8

Mali, 112, 121

management systems, 48
manufacturing industry, 46, 54, 58–60, 101, 119
Mao Zedong, 17–23
marginalization, of Africa, 8
Mariam, Mengistu Haile, 25
markets, for exports, 11, 28, 89
marriage, 94
meat industry, 100
media, 122
medium-scale firms, 65
Meiji transformation, 19
Mekelle, 103
Merkato, 65, 93
methodology, 15
middle-income nation, goal of becoming, 34–36, 46–49, 56, 111, 117
migration: of labor force, 94; root causes of, 96
military assistance, 88
military bases, 5–6, 31, 42–43, 90, 123
military cooperation, 4–5, 27–28, 30, 36, 77–78, 118
military regime, 23–25, 31–32
Millennium Development Goals, United Nations, 6, 46, 66, 98
mineral resources, 28
mining, 93
Ministry of Foreign Affairs and Commerce, Chinese, 84, 121
minority rights, 110
modernization, 2, 43–50
Mogadishu, 35
Mombasa, 105–106
Mombasa-Nairobi Railway, 97
monopolies, 46, 85, 90
mortgage slaves (*fangnu*), 94
most-favored-nation status, 3, 26, 32, 77
Mugher Cement Enterprise, 84

Index

multilateral diplomacy, 9–10
multilayered cooperation, 6, 76
multiparty elections, 27
mutual benefit loans, 69
Mutual Defense Agreement, Ethiopia-U.S., 18, 21, 24, 31, 74, 82

Nakodok, 97, 106
Nasser, Gamal Abdel, 21
nationalism, 21, 122
nationalist liberation fronts, 20
Nationalist Party (Kuomintang), 19
nationalization, of economy, 64
natural resources, 1, 11, 84, 90, 121
naval bases, 6, 31, 123
neo-imperialism, 8
New Partnership for African Development (NEPAD), 28, 35, 37
Nigeria, 109
Nile River, 5, 21, 36, 56, 102, 111
Nixon, Richard, 17, 22
Nkrumah, Kwame, 20
nonaligned movement, 19–20, 33
noninterference policy, 5, 13, 27, 35, 39–40, 47, 56–57, 79–82, 113–115, 118
North to South relationships, 6

Obock, 43
Ogaden Liberation Front, 41
Ogaden region, 24–25, 32, 41, 49, 54–55
oil development, 4, 41, 54–55, 67, 86, 90, 97, 121
Oman, 5, 98
one-China policy, 10, 28–30, 35, 38–39
one-party rule, 27, 44, 47, 117, 122
"opening up" program, 26
Organisation for Economic Co-operation and Development, 37

Organization of African Unity (OAU), 18, 30, 49, 74. *See also* African Union
Oromia, 52, 60, 110, 119
outsourcing, 66, 100

Palestine Liberation Organization (PLO), 20
Pan-Arabism, 20–21
PASDP. *See* Poverty Alleviation and Sustainable Development Program
peace: negotiations, 13, 78, 86; security and, 57
Peace and Security Council, African Union, 78, 88
peacekeeping operations, 1–2, 5, 49, 87–88, 112
People's Democratic Republic of Ethiopia, establishment of, 25
pipelines, 41, 97
piracy, 6
PLO. *See* Palestine Liberation Organization
policy banks, 11–12
political resources, 1, 117
political stability, 6, 24, 109, 122
population growth, 122
port facilities, 41, 97, 106
Port Sudan, 36
poverty, alleviation of, 2, 13, 66, 117–118
Poverty Alleviation and Sustainable Development Program (PASDP), 84
power generation, 102
pragmatism, 7, 18–23, 26
predatory lending, 57
primordial realm, 81
private realm, 81
productivist approach, 9
productivity, 102
public realms, 81

Qatar, 4–5, 7, 91, 112, 123
Qian Qichen, 27
Qiao Zonghuai, 42

railway construction, 16, 48–49, 52, 60–64, 89, 96–98, 102–104, 119
raw materials. *See* natural resources
RECs. *See* regional economic communities
Red Sea, 5, 6, 7, 15, 31, 42, 90–91, 111–112, 115, 123
reform, economic, 77
regional conflicts, 7, 85–86
regional economic communities (RECs), 104, 105
regional organizations, 78, 120
regulatory institutions, 109
renewable energy, 55–56
responsible states (*fuzeren guojia*), 78
retail sector, 54
revitalization, 97
revolutions: Chinese, 17–18, 43; Ethiopian, 74
Rhee, Syngman, 34
road construction, 24–25, 45–47, 58, 85
rural Ethiopia, 51–52
Russia, 5–7, 26, 90, 121–123. *See also* Soviet Union
Ruvu Station, 97

Saudi Arabia, 4–5, 91, 111–112, 123
scholarship programs, 73
"scramble for Africa" paradigm, 11
Sebeta, 103
sectoral distribution of gross domestic product, *101*
security: alliances, 123; challenges, 86; gaps, 96; regional, 85–86
Security Council, United Nations, 4–5, 23, 39, 112, 121

security interests, 15, 40–43, 49, 57, 90–91
Selassie, Haile, 18–23, 31, 118
self-determination, of nationalities, 122
self-directed development, 34
self-employment, 70
service sector, 56
sesame seeds, export of, 68
Sharia courts, 87
Sharm El-Sheikh Plan, 87
shoe industry, 64–65, 119
Silk Road Economic Belt, 96–98
Silk Road Stations, 43
Singapore, 34
Sino-Ethiopian Trade Agreement, 69
small-scale firms, 65, 70, 100
social challenges, 86
socialism, 74
socialist market economies, 7
social responsibility activities, 38
social services, 12–13
soft power, 8–9, 26, 54, 73, 82, 120
solar energy, 55
Somalia, 4–7, 22–24, 32–35, 41–43, 74, 78, 86–89, 96, 103–106, 121. *See also* Somaliland
Somaliland, 5, 35, 41–42, 49, 74, 96, 123. *See also* Somalia
Somali Liberation Front, 23–24
South Africa, 93, 109
Southern Region, 26
South Korea, 34, 47
South-South relationships, 6, 9–10, 16, 28, 31, 34, 37, 54, 94, 117
South Sudan, 4–7, 35–36, 78, 86, 89–90, 97, 103–106, 120. *See also* Sudan
sovereignty, of internal affairs, 9, 95
Soviet Union, 15, 18, 21–25, 30, 32, 82. *See also* Russia

special economic zones (SEZs), 16, 62–66, 97, 102. *See also* Chinese Overseas Special Economic Zones (COSEZ)
sphere-of-influence politics, 19
stability: political, 6, 24, 109, 122; regional, 35, 49
standby brigades, 88
state capture, 2, 14
State General Reserve Fund, Oman, 98
state-led development, 43–46
strategic interests, 16, 119–120
structural power, 80
student exchanges, 30
Suakin Island, 5, 112
subsectors, economic, 100
Sudan, 5–7, 24, 35–36, 41, 86, 103, 112. *See also* South Sudan
Suez Canal, 112
Swaziland, 38
Syria, 21

Taiwan, 8, 20–22, 27, 32–38, 118
Takeze Dam, 82
Tanzania, 89, 96–98, 106, 109
Tanzania-Zambia Railroad Project (TAZARA), 8, 96, 98, 102
tariffs, import, 70
TAZARA. *See* Tanzania-Zambia Railroad Project
teacher exchanges, 30
Technical and Vocational Education and Training (TVET) institutions, 30
technology institutes, 100
technology transfers, 13, 26–27, 44
telecommunications sector, 38, 44
terrorist organizations, 87
Teshome, Mulatu, 39
textile industry, 64, 100, 119
tied assistance, 85

tied loans, 10, 90, 109, 125
tourism, 48
trade: balance of, 68–71, 69, 124; China-Africa, 9; Ethiopia-China, 66–70; liberalization of, 11, 13; regulations governing, 119; unfair, 85
traditional donors, 2, 16, 80, 95, 112, 120
trans-border infrastructure, 107
Transitional Government of Ethiopia, 25–26
Transitional Government of Somalia, 87
transmission lines, 37, 56
transportation bottlenecks, 11
Treaty of Friendship and Cooperation, Ethiopia-Soviet Union, 25, 32
Trump, Donald, 123
Tsinghua University, 48
Turkey, 5–7, 37, 91, 112
TVET. *See* Technical and Vocational Education and Training institutions

UAR. *See* United Arab Republic
Uganda, 4, 41, 106
Uhuru Highway, 98
UN. *See* United Nations
unfair trade, 85
United Arab Emirates, 5, 91, 111, 123–124
United Arab Republic (UAR), 21
United Nations (UN), 4–5, 8, 18–23, 28, 33–35, 39, 74, 87, 98, 121
United Nations Transition Assistance Group (UNTAG), 88
United States: aid to Egypt, 21; assistance from, 88–89, 96; China as rival to, 40, 82; containment of Soviet Union, 18, 30; development policies of, 112–113; foreign policy,

74, 114–115; investment in Africa, 123; military bases, 6, 42–43, 90; rapprochement with China, 22; Selassie's visit to, 22. *See also* Ethiopia-U.S. relations
UNTAG. *See* United Nations Transition Assistance Group
urban guerilla warfare, 24, 32
urban poor, 46
US. *See* United States
USSR. *See* Soviet Union

veterinary research, 82
vocational education, 30, 38
"voracious dragon" paradigm, 11

Wang Yi, 49
Washington Consensus, 56
Wen Jiabao, 28, 34
Western Somalia Liberation Front, 24
wind energy, 55–56
win-win relationships, 6, 9, 12–23, 16

Woldeya-Kombolcha-Awash Railroad, 104
Woldeya-Woreta Road, 25, 47, 82
Woreta, 25
World Bank, 2, 21, 34, 54, 117
World Trade Organization (WTO), 11, 70

Xi Jinping, 75, 88
Xinhua News Agency, 23, 25

Yemen, 5, 112

Zambia, 93, 98
Zenawi, Meles, 2–3, 26–28, 32–34, 77
Zhenbao Island, 22
Zhong Jianhua, 78
Zhongyuan Petroleum Exploration Bureau, 41
Zhou Enlai, 13, 20–22, 47, 79
ZTE Corporation, 48, 60

www.ingramcontent.com/pod-product-compliance
Ingram Content Group UK Ltd.
Pitfield, Milton Keynes, MK11 3LW, UK
UKHW041855120325
456170UK00014B/84